Jefferson's GREAT GAMBLE

THE REMARKABLE STORY OF JEFFERSON, NAPOLEON AND THE MEN BEHIND THE LOUISIANA PURCHASE

CHARLES A. CERAMI

SOURCEBOOKS, INC.
NAPERVILLE, ILLINOIS

Published by Sourcebooks, Inc.

P.O. Box 4410, Naperville, Illinois 60567-4410

(630) 961-3900

FAX: (630) 961-2168

www.sourcebooks.com

Library of Congress Cataloging-in-Publication Data

Cerami, Charles A.

Jefferson's great gamble: the remarkable story of Jefferson, Napoleon and the men behind the Louisiana Purchase / by Charles A. Cerami.

p. cm.

Includes bibliographical references (p.) and index.

ISBN 1-4022-0240-7 (alk. paper)

1. Louisiana Purchase. 2. Jefferson, Thomas, 1743-1826. 3. United States—Territorial expansion. I. Title.

E333 .C465 2003

973.4'6—dc21

2002153440

Printed and bound in the United States of America

QW 10 9 8 7 6 5 4 3 2 1

For
My Incomparable
Mary Ann

ACKNOWLEDGMENTS

Not for the first time, my friend and agent, Bob Silverstein, has done something more than either of those roles encompasses. In helping to refine my original thoughts before they became a project, and then helping to resolve moments of doubt, he has been an indispensable partner.

Having Hillel Black as my editor was an educational experience. He has a sensitivity to the sound and value of words that forces me to forget the interim distress his innumerable suggestions caused me. For the quality of his effort and its uplifting effect, I can be nothing but grateful.

The diligence and expertise of Peter Lynch and his staff in the last phase of the process made it a real joy to see this volume take shape. Especially creative was Tressa Minervini's internal and cover design, making my twelfth book the most beautiful of all.

Many libraries in New York, Philadelphia, and Baltimore were very helpful, but four in Washington, D.C., outdid themselves for me in many ways that include the following examples.

In the Martin Luther King Library, the Washingtoniana Room was an unfailing resource, which was no surprise, since I had been similarly helped when I researched previous books. But it was Kenneth Whisenton, of the library's Government Desk, who startled me by finding points about executive privilege that I knew to exist, but had almost despaired of proving.

At my own old school, Georgetown University, the seemingly endless collections of books on diplomatic history enabled me to pinpoint facts that were said to be totally obscured by time. As an example, I had been told by a foreign government that the career facts about one of its diplomats who appears in this book could no longer be found. An afternoon at the Georgetown University Library turned up a wealth of details that played a part in making the man come to life in these pages.

At the Library of Congress, Alexander LoBianco, a technician in the Law Library section, gave me painstaking attention that turned hard searches into swift discoveries.

And in the much less famous Senate Library, Zoe Davis made short and pleasant work of several painful searches that had eluded all other sources. She also upheld my contention that the people of Capitol Hill, contrary to the media's gibes, are Washington's brightest and kindest.

CONTENTS

PREFACE

It is my impression that books dealing with great historical events are hardly ever as compelling as biographies. Focusing on a single person's life often provides a peripheral view that clarifies surrounding events; works that tell how several leaders combined to produce a world-altering result seldom give us more than surface facts. Be it a war, an exploration, or a treaty, the teamwork or the antagonism that brought it about is usually skimmed, and it may read as if a number of men in dark suits gathered solemnly to initial the preordained pages.

These shortcomings have been especially unfortunate in the case of the Louisiana Purchase, for the emphasis on a certain number of square miles and a remarkably low price made it seem to be merely "the largest real estate deal in history." Not only its drama but some of its significance is lost if we know only that no nation has ever acquired so much territory in a single stroke and without resort to arms.

I believe that new meaning is added in seeing the lively words that were exchanged during thirty months of blandishments, posturing, and infighting among nine principal players, American and French. When they signed, they knew, almost unbelievingly, that they were totally transforming the size and prospects of the United States of America. Napoleon even saw that his withdrawal might transform the world.

Early in April 1803, the Union had been primarily a strip of states along the Atlantic seacoast; as the month ended, it was doubling in size and clearly reaching out to grasp the entire continent. Now, at the bicentennial of this unique happening, its place in American—and world—history seems more significant than ever. Without owning an entire continent free of other great powers, not only would this nation's global influence have been unthinkable, but the United States might never even have attained a place among the world's major countries. My aim in this book is to give life and voice to the diverse group of men whose talents, weaknesses, and motivations interacted to produce what has been called the greatest event since the nation was founded.

Chapter One

TOWARD
THE GREAT RIVER

The new country was just a few years old when a wild, stomping rush toward the west gathered alarming speed and force in the 1790s. It had started years earlier, slowed during the war, then surged late in 1781, after the British surrender signaled freedom. And it never let up.

Even before a nation had been established, the Declaration of Independence—and the special word "united"—seemed to signal the right to go anywhere. It echoed the pre-Revolutionary words of Patrick Henry in 1774: "Where are your landmarks, your boundaries of colonies? We are in a state of nature....The distinctions between Virginians, Pennsylvanians, New Yorkers, and New Englanders are no more. I am not a Virginian, but an American."

Most people still felt that they belonged to one of the original colonies—or states—and for some, that old tie would never snap. But now, more Americans than anyone had imagined possible were caught up in the urge to take virgin land. By the thousands, they were talking with neighbors, hearing stories about wide-open opportunities, and studying maps. In earlier years, the lines of travel had most often been to the north or south, where one would find established roads facilitating contacts between colonies. Communities that wanted to grow sent word along those routes, luring new people with offers of land. French Huguenots in Pennsylvania were attracted to Richmond, then drawn further south to North Carolina. Scottish teachers and clergymen were invited to extend their discipline and classical training both northward and southward. But in the 1780s, many more with only good health and ambition to offer began spreading wider maps and looking to their left—westward.

Some drew their pencil lines past Albany, then through the lakes and into the Ohio country. Others further south approached the prized Ohio River area by way of Fort Pitt, which was already on the verge of industrial renown as "Pittsburgh." Virginians, more simply, moved within their own state to the county called Kentucky, and North Carolinians did the same to start populating their Tennessee County. People from all over the east thought of ultimately moving between those two counties—through the Cumberland Gap, an old Native American passage that had been rediscovered only a few decades before—and so breaking through the Appalachians into the lush Mississippi Valley. Probably millions made these trips in their minds or at their kitchen tables, and a surprising number of them actually began the trek to unknown places.

Crude roads those were, not at all like the ones that many state legislatures were requiring towns to build between themselves and neighboring communities. These westward routes had mostly begun as Native American trails and had been expanded haphazardly by traffic. Their condition forced many of the travelers to turn back. The real story, however, was how great a horde did keep going west, staking out land and starting to farm.

The travelers were mostly hopeful, optimistic, and good-natured at first, even though most of them were on foot. Their feelings went beyond practical ambitions, for they were caught up in the timeless fact that, as current travel writer Sam Howe Verhovek has put it, "America has always had something of a Great Beyond in its national psyche, a far end of the wilderness dreamscape." One of these pioneers spoke for them all when he wrote, "A field is a wonderful place," and they were uplifted by seeing what a beautiful country they had, with bursting, luxuriant growth on all sides. It seemed incredible that they were headed for places where they could claim acres and acres like these as their own.

Some of the travelers were frontiersmen at heart who were captivated by tales of Daniel Boone, a lone hunter who went on into very old age, roaming with only a rifle as his best friend. Men of this type, and more than a few women, loved movement for its own sake—always determined to find out what was beyond that forest or over that next hill. They even made rafts and crossed the Father of Waters, the majestic Mississippi, not caring that it was the country's western boundary and the other side was off limits because it was owned by Europeans.

But many more of the migrants consisted of families who had grown tired of hearing about this "land of opportunity," for they foresaw years of drudge work for small wages before a better life could be expected. It seemed to them that the "new world" they heard so much about was already owned by others. Why not try to make a really new world where they would be the property owners? The idea of moving brought excitement. They struck out for rich, untitled land that they might claim as "squatters." And there were a good many well-to-do financial adventurers, usually on horseback, who were enticed by battalions of speculators into investing their savings in acreage that might make them rich.

This initial joy abated a bit when departing travelers began to feel the disapproval of those who stayed behind. They would say good-bye to neighbors and get the barest smile in return. Or, "We'll try to get word back to you," and receive only a silent, glum nod. Accounts of early travel give the impression that people who told neighbors about projected moves often found that the less-adventurous persons felt threatened by their plans. After such a leave taking, the first few days on the move were tinged with resentment—a feeling of being misunderstood.

By the early 1790s, this mass migration was seriously dividing the country. Even those who had no intention of moving felt forced to choose between considering themselves to be "easterners" or "westerners." It was not just a matter of location; it was also a mind-set about the nation's future. The westward flight was frightening and infuriating to many in the original thirteen states, especially those in the north. Many of their laborers were being pulled away, forcing employers to pay higher wages as workers grew scarce. Worse yet, the easterners feared that the mad westward push would involve them in expensive wars. The old European powers, whose landholdings covered most of the continent, would surely resent the threat of encroachment and move to block the Americans before they converged on the Mississippi area in greater numbers. "What then?" the eastern people wondered, fearing that their own young men might be called to defend the west.

Many Americans, especially in New England, saw no reason for the United States to be stirring up trouble with this further growth. "The frontier should stop at the Appalachians!" had become the easterners' insistent cry. Tensions ran so high that some were seriously suggesting that a small group of northeastern states should form a new nation with people who had more in common:

anti-expansion and anti-slavery beliefs. The other core conviction of this group was one that might seem surprising so soon after the Revolutionary War: they thought that the congenial states should favor Britain in its war with France. They knew America owed the French a debt for having helped in the fight for freedom, but the mother country was still the major source of America's income. Great Britain, the country that the U.S. had spurned and defeated, still provided three-fourths of its world trade, and most of the U.S. government's funds came from the customs duties on that trade.

A sharp portrait of how easterners saw themselves in contrast to westerners was drawn later by American historian Henry Adams, who pointed out that most of the original colonies had prided themselves on living by great moral and civic purposes. With irony, he went on to say, "It is no wonder that foreign observers, and even the educated, well-to-do Americans of the seacoast, could seldom see anything to admire in the ignorance and brutality of frontiersmen and should declare that virtue and wisdom no longer guided the United States!"

Yet, no rule is secure without its exception. Thomas Jefferson, a universal symbol of refinement, was a dedicated westerner at heart. For a time, when he was American minister to Paris, he had become very "French," dressing in the latest mode; taking pride in his knowledge of France's foods, wines, and culture; and visiting the greatest salons, where he paid compliments to ladies with a Gallic flair. Since his intellectual interests were genuine, he kept them up after returning home. However, he realized that stylish dress and manner would be a political handicap in America, so his appearance swung in the opposite direction. From then on, he would never wear a proper wig, often appeared in slippers, and gave the appearance of being carelessly dressed. Somehow, with his fine features and intellectual brow, this casual look was taken to be a sign of elegance. But *poseur* that he was, he had some core interests that never slackened. Regardless of pretenses, no "brutal frontiersman" was more committed to the idea of expanding to the west than this son of Virginia was.

Jefferson had been attracted to western lore since his boyhood. Growing up, he had thought repeatedly of the land beyond the Blue Ridge, though he had never traveled there. He had been dazzled by reading that a young Frenchman, Pierre Radisson, after years as a captive of Native Americans, had told of lakes as great as oceans and a massive river the origins of which no one knew. And then, closer to his own time, were the reports that La Salle's journey down the Ohio River had produced rapturous descriptions of lands "so beautiful, so fertile, so full of meadows, brooks, and rivers, so abounding in fish, game, and venison…The soil will produce everything that is raised in France….There can be no doubt that colonies planted here would become very prosperous." Moreover, the ill-fated young La Salle had estimated, in 1682, that the total drainage area of the Mississippi River, which he claimed for France, was some 1,240,000 square miles. Since only 240,000 of that was thought to be on the east side of the river, this meant there might be one million square miles west of the Mississippi. It was the size, the vastness, that captivated Jefferson then and into the future—and the fact that nothing was being done with it.

As a young Williamsburg lawyer, Jefferson had been quick to become a revolutionary. But immediately after the war, despite a pressing need to care for his Monticello property, he went back to active research into the western country. A notation in one of Jefferson's papers mentions "the great salty sea on the other side." He could not have known much about the Pacific Ocean, for the western part of the continent had barely been approached. Sir Francis Drake had sailed along the Pacific coast without landing. Spanish priests and monks had set up missions inland, and a few thousand Spanish settlers were living around Santa Fe and Albuquerque, mostly doing business with the Pueblo Native Americans, who had developed a new demand for horses. To the south, Spain had succeeded in countering La Salle's claim to Texas by sending in military men to accompany the intrepid Jesuits in the 1690s, but the province remained wild and little changed for more than another century.

The bits of information from such sources did not combine to answer what Jefferson wanted to know about the Mississippi and what the travel beyond it would be like. What directions could a raft go along various other rivers he had heard of—the Arkansas, Missouri, and Red Rivers? The center of the continent was largely conjecture; neither its size nor shape could be reliably envisioned. Then, in 1778, when Jefferson was well into his thirties, an amazing new volume came into his hands.

Jonathan Carver, who had been a British army surveyor in America, had failed in searching for a route that would link Hudson's Bay with the Pacific Coast, but he had covered so much uncharted ground that he wrote a remarkable book about the New World. After eight years of trying unsuccessfully to find a publisher, Carver was a penniless dying man when one printer finally risked a small press run—and made a fortune. It led to one of the most successful travel books of all time, *Travels through the Interior Parts of North America in the Years 1766, 1767, and 1768*, reprinted some forty times and in every modern language. It might also be said to have led to the Louisiana Purchase, for the impact of a book depends as much on who reads it as on what it says.

What struck Jefferson was that Carver's map made the North American continent seem more than three thousand miles wide, a great deal larger than others estimated. Carver gave the impression of being such a reliable observer that Jefferson's old absorption with that huge river and the great expanse beyond it was fired again. For now, he filed the map in his memory bank, certainly thinking grimly what a giant empire either Spain or France could develop next to the smaller United States. Five years later, Jefferson saw corroborating facts in a book by John Ledyard, who had sailed with the famous Captain Cook. This volume also estimated that the land west of the Mississippi must be very wide, based on a new method of calculating longitude.

Jefferson began to think more positively of how the U.S. might move faster to expand westward before traders or troops from Britain, France, or Spain began to block any hopes for the young nation to gain a firmer hold on the continent. Among other things, Jefferson saw something suspicious in the reason the British offered to hold on to its forts in the west long after the date of departure that a treaty had specified. Their excuse was the false accusation that the U.S. was not living up to its own treaty obligations. But Jefferson harbored a suspicion that the U.S. had not seen the last of British attempts to rule the new continent. Even when he was in Paris as the American minister in 1784, Jefferson was so concerned about this menacing behavior that he had asked James Monroe, then a young Virginia legislator who had studied law under Jefferson's guidance, to explore the land during the vacation months. In August 1784, Monroe wrote back, reporting on a projected observation trip westward "to acquire a better knowledge of the posts which we should occupy, the cause of the delay of the evacuation by British troops...the temper of the Indians toward us, as well as of the soil, waters, and in general the natural view of the country." It raises the question: Was Jefferson thinking, even then, of a possible expansion beyond the Mississippi into territory that belonged to Spain?

Whether or not that was the case as early as 1784, it was certainly true nine years later, when Jefferson heard that a famous French botanist, Andre Michaux, was trying to persuade directors of the American Philosophical Society to let him attempt an exploration across the Continental Divide to the Pacific Ocean. Jefferson was instantly enthusiastic about the plan, saying that its scientific nature could rule out any charge of illicit trespassing in foreign territory, and he raised a substantial sum of money for it, including a donation from George Washington. The detailed letter of instructions that he prepared for Michaux showed that Jefferson had, by then, learned enough about the still barely explored territory to give meaningful directions. For instance, he asked Michaux to find "the shortest and most convenient route of communication between the United States and the Pacific, within the temperate latitudes," to give special attention to the Missouri River as the route of unquestioned preference (for much of the money subscribed had been based on this hope), then to find the shortest route to some other river that would enter the Pacific Ocean. And on that subject, he mentioned that the latest maps seemed to show "that a river called Oregon interlocked with the Missouri for a considerable distance and entered the Pacific Ocean not far southward of Nootka Sound."

In addition to specifics such as soil, rivers, mountains, crops, animals, inhabitants, numbers of dwellings, and the state of society, arts, and commerce, Jefferson commented on the need to avoid Spanish settlements, and to preserve any observations on birch bark and other secure materials that would not excite suspicion. However scientific the purpose might be, it was clearly clandestine. These inquiries, he wrote, "are for the enlargement of science in general, but of the United States in particular, to whom your report will open new fields and subjects of commerce, intercourse, and observation."

All of Jefferson's feelings for the westerners' cause were fully reciprocated. Much of the world might have admired him for his taste and intellect, but the frontier people cherished him for his tireless work on their behalf. Many a mug of ale was raised to his health, for they knew about some of his practical accomplishments that were major victories in the struggle against the stand-pat easterners. During the past several years, even when his own political party was out of power, he had headed a committee that gave 350,000 square miles of unused state property between the Appalachians and the Mississippi to the government as public land for future settlers. This expanse would eventually become the states of Indiana, Illinois, Ohio, Michigan, Wisconsin, and part of Minnesota. He also had a hand in making it amazingly easy to get a new state started. A ruling called the Northwest Ordinance of 1787 promised self-government to any new territory that had a population of at least five thousand, and full-fledged statehood would come when a population of sixty thousand was reached. With these lures, the speed of growth in the western areas was astonishing; Virginia's Kentucky County already had 140,000 residents.

The frontier people also loved what Jefferson wrote. When the country's fifteenth state was being formed, he contributed the rousingly free-spirited Kentucky Resolutions, writing:

> Resolved, that the several states composing the United States of America are not united on the principle of unlimited submission to their general government.... That the government created by this compact was not made the exclusive or final judge of the extent of the powers delegated to itself....Each party has an equal right to judge for itself....

Nor was it a political handicap that Jefferson openly mistrusted the leaders of commerce and finance, feeling that they tried to influence governmental affairs just as selfishly as the aristocrats of Europe did. So he pressed the idea of promoting an agricultural society, urging the government to help worthy people to acquire land, even if they lacked the money to do so. As he saw it, however, a society that was primarily based on agriculture need not preclude a close, profitable, and enduring union with parts of the country that were devoted to commerce and industry.

As if they were trying to prove the easterners' point that expansion could lead to war with Europeans, the Spanish made repeated threats to close the Mississippi to American traffic. Spain had only acquired the Louisiana Territory in 1762, in a strange transaction that showed how unimportant these distant possessions could seem to those who reigned over some of the world's leading nations.

Louisiana had long belonged to France because early French explorers had claimed it for their king. Attempts to colonize it profitably had failed miserably, and the territory was a steady drain on the royal treasury. The Duc de Choiseul, the cleverest minister in the cabinet of Louis XV, had an idea for getting rid of it while appearing to pay a debt of honor at the same time. In 1762, he convinced a young Spanish king, Charles III, to accept this huge white elephant as a repayment for the losses Spain had suffered a year earlier when, loyal to a pact of the Bourbon family, it had joined France in a war against England. The British had taken both Cuba and the Spanish Philippines away from Spain, and were demanding Spain's holdings in Florida as the price of giving them back. A secret treaty between France and Spain signed at Fontainebleau on November 3, 1762, left many property rights in an unsettled state, but it was clear that the huge Louisiana Territory west of the Mississippi would henceforth belong to Spain. The demoralized Spanish had only vague ideas about what use they might make of the vast lands. However, they realized they could dominate a great expanse with just a small force stationed in the key city of New Orleans, which could easily pinch off traffic into and out of the Mississippi River.

In 1784, Spain's first minister, Count Floridablanca, announced that he would close off U.S. shipping on the Mississippi, cancel the right of American shippers to store goods in New Orleans for trans-shipment to the world, and establish river patrols to make sure the new orders were carried out. Fortunately, when Spain was involved, such things were usually discussed at great length before going into effect. A new Spanish ambassador would be coming, and John Jay, whom some considered the country's shrewdest negotiator, was named as the American who would debate the issue with him.

Jefferson was just leaving on his assignment as American envoy to Paris, where events were also at a delicate point. Even from far away, relying on news that was two months old, Jefferson followed the progress of events with misgivings, for he knew Jay to have a strong leaning toward the eastern business and financial interests. When Jay's proposed trade treaty with Spain was made known in 1786, it was even worse for the westerners than Jefferson had expected. Newspapers that sided with Jefferson referred to it as "the infamous treaty." Jay had concentrated on gaining lower tariffs for American ships carrying goods to Spain, which would almost entirely benefit the eastern shippers. But he had won these concessions by agreeing that Spain could close off "for twenty or thirty years" the rights of navigation and the privilege of depositing goods in transit at New Orleans. It was like draining the lifeblood away from the west and using it to give a grand transfusion to the eastern shipping interests. The ships from New York and New England would have enjoyed a business surge, but farmers in the Mississippi area and shippers who handled their products would have seen their business wither. The treaty was so one-sided that it died after an explosion of anger in Congress, falling short of ratification by two votes.

Nothing would ever be the same again, as Jefferson had foreseen in a burning letter to James Madison, sent from Paris in January 1787.

Simply put, he made it clear that the frontier people now held the power to kill the Jay Treaty without help from the rest of the nation. In these words, he predicted that they could secede from the Union and that other Americans would never take up arms against them:

> The act which abandons the navigation of the Mississippi is an act of separation between the eastern and western country. It is a relinquishment of five parts out of eight of the territory of the United States....If the frontiersmen declare themselves a separate people, we are incapable of a single effort to retain them. Our citizens can never be induced, either as militia or as soldiers, to go there to cut the throats of their own brothers and sons....They are able already to rescue the navigation of the Mississippi out of the hands of Spain and to add New Orleans to their own territory.

No matter how this came out, the botched treaty had made far more Americans aware that the nation was seriously divided. If the U.S. accepted Spain's terms, the frontier Americans who were being treated like aliens would simply arm for battle and arrange their own version of free navigation. What troubled Jefferson most was not whether the frontier people would win, but whether the original states could bring the furious "Kentuckians" (as all the people of the river area were often called) back into the national fold. They were being besieged with offers of partnership from many European powers, but, in fact, they were numerous enough to survive independently, if they chose to do so.

This point was demonstrated when self-appointed leaders in the areas that were to become Kentucky and Tennessee roused thousands of followers—settlers who had a lot at stake and frontiersmen who would relish a fight—to abandon an America that did not seem to know they existed. They were listening seriously to the offers that British secret agents were making to them—to leave a flimsy confederation that seemed powerless to defend its members. The offer to rejoin England not only promised active support for the westerners' ambitions, but actually invited them to name their own terms.

The western parts of many states had Americans who were interested in such a proposal. A few even listened to Spanish offers to cross the Mississippi to Spanish Louisiana, where the "legitimate owners of the land" vowed to resist both the English and the Americans. And some adventurers claimed that they already owned sufficient acreage to declare themselves independent states, and then see which country would make them the best offer. One wealthy man was purported to have set up a viable state, with the universally respected name "Franklin."

Other histories have said enough about strong secessionist movements to indicate that the several years surrounding this moment were the time of greatest peril to the nation's survival. At other serious times—as when the legality of a president was challenged or even when a civil war was fought—the traditions and the spirit of belonging that had been built up made a majority of Americans determined to hold on to the citizenship they had grown up with. But when the nation was just a few years old, there was no such unifying compulsion.

No one can be sure how badly out of control things might have spun if the Constitutional Convention had not been convened in 1787. News of the convention had come as a thunderclap—it was a political miracle. With Jefferson in Paris, two other great political warriors had to set their long enmity aside to make it happen. Alexander Hamilton would prove that he did not want his pro-eastern, pro-British leanings to tear the country apart. And Jefferson's great friend James Madison, whose quiet, concise words so often contained the kernel of how any issue would be resolved, would supply the basic ideas that were to form a constitution for the ages. When those two enemies made the sacrifice of coming together, everybody knew a lasting compromise was possible.

From their estates, plantations, and major cities, the other patriots who had been through so much together rode to Philadelphia for one more meeting. The news of this great gathering became widely known. The presence there of so many leading citizens, who possessed the national and international prestige of having defeated England, momentarily quieted the secessionist clamor. The world stood still, waiting to see whether the unstable confederation would really make itself into a forceful union.

As soon as it was learned that a strong constitution had been agreed on, and especially when it became apparent that the extremely popular George Washington would become president, talk of deserting the United States evaporated. Leaders in Kentucky and Tennessee who had been flirting with thoughts of secession were grateful when they were given the chance to work toward statehood. Kentucky entered the union in 1792 and Tennessee in 1796—the first trans-Appalachian states. Luckily, the world didn't imagine that Washington's government had less than a thousand men in uniform when he let it be known that he would move on New Orleans if anyone tried to interfere with Mississippi traffic. If George Washington made such a threat, who could question it?

Now that the United States possessed a respected constitution, there was a gradual improvement in the way Europeans treated the country. Even the sleepy government of Spain—though it took nearly a decade—finally awoke to the fact that the Mississippi issue had been dangling alarmingly and the western Americans were becoming infuriated at the uncertainty of their status. A new first minister, Manuel de Godoy, decided in 1795 that he would be happy to open talks on the subject with President Washington's envoy, Thomas Pinckney.

The very competent Pinckney waited patiently in Madrid as dozens of tiny points kept being introduced and the talks dragged on. However, when two months had passed in that way, he suddenly asked Godoy to return his passport so he could go home and "report to President Washington." This, in diplomatic language, would mean that the talks had broken down.

Pinckney reported that at the mere mention of the president's name, Godoy said he had an agreement upstairs waiting to be signed. It gave American ships the right to navigate the Mississippi freely for a minimum of three years and foresaw the likelihood of extension. On the following day, Pinckney signed, toasts were drunk, and the Senate later approved the treaty without a dissenting vote.

In a flash, the Louisiana crisis appeared to be over. The Mississippi River, although still the U.S. boundary of which the west bank was technically foreign, was wide open for use as America's "west coast."

A sense of relief swept over the country, as United States foreign relations were seen as being in a more settled condition. It was soon apparent, however, that Spain's accession to America's demands had been only the first act of a longer play, in which a daring European leader unlike any other would take center stage.

On 12 Fructidor, Year III (August 29, 1795), an inexperienced officer of the shaky Directory government was trying to put down the royalists and revolutionaries who were vying to take over the streets of Paris. He nervously asked for someone with artillery training to help him subdue the multiple threat.

"Call Buonaparte!" shouted an officer named Turreau, who had seen Napoleon's mastery during the siege of Toulon, using the four-syllable Italian pronunciation of the name that Napoleon had brought from Corsica. Napoleon, "an odd little chap whose penury was still evident in his disorderly dress, his long unkempt hair, and the antiquated look of his clothing," as biographer Andre Castelot memorably put it had been brought forward. But that impression was wiped away within seconds, for it was the brevity of his words, the decisiveness, that riveted every man and speeded each one's reactions.

"How many troops do you have?" Napoleon shouted.

"Five thousand."

"And your artillery?"

"There are forty cannons."

"Where?"

"Plaine des Sablons."

Without a pause, Buonaparte called for a cavalry officer, who turned out to be a large, handsome man named Murat, and told him, "Take two hundred horses. Go immediately to the Plaine des Sablons, and bring back the forty cannons. Use your sabers, if you have to, but bring them here. You answer to me if you don't! Go!"

The Convention that was trying to set up a stronger government was saved. Five days later, the commanding general of the Army of the Interior, Barras, named Napoleon his deputy commander. By October 26, Barras had resigned, and Buonaparte was the commanding general and also one of the five Directors.

Napoleon Bonaparte (he had dropped the "u" to make the name sound more French) was soon given command of the Army of Italy, a rag-tag group that he inspired and turned into a free-wheeling victory machine. Together, they appeared to reinvent geography over the next four years of marches through Europe and even into Egypt, giving the impression of an imperialist and conqueror who recognized no limitations. As the American presidential election year of 1800 approached, Napoleon's stated interest in creating a separate French empire in America had become a subject of conversation in the new capital city of Washington, D.C., with a place on the congressional agenda.

The French had been America's wartime friends, helping the country gain independence. But the true meaning of that independence was being questioned when America's foreign commerce with England was its lifeblood and while both England and France were often capturing American ships that each suspected of carrying goods to the other.

A candid series of letters written by Congressman Joshua Coit of Connecticut to his brother Daniel provides a years-long account of the anger that raged between northerners and southerners, between those who were pro-British and those who were pro-French. At one point, Coit wrote "One would have expected a different complexion from these owners of slaves and men of large fortunes." [He meant that slave-owning aristocrats would not have been expected to seem so approving of the anti-aristocratic and bloody French Revolution]. And again, "Some of our southern gentlemen, Virginians especially, have a most unconquerable aversion for the British nation, and partiality for France."

Over and over, he wrote of the wrangling in Congress as so nearly hopeless that, as he put it, "It is a doubt with many whether our present form of government continue many years." And his fear of being caught up in the war between England and France led repeatedly to the thought: "Should a war take place, I think we have scarcely ground to hope a continuance of the Union." But with or without war, this reasonable, normally quiet legislator felt duty bound to apprise his brother: "The jealousies which exist in the

Southern States...added to some strange and fantastical notions about liberty which they entertain...render the continuance of our Union for many years...doubtful."

Such talk had been common under the weak Confederation, but it was shocking to hear it now. Though trying to move together in harness, the states were determined to be themselves. In the capital city, the political differences seemed unbridgeable. But when observed from a distance—from Europe, for instance—it could be seen that the unruly team was moving boldly forward. Growth and prosperity restrained even the hottest tempers and added comforts that made conflict bearable. The easterners, their industries, and their financiers were thriving. The country's credit was so good that every foreign money house was eager to offer loans at low rates. The frontier people were doing equally well, for the nation's much-debated expansion was an insubstantial issue with little foundation. Westward expansion was an ongoing fact of life. Following on the recent statehood of Kentucky and Tennessee, several other communities were building populations that would soon qualify to join them.

But so much success made it all the more dreadful to envision a possible collapse of true American independence, for prosperity did not guarantee the physical ability to bar Napoleon Bonaparte from sending boatloads of battle-tested troops to make himself America's unwanted neighbor in Louisiana. Nor was there any certainty that the British, who clearly coveted the prime location of New Orleans, might not make a sudden move to possess it.

Vice President Thomas Jefferson narrowly won the presidency from his estranged friend John Adams in the fall of 1800. And as he looked ahead to the perils he would begin to face the following spring, he feared Napoleonic France the most. Napoleon had been known to say that he dreamed of a new French empire in America.

True, France had made a grand gesture in giving Louisiana to Spain in 1762. But if Napoleon, now known as the First Consul, had shown the world anything in these scintillating fifty months, it was that the only treaty he respected was the one he was hastily writing at the moment. He already dominated the Spanish government, so forcing it to give Louisiana back to France would be easy to do. He also had part of a large, rich, and productive island called Saint Domingue (which Americans have usually called Santo Domingo because another half of the same island was Spanish-owned) in the Caribbean, which could be used as a springboard for a troop movement to the mainland. And he held scattered French trading outposts in remote parts of the American continent that had better ties to the Native Americans than other nations had been able to achieve.

The United States had almost no defense in place to oppose such a Napoleonic adventure—less than a thousand men in uniform and no navy. Against them might suddenly come many thousands, directed by the man who had roused a tattered and hungry French army in Italy in 1796 and destroyed a succession of enemies with a speed that was without parallel in military history. And, if he had convinced the pliable Spanish to give him back Louisiana, he would have a technical right to be there, controlling the Mississippi River and most of the continent that lay beyond it. How could a new nation dedicated to the rule of law defend itself against a "legal" neighbor whose intentions it regarded as far from legitimate? What arguments or what forces would it use?

American newspapers, which were especially taken with the glamour and excitement of news from France, carried innumerable items about Napoleon. Not only the French-language *Le Moniteur de la Louisiane,* but *The New York Morning Chronicle, The New York Evening News, The Alexandria Gazette,* and many others gave more space to French items—Napoleon's moves against press freedom, his dispatch of a warning squadron to Tunis, his discussion of a possible successor, and most of all, his interest in Louisiana—than to British ones.

As president-elect Thomas Jefferson waited to take office, his chief preoccupation was to search for a way to bar this unwanted neighbor.

Chapter Two

FRIENDLY FRANCE THREATENS AMERICA

E ven months before his inauguration in March 1801, Thomas Jefferson had anxiously sifted through reports and letters from friends abroad for signs that might indicate whether his fear of Napoleon's threat to America was justified. He had a hunch, rather than a specific reason, for believing the French might suddenly move into Louisiana, turning America's world upside down. Learning that such a move was under way might not bring a means of counteracting it, but it was normal to feel that there might be some advantage in being forewarned.

Then, as now, other countries knew much more about what was happening in America than Americans knew about what the other nations were up to. The transparency of American society, contrasted with the opacity of what went on in the Old World, created a curious imbalance when it was desperately important to know what the dictatorship in France was planning. Informed guesswork was the chief source of the American government's advance planning, and it was a frighteningly shaky platform on which to build a nation's future.

After having had just one coastline—the Atlantic—the westward migration had led to so much productivity and world trade along the Mississippi that the United States now possessed the equivalent of a second seacoast. But it was clear that possession of New Orleans could open or seal off so great a waterway. Against this threat was the fact that thousands of Americans who had been lured westward to see the Mississippi would defend their rights to it. But the nation's unity depended on whether their fellow Americans in the east would see this great waterway as their Mississippi, too.

On the brink of the new century, when he was still unsure whether his run for president would succeed, Jefferson's concern about New Orleans, the Mississippi, and the west reached a new height. The altered style of French leadership was clearly a potential threat to America, a jarring change from the friend and ally that France had always been. Napoleon was one of three consuls, but the names of the other two were hardly worth noting. It was already clear that Napoleon virtually dominated Spain. Would he, at some point, simply order Spain to hand the Louisiana Territory back to France and proceed with the dream of a new empire in America?

The United States, although troubled by Spain's occasional interference with Mississippi traffic, considered its acts more a bother than a serious threat. The Spanish had mainly abided by a comfortable arrangement for American shipments that traveled down the great river to be warehoused at moderate cost and then exported to the outside world. Spain had twice threatened that it might act to stifle the burgeoning Mississippi River traffic, but that had created only excitement, not panic, for the Spanish had fallen into a comic-opera way of doing things. Their threats or edicts usually carried distant extended dates. It would be a different matter if such a threat were to come from Napoleon Bonaparte, for his actions could be explosive and devastating. Or he might even act without the courtesy of a threat. The clearer it became that Napoleon was giving orders to Spain, the more agitated Jefferson grew about his early insight that the French dictator might simply insist that the Spanish give the whole Louisiana Territory back to France, allowing him to go forward with extensive colonization. To the Spanish, such an order would have been an embarrassment, but not a great shock, for it will be recalled that Spain had acquired the title as a royal gift and held it for only a few decades.

Few examples of bad government have ever been as egregious (fortunately so for the United States) as Europe's disinterest in and mismanagement of the vast wilderness in the heart of North America. However much the French and Spanish explorers had exulted about the grandeur and richness of the limited areas they had seen, the rulers asked them mostly, "Is there much gold?" Invariably, the explorers would reply in the affirmative, because it was the only way they could obtain funds for new explorations. Both these countries concentrated on sending mostly adventurers and missionaries to search for gold or convert the natives. Only the British colonists looked at the land and saw all the ways that hard-working people—creating farms, shops, services, and whole communities—could earn more "gold" in the North American wilderness than the Old World had ever offered.

Now, however, Jefferson and Madison saw that France was ruled by a determined conqueror whose talents extended far beyond the military. He was known to be a skilled administrator over the areas he controlled. Even in his ill-fated invasion of Egypt in 1798, he had shown some "Jeffersonian" traits, for he had taken along artists, scientists, and historical scholars. What if this man should come into New Orleans with the right and title to rule as he pleased, with a plan to send troops and colonists to reassert the French identity of the city, take up old French ties with Native American tribes far to the north and west, and move to control the Mississippi? After America had been unopposed for so long that the presence of other powers on the continent had been largely forgotten, it came as a shock that Napoleonic France would probably try to impose a heavy price on United States shipping, and ultimately aim to be master of lands stretching to the Pacific. The British, with troops in Canada, would surely clash with the French, and that would force the United States to choose between the mother country and the former wartime ally—either of which would expect to dominate the newer nation. It became clear how fortunate the United States had been to have such indolent neighbors in its enormous, mysterious backyard throughout the eighteenth century's formative years. But those happy days might be slipping away.

In the mind games to come, President Jefferson would have more than just Napoleon to contend with. As knowledgeable as he was about France, he realized that Napoleon's own ambitions were enhanced by at least two first-class ministers, whose strategic brilliance and keen understanding of the Americas could well mean that shrewd plots aimed toward the New World were already under way. One was the legendary foreign minister Charles Maurice de Talleyrand-Périgord, whose ethical principles Napoleon questioned but tolerated because of his diplomatic adroitness and creativity. The other was France's impeccably honest finance minister, François de Barbé-Marbois, who had served in Philadelphia as secretary of the French Legation when he was just over thirty years old, loved America almost as much as he loved France, and retained a great many devoted American friends. Still, he was a loyal Frenchman and undoubtedly faithful to his ruler. France would come first in his thinking.

Jefferson faced a dilemma, for he had long regarded France as America's perpetual ally. Favoring France over England was one of his Republican Party's firm principles. But he was determined not to allow America to become another victim of Napoleon. Almost as feverishly as Napoleon himself did, Jefferson solicited the views of his many friends, especially those who traveled frequently to Europe, and examined their responses for clues to French planning.

On the official side, the president's principal source of help and support was James Madison, the close friend he would select as his secretary of state. So small, pale, and weightless that he seemed hardly there, and always in delicate health, the five-foot, four-inch Madison was fighting an intestinal illness when the new administration took office. He therefore worked from his Virginia home, Montpelier, about thirty miles from Jefferson's Monticello. But he invariably made Jefferson's concerns his own, so he turned his penetrating intelligence to divining the enigma of the Napoleonic mind. Already, there existed frequent courier trips between the two homes, a custom that would continue throughout the Jefferson administration.

New Orleans was far and away the overriding subject on the administration's mind. Any number of highly charged cabinet decisions had to be made, congressional tangles unknotted, and inter-party feuds smoothed over. But to Jefferson, the success of his presidency and the destiny of the nation would depend on whether he could keep America essentially free of foreign intrusion. Jefferson's elation about the western country was almost forgotten in a climate of fear. As late as 1802, he and Madison were seeing Louisiana mainly as a threat, not as an opportunity. They were mostly concerned about ways to keep it from growing into a great French empire and turning the United States into a battleground, perhaps caught between the rivals, France and England.

As much as Jefferson and Madison agreed on nearly every subject, the pair did have divergent views on how to deal with the Napoleonic threat. Some signs now seem to point to a difference between the two men about strategy. It is not clear why, but Madison appears to have been less concerned than Jefferson about France's possible moves into the New World. Repeatedly, one finds notes he wrote on the subject that seem to take a rather relaxed attitude, in marked contrast to Jefferson's show of great anxiety.

But Madison was so clever—as is seen by his skillful spreading of falsehoods to confuse the French in the subsequent two years—that this unworried manner could also have had a strategic cause. Whatever the reason, any difference of opinion with Jefferson was kept far short of hostility, probably because of exceptional prudence and self-control on Madison's part. One of his many rare qualities was an ability to endure with equanimity any amount of disagreement in a dispute. Even a member of the opposition Federalist party who expected to be recalled from his post overseas said, "If Madison be Secretary of State, there will be more justice and liberality of opinions....He is the best of them all." As rare as it was to enjoy such esteem from opponents, it was perhaps even more astonishing that a man could be so close to the often-tempestuous Jefferson and yet keep the relationship stable.

James Madison, in short, stood apart from the other participants. Some were masters of strategy, others of language, but none were as incisive and decisive, so that a quiet and modest sentence often made it seem that there was nothing more to be said on the subject. It was a special talent, over and above mere intelligence, much as a great musician or artist might accomplish feats of beauty with a naturalness that he or she can not explain. Facts that seemed murky to others were immediately clear to him. Even though Jefferson was often in the habit of making statements that might not survive until the next day, he was probably sincere—and not so very far from the mark—when he said, "James Madison is the greatest man in the world."

Where Jefferson repeatedly warned that the U.S. might join with Britain to block France, Madison felt certain that the French already had that fear in mind, so he made the point stronger by leaving it up to Napoleon to make the conclusion on his own. Madison's opinions, although never fervently stated, were exceptionally strong. On the American worry that an East-West split might break up the union, for instance, Jefferson was distinctly of two minds, but Madison saw no reason to doubt the outcome. "The Western people believe, as do their Atlantic brethren, that they have a natural and indefeasible right to trade freely through the Mississippi," Madison wrote. "They are conscious of their power to enforce this right against any nation whatever."

Even Jefferson's approach to risk-taking lacked the authority of Madison's direct aim on a target; the two of them together formed a superb team. Jefferson, though he had to work at it, managed to exude the confidence that Madison truly felt, and his presence, his exalted language, made everyone quickly feel that he was expressing just what they all believed. Madison, because he was so small and pallid, was nearly always underestimated by those who were first making his acquaintance. But the wisest persons soon realized that he was the greater statesman in the room, and some even said "a giant." Over time, good observers saw that whatever the issue, he was likely to end on the winning side. This might occasionally be slow to develop, as when "the rights revolution of the 20th century fulfilled Madison's original vision of 1787," in the words of one of Madison's biographers. Another, looking at the rare teamwork between Madison and Jefferson, wrote, "The effect was to put Madison's reasoning behind the combined projects, with the force of it coming from the temper of the American people."

Madison's rocky start as secretary of state stemmed from a serious attack of "bilious fever"—to which his delicate body was subject—and doctors talked of how much better he might be if he were in the "pure air he breathed at home." Actually, he felt that "the application of his mind to things more congenial to it than the vexatory details of a farm" did him an amazing amount of good. To a man of his cerebral interests, the play of problems and strategies called for by international diplomacy was pure recreation compared to the rude challenges of the farming life.

Despite his preference for his duties in the administration, there was a malaria season in humid Washington that really had to be avoided. So Madison and Jefferson both set up a custom of withdrawing to their country places year after year. At such times, they made numerous personal visits to each other, supplemented by a steady stream of notes. Their work actually seemed to go more smoothly in the country than in the new capital, for they were less troubled by interruptions, and the special couriers did double duty in arranging for virtually every important paper to be seen by both and often reviewed more than once as changes were inscribed.

The new secretary of state had selected fewer than a dozen men who would make up the professional core of the State Department, most of them experienced because they were holdovers from the past administrations of John Marshall and Timothy Pickering. As serious as the situation often seemed, the administration had its light moments, as was shown by the humorous nicknames that Jefferson and Madison gave to State Department aides, based on the history of their employment. Those who had worked under Secretary Pickering were called "picaroons," which was also a slang word for thieves. One was damned as a "Hamiltonian," because he had come in under a Federalist administration, and Alexander Hamilton was that party's leader. Those who had no strong affiliation were nonetheless slurred as "nothingarians" or "nincompoops." The obvious good-naturedness of this banter is confirmed by the fact that Daniel Brent, although called an absolute nincompoop, still worked

for the department in 1837 and showed his relish for the Madisonian days when he complimented President Van Buren on one occasion by saying that his message to Congress "reminded me of Mr.
Madison, who understood the use and value of words better than
any other man."

When it came to dealing with the diplomats of long-established
nations, the infant American government was surprisingly adroit.
Any impression that Franklin and Jefferson were the only exceptional men who had quickly adapted to dealing with the Old World
on its own terms is misleading. There were less than a dozen persons
with diplomatic status in America's foreign service, but most quickly
established themselves as the cultural equals of the British and continental diplomats they were sent to deal with.

In a day when northerners tended to think that most well-to-do
southerners must be crude, slave-driving boors, the administration's
minister to Madrid was Charles Pinckney, a polished South Car-
olinian, who had been a success on several diplomatic missions, as
had his cousin, Thomas Pinckney, some years earlier. Rufus King,
from Massachusetts, the American envoy to London, would one day
become a serious candidate for U.S. president. He once beguiled
Lord Hawkesbury, the British foreign secretary, by quoting Mon-
tesquieu's observation that "It is happy for trading powers that God
has permitted Turks and Spaniards to be in the world, since of all
nations they are the most proper to possess a great empire with
insignificance." The Englishman understood this sophisticated slur
to mean that the United States felt safe with the insignificant Spanish in control of Louisiana, but would not welcome a change to
more aggressive French ownership. By agreeing with the quotation,
he implied that England felt the same way about Louisiana, and
both men were clearly pleased at having a meeting of the minds
without any need to speak bluntly. Since America and Britain were

alike in wanting to block a Napoleonic seizure of New Orleans, they could exchange subtle opinions on this subject, even at a time when they were at swords' points on other issues.

Several of the departmental aides in Washington and all the diplomats abroad had been specially briefed on the arcane Louisiana matter that could mean peace or war—indeed, open horizons or encirclement—to a nation that had never known such a fear or limitation in its short history. But they, like President Jefferson in all his personal inquiries, failed utterly in the opening round of hide-and-seek with Napoleon.

The new administration thought it was leaving no avenue untried in its search for foreign-policy information, but in fact, it was guilty of a serious oversight. While its small diplomatic staff was first-class, the related area of intelligence and espionage was almost entirely ignored. It is important to keep this subject in mind because as the Louisiana negotiations proceeded, intelligence, counterintelligence, and especially what is now called disinformation (then simply thought of as misleading the other side) played a vital role in the outcome. Napoleon began with the advantage of knowing beforehand that the U.S. would strongly oppose any French move to occupy New Orleans, leading him to be especially secretive, to make extra arrangements in preparation for trouble, and to fool the Americans with an elaborate deception early on. The new administration was slow to counter these moves, not realizing that harvesting important secrets is a separate activity, requiring its own skills and methods. So the very thing it wanted most to know—France's plan for New Orleans—was a blank page.

The State Department's failure in this area came from overlooking the fact that information is worth money. Only those who were known to pay for it got timely facts. Madison was notably slow in offering modest amounts of cash to potential informers who were working in various embassies abroad—such as the British, French, and Austrian missions. Only after a shocking situation in 1801 revealed that America had been very late in learning a crucial fact about Napoleon's plan for Louisiana did the secretary set up a small discretionary fund that he could disburse in exchange for information. Madison was very careful in managing it, for George Washington's example of Revolutionary War expenditures, minutely recorded in his own hand, had left a lasting impression.

Struggling to raise and organize a military force, Washington had not immediately been able to start a plan for gathering information. But he had spent his first money for intelligence in July 1775, even before hostilities with England had formally begun. He disbursed $333 for "someone to go into Boston and establish secret correspondence." Not long after that, he engaged a few spies to report on the movements of British vessels, and their reports enabled a little flotilla of six American ships known as "George Washington's Navy"—including the seventy-eight-ton *Hannah*—to overtake and plunder the slower English supply vessels. More serious planning for a team of spies had begun in 1777, and it grew as the Revolutionary War intensified through 1781. General Washington had first asked for special information on the health and spirits of the British army and navy men seen in New York, the number of men allotted to the defense of the city, the guarding of transports, what equipment was crossing at various key points, such as the Harlem River and the East River, and the nature of the defenses. He stressed the importance of details and absolute accuracy, and was quick to discount rumors. In an analysis after the war, Washington revealed not only how important intelligence had proved, but also how the modern-sounding science of disinformation had succeeded, for the British had been thrown off the track when Washington gave them the firm impression that the Americans and French had a fixed intention of joining together in a main attack on New York—which was never even remotely a part of their plan. He said with pleasure how he "even deceived our own army" into believing that Virginia was the object of his next move when, in fact, his troops were already on the march toward Yorktown and victory.

All these clandestine maneuvers were well known to Adams and Jefferson when they followed George Washington into the presidency. They made exceptional use of their own social contacts to learn even the smallest bits of information that could be combined into helpful insights into world affairs that might affect the United States. However, they made no immediate move to establish an effective intelligence operation. In this, as in so many things, they followed the British custom of discontinuing such activities between wars. England's first prime minister, Sir Robert Walpole, in office from 1721 to 1742, said he wanted to be sure no gun could be fired in Europe without England knowing why, and he really meant to maintain a permanent operation for that purpose. But his successors ignored his advice. Even when Britain was fighting the war against the American colonies, they were so careless about intelligence that they were surprised to learn that most of the states in Europe had formed a League of Armed Neutrality against them. An old feeling persisted, shared by both English and Americans, that espionage was an immoral activity.

Not so in France. Even before the French Revolution had everybody watching everyone else, there had been a practical feeling that knowing as much as possible was a basic part of security and self-preservation. So during the so-called Peace of Amiens between England and France—the treaty that held for only fourteen months at the start of the 1800s—the flood of English tourists who went cheerfully back to Paris couldn't help noticing the virtual orgy of secrecy and snooping that pervaded the city. Some of these British visitors were officers who were stunned to learn that the French War Ministry had a special Bureau d'Intelligence and that a select group of over one hundred men had been given special training and status as Guides-Interprêtes de l'Armée d'Angleterre, meaning that they were assigned to specialize in spying on the British Army. The touring officers quickly returned home to set up the Depot of Military Knowledge on the top floor of Horse Guards—to be ready for the resumption of war that they now knew to be inevitable.

Almost as much as the British did, the new American administration run by Jefferson and Madison finally realized the urgent need of first-class intelligence in order to safeguard the country against France's wily and professional operation. Madison seldom repeated a mistake. Although the new secretary might be faulted for not having acted on espionage sooner, it must be said that once Madison realized how many facets of intelligence required attention, he became a master of the game. His personal skill at the art of misleading the adversaries made a major difference in Napoleon's planning. And despite Madison's natural thriftiness, he came to realize that making the presence of hard cash known in the appropriate quarters was like cheese in a mouse trap, often promoting action. After that, the information did come in—most of it ominously pointing toward the likelihood that Jefferson's hunch about Louisiana was appallingly correct.

To Madison, there was little need for inspiration on this main point. He had studied the adversary's personality in detail, and it seemed clear to him that Napoleon would take back Louisiana. The idea that a First Consul had to be careful about cancelling a gift that France's King Louis XV had given to Spain's King Charles III seemed ludicrous to him. Napoleon would enjoy such a gesture immensely. The only question Madison considered worth asking was, "When will he move troops into action?" And on that point, he thought (wrongly, it turned out) that it would be sooner than expected, for Napoleon had always appeared before he was looked for. And further, he knew that Britain might otherwise try to head him off by seizing the territory first.

But even coming from Madison, all this circumstantial evidence did not give Jefferson confidence enough to make an open declaration against Napoleon. France's image as the great friend that had helped America to win its freedom was still powerful. If France were to deny convincingly that it had any designs on the Spanish holdings in America, the Jefferson administration would be making a very poor start, giving the Federalist opposition a chance to ridicule the Republicans as warmongers. The agony of fearing a sudden move on New Orleans and yet finding it impossible to act defensively was nearly maddening to Jefferson, whose growing agitation put great pressure on Madison. The president seemed to consider it his personal responsibility to learn the facts. As 1801 went on, there was a steady drumbeat of Jeffersonian queries, many of them to personal friends who were traveling abroad, and many questions posed by Madison, in a variety of guises, to foreign diplomats.

Madison also arranged for two of America's ministers abroad to ask separate questions that might cause either the French or the Spanish to give an answer that would reveal whether there was a secret deal between them giving Louisiana back to the French.

Robert Livingston, a New Yorker who was then American minister in Paris, was to ask France to sell West Florida to the United States. If France denied owning the area, he was to ask Talleyrand for assistance in buying West Florida from Spain. It was hoped that the nature of the answers to the two queries would offer a clue. (West

Florida was used as a way to avoid direct mention of New Orleans because it was thought to be a part of the Louisiana territory, as Spain and France defined it.)

Simultaneously, Charles Pinckney, in Madrid, was to try to buy West Florida from Spain. If the Spanish seemed evasive about whether the land was theirs, it might help to confirm what had been learned from the French.

But the attempted cleverness failed, and the trap netted nothing. The French denied owning West Florida, and the Spanish simply failed to answer. The Jefferson administration had not yet attained the diplomatic skills it would display later.

Nonetheless, before 1801 was half over, the belief that France was preparing to become the master of New Orleans, all of Louisiana, the Mississippi, and probably the Floridas grew steadily stronger. It is sometimes said, imprecisely, that the Louisiana negotiations began at that time. In fact, nothing that could be called negotiations occurred until early 1803, for the period between those two dates saw France making extensive preparations to occupy New Orleans and Florida, while hoping to keep the details secret in order to lessen the likelihood of armed resistance by western Americans. Neither France nor America had negotiations in mind. Napoleon was stealthily preparing for a substantial occupation, and Jefferson was considering threats that would discourage such a move.

What did appear on March 29, 1801, was a letter from Rufus King, the American envoy in London, to Secretary of State Madison. It was the first document in an invaluable collection of papers later prepared for the Congress, entitled "State Papers and Correspondence Bearing Upon the Purchase of the Territory of Louisiana." In that letter, King reported a "credible rumor of the day" that the French government had probably succeeded in convincing Spain to cede Louisiana and the Floridas to France. He added that "certain influential persons in France believed that nature has marked a line of separation between the people of the United States living upon the two sides of the range of mountains which divides their territory," apparently leading the French to expect that eastern and western Americans would not be united in their opposition to the arrival of French troops and colonists. And while King wrote that he considered this view false, he cautioned that this cession "may actually produce effects injurious to the Union and consequent happiness of the people of the United States."

King's report exacerbated the nerve-wracking situation, for it fed a growing fear that a French seizure of New Orleans might come at any moment. Although it was not published, the report became known to members of Congress, and some urged that American troops be moved into New Orleans as a preemptive measure. But that would have required a call-up of more men, and Jefferson was reluctant to consider such a warlike act. An enlarged army would have appeared to be a threat against Spain, when there was no way to prove that it was actually intended to counter a French move that was not known to have occurred. Every proposal for action or protest seemed unthinkable without being able to define just what the Americans were protesting, and what legal justification they had for trying to block a peaceful transfer of land between two friendly powers.

Such was the awkward position when Madison—undoubtedly prodded by the impatient president—felt it was time for Robert Livingston, in whom he had little confidence, to start letting Napoleon's inner circle know how seriously the United States would view any French attempt to make itself mistress of the Mississippi. Again, the administration made an awkward, stumbling move. The hypothetical nature of the complaint he wrote about clearly made Madison uneasy. He must have felt that it was arrogant and unseemly to protest a change of ownership that might be denied or that would surely be made to seem legitimate. His letter on September 28, 1801, which did not sound like a Madison product at all, gave Livingston a catalog of convoluted ideas to be conveyed to the French. The simple points were clumsily worded, possibly showing that Madison was uncomfortable with the underlying logic of the American position. Reading the letter is almost like hearing a torrent of words that Jefferson must have uttered during a *tête-à-tête* and that Madison had tried to dampen and soften. Similar letters went to Rufus King in London and Charles Pinckney in Madrid, for their conversations in those circles often found their way back to Paris, and so were another route to the First Consul's attention.

The letters would have been confusing regardless of who their author was; coming from Madison, the clearest of men, they were unbelievably tangled. After needlessly announcing that Washington had clandestine methods for learning such facts ("From different sources information has been received that a transaction concluded or contemplated between France and Spain…"), Madison proposed that Livingston remind the French government (and that King and Pinckney make similar attempts through their contacts) of the effects that France's occupation of New Orleans would have. As an example, Madison pointed out how the frequent hostilities between France and England made it likely that control of New Orleans, the Floridas, and the Mississippi by France would so upset the Americans in those vicinities that they would "inspire jealousies and apprehensions which may turn many of our citizens toward a closer connection with France's rival." Suddenly, however, he veered sharply to remind the three envoys that if they should meanwhile find that the cession from Spain to France had, in fact, taken place, "nothing should be said to unnecessarily irritate our future neighbors."

In short, Madison's usual clarity had so far deserted him (or he deliberately wrote in this ambiguous fashion to placate an insistent

President Jefferson) that he reversed course in mid-letter, first asking his ambassadors to issue warnings based on his supposition of a Franco-Spanish deal, then telling them not to make any irritating complaints in case there had really been such an arrangement. In that case, the letter should never have been sent, for its curious message is that action is called for only if there is no known cause for it. Not surprisingly, neither Livingston nor the other two American diplomats who received this letter were able to turn it into an effective warning message that had any chance of influencing French policy.

The dreaded truth was finally confirmed, and what had really happened between France and Spain had humbling and embarrassing aspects, even though it was no longer a surprise. Napoleon, as it turned out, had already made the feared move over a year earlier, then kept the whole world in the dark about it. France had owned the Louisiana Territory—on paper—for all that time, though without any hint of taking possession. It was exactly the reverse of any move Napoleon had made before. The master of lightning troop movements had simply ordered Spain to give him back the title to the great property, but to leave Spanish troops in place until further notice. History, in concentrating on Napoleon's military strategies, has paid too little attention to his cleverness in setting up complex treaties that sometimes transferred big chunks of real estate even more rapidly than battlefield triumphs could accomplish.

In this case, as if conducting a giant magic show, Napoleon had created a distraction by making what looked like a great pro-American gesture on September 30, 1800. After years of rebuffing U.S. protests about the French capture of American merchant ships and serious mistreatment of the seamen, France had received a three-man American delegation in Paris, quickly agreed to terms, and signed a treaty that promised to end the abuses. With all the good feeling surrounding this success, these three diplomats could hardly have imagined that a seemingly anti-American move was one object of the exercise. On the very next day, October 1, 1800, the First Consul had signed a secret treaty—usually known by its Spanish name, the Treaty of San Ildefonso—with Spain that gave "the colony or province of Louisiana" back to the French republic. Jefferson, who had not even been sure of his own electoral victory when that happened, had nonetheless been making inquiries on the subject of New Orleans from every possible informant. He and Madison had been determined not to let Napoleon's surprise tactics win in the New World as they had in Europe. Yet, the dictator had carried out the whole affair without their knowing it.

Now, some sixteen months later, the new administration was finding out that Napoleon had not only made the ominous move Jefferson had been fearing, he had proved his bad faith by making it secretly while France was still accepting words of gratitude for having helped the United States to break free from Britain. Napoleon, perhaps offering some promise of future benefits in return, had used his almost hypnotic power over the weak-willed Spanish to make them give back the entire Louisiana Territory to France, defining this as not just New Orleans, but the two Floridas and a third of the continent as well; only on the subject of relinquishing Florida did Spain dare to disagree mildly. The secrecy had to be considered decidedly anti-American, although it could also be seen as a defensive measure to keep Britain from making a preemptive grab for New Orleans.

It was not a serious reflection on Robert Livingston that he had not brought forth the information that finally proved the French had taken title to Louisiana, although Livingston and all the other American ministers abroad could have been faulted for not suggesting the kind of source that finally revealed the secret. A paid informant who worked in the Spanish Foreign Ministry—the sort of person who could have been employed two years earlier—had sent word to Madison about the treaty of transfer that had been signed. It happened that the British foreign secretary, in a belated goodwill gesture, had also given a copy of the secret treaty to Rufus King, the American minister in London, at about the same time. This was the haphazard nature of intelligence work, and the reason that the U.S. learned that many avenues had to be tried before information could be found.

In any case, Lord Hawkesbury said consolingly to Rufus King, "Since France would be coming into possession of Louisiana subject to all the engagements which appertained to it at the time of cession...the French Government could allege no colorable pretext for excluding His Majesty's subjects, or the citizens of the United States, from the navigation of the river Mississippi." The words that could be so easily said from across the Atlantic did not in the least reduce Jefferson's apprehension. The way this French move had been made seemed proof of a malign intent.

After this, French ships loaded with troops were seen at sea and were at first thought to be headed towards New Orleans. The movements had prompted Livingston to ask Talleyrand directly if France was taking back New Orleans. The foreign minister flatly denied it, which was thought to be clearly a lie, for why else would the French be sending troops to a Louisiana city owned by Spain. The secrecy and deception made France's ultimate motive seem even more menacing, but it turned out that New Orleans was not the immediate destination. The conqueror who had once brashly said, "If you start to take Vienna—take Vienna," was learning that distant New Orleans was not the same as Vienna.

It will be remembered that Madison had expected Napoleon to

take possession of Louisiana with his usual speed and surprise. Why had he done the reverse, letting a year and a half go by after he actually owned Louisiana? It is often said that the First Consul was delayed by the laborious process of setting up a new kingdom, to be called Etruria, in a tiny part of the Italian boot. Its sole purpose was to provide a realm for the son-in-law of the King of Spain, an act needed to complete the Franco-Spanish Louisiana deal. But it is hard to believe that the impetuous Napoleon would have let that bit of diplomacy and minor mapmaking delay the hard reality of occupying a key place that might otherwise be suddenly taken by the Americans or the British. This risk had certainly been clear to Napoleon. Louis-André Pichon, the French *chargé d'affaires* in Washington, had warned of it in his reports. "I am afraid they [the Americans] may strike at Louisiana before we take it over," he had written, sending along new figures that showed a tremendous population explosion in the west and the imminent formation of several new states. With all that, why had Napoleon not acted?

The First Consul had had two serious reasons not to do so. For one thing, he needed the extra time to hide a different kind of surprise—the decision to make this move not with his usual speed, but with more elaborate execution. Instead of rushing a small token force to New Orleans for the formality of taking possession, he apparently realized that America's determined westerners might crush such a flimsy action. He had foreseen those determined thoughts of Jefferson's and had arranged a major troop movement. This took on a more menacing look when Livingston learned that *two* separate military and colonial efforts were under way. First, Napoleon's brother-in-law, General Leclerc, was indeed off to the Caribbean with as many as forty thousand troops. And a back-up effort, with more troops and colonists, was being prepared to sail later from the Netherlands.

But the other reason was one troublesome detail that would make the time of arrival in New Orleans uncertain: Leclerc was first expected to put down a slave rebellion on the key island of Saint Domingue in short order, before moving on to Louisiana.

Chapter Three

THE
FATEFUL ISLAND

The western half of the lush island that Spain called Santo
Domingo had been ceded to France in 1697, and its productivity had made it a crown jewel among France's colonial possessions. Very substantial fortunes had been built up by the *grands
blancs,* as the wealthiest whites were called, and even after rebellious
groups had created a dozen years of disruption, the basic tropical
richness of Saint Domingue, as the French called it, convinced
Napoleon that he could soon be counting on it as a point of departure and supply center for the forces that he would send to take control of New Orleans.

It happened, instead, that France's misadventures in Saint
Domingue would change American history and help to save the
heart of the continent for the United States. Unbelievably, some
French biographies of Napoleon Bonaparte, apparently preferring to
overlook events that resulted in the loss of French property, make no
mention of the island, the sale of Louisiana, or the Caribbean mis-
ery that was to signal a change in the First Consul's plans.

The island's revolutionary troubles dated back at least to 1788, when Louis XVI was still on the throne and had announced the meeting of the Estates General. It was this political turbulence in the mother country that signalled an outbreak of disorder in Saint Domingue, with "great whites" and "little whites" taking sides against each other and some of the whites also arrayed against free blacks. (At that point, the slaves were bystanders.) The *grands blancs,* as major landowners, sent representatives to the Estates General, and these were actually admitted to the National Assembly in Paris—the first time representatives of a colony had ever been accepted as members of a European legislature. Briefly, this seemed to be a new high point in the colonists' power.

But when the French Revolution burst into full force in 1789, its reverberations again echoed in Saint Domingue. Many of the slave-holders wanted to separate from France and become an independent nation, in order to retain their race-based superiority and their slaves. But a French society—Les Amis des Noirs—was represented on the island, and it won a compromise law that gave voting rights to certain people of color, which only increased the factional fighting.

The great bloodshed began on a night in August 1791, when slaves, who had remained passive up to that time, burst into action against their masters, killing thousands and destroying much of the property. Within a few months, the French legislature declared full legal equality among all free men, regardless of color, but appeared to leave the institution of slavery intact. A commission that it sent to the island to enforce this edict was backed by seven thousand troops. The commission was headed by a firebrand named Leger Sonthonax, who caused great bloodshed, but left the situation as turbulent as it was in the mother country. And some of this disorder inevitably prevailed on other French Caribbean islands as well, such as Guadeloupe, Martinique, and St. Lucia.

A new turn came in 1793, when Britain, seeing a chance to make a great acquisition during France's disarray, invaded Saint Domingue. For a time, the English were so successful that they appeared poised to take over the entire French West Indies. But the complexities that France had faced soon reemerged, and the critical islands turned into a disaster for their new masters. The British lost great amounts of money and thirteen thousand men—mostly to malaria and yellow fever—while slave rebellions erupted in nearly all the islands. The belief, especially of some African critics, that blacks in the Western Hemisphere were usually passive in the face of persecution should be viewed with suspicion; some bided their time, but many slaves and free black planters eventually showed great leadership skills and set up independent rule with considerable promise until the British, French, or Dutch suppressed them at great cost.

It was in 1791 that a slave named François Dominique Toussaint (Louverture, meaning "The Opening," was an assumed name generally thought to symbolize his destiny, although some fellow slaves said they first called him that because Toussaint had a gap in his front teeth) politely informed the family he had served all his life that he had decided it was his duty to enlist in the French forces. He wanted to see Saint Domingue free, but thought its best chance was as a semi-independent part of France. The family had educated him and put every book in the house at his disposal. He, in turn, took great care of them until the day he left. Everyone around him had noticed his exceptional skill at managing others. In the military, this was quickly seen to be genius.

Already in his forties, Toussaint introduced discipline and tactics that not only riveted the men he commanded, but even helped to upgrade the performance of his superiors. From watching him, untutored chiefs are said to have learned subtler ways of dealing diplomatically with conflict situations. How he had developed such skills from simple book learning while working at a slave's household duties can only be explained by Toussaint's inherent talent for leadership. Toussaint was soon the head of his own troop, and—in the course of chaotic changes of loyalty that various commanders were undergoing—found himself in charge of a Spanish unit that was attacking the French. That Napoleon expected Leclerc to deal with such a murky situation in a few weeks indicates why his formula for success proved ineffective.

Toussaint had taken a force of four thousand black troops that he had disciplined and trained in guerrilla warfare and began working to recapture Saint Domingue, without specifying in whose behalf this would be done. He was, as one historian has written, "a master of constructive duplicity." His original intention was to act in the service of France, but he later opted for the creation of an independent state. With brilliant generalship that he had learned in part from reading and then adapted to his own needs, he used both guerrilla tactics and classic assaults to confound the British, who were also contesting for the island. He gradually captured the north and west provinces from Britain, and finally the south in 1798. The British general was forced to sue for peace. Then, to make sure that the Spanish were not going to be troublesome, Toussaint even subjugated their part of the large island, Santo Domingo, in a three-week offensive.

Toussaint found himself the ruler of an independent nation, and, considering the shattered condition of the land he controlled, he was as brilliant at governing as he was at warfare. But even that was not enough. There was nothing around him but desolation. Roving bands of hopeless men roamed the island. Slavery had been abolished, but all standards of behavior had been destroyed, and there was no discipline anywhere except in the army. Toussaint realized that his new nation could not pay wages to free men and hope to export sugar and coffee at competitive prices while the nearby islands were still using slave labor. He invented a system of forced labor that was harsh, but not brutal. His plan for having half the profits go to support the government, one-fourth to the owners, and one-fourth to the workers began to show results in stimulating the dormant economy. But black workers who had hoped independence would give them small separate farms, where they would live as they pleased, were alienated when they found themselves forcibly put to work. This was too much like the army—or like slavery. Toussaint had hoped to have a strong enough population to fight off the new French invasion that he knew would come. But most of the slaves Toussaint had liberated had lost the incentive to follow him. When the troops from Napoleonic France landed, they found little resistance.

In assuming that his brother-in-law, General Charles Leclerc, would quickly restore order in Saint Domingue and be free to proceed to New Orleans, the First Consul was engaging in some of the audacity that he recommended as a prescription for success. He knew that the island's problems were actually of long standing. It had been a graveyard for European ambitions for a dozen years. But Napoleon considered this to have been caused by the sort of mismanagement that he had so often cured in other venues. He felt sure he had the formula to quickly pacify this island, and he wrote it out for Leclerc on a few sheets of paper.

General Leclerc had come with some of Napoleon's best troops, many of them battle-tested Swiss and Polish conscripts. He obediently consulted the detailed set of typically Napoleonic instructions on just how to conduct the pacification of Saint Domingue. There were to be three phases: first, occupy the coastal towns in fifteen to twenty days; second, deliver rapid and converging blows into the interior to shatter organized resistance; third, disarm everybody. The First Consul's note continued:

> Then treat with Toussaint and promise him everything he asks for. As soon as you establish yourself in the country, you will become exacting. All Toussaint's chief agents, white or colored, should be loaded with attentions and confirmed in their posts; but in the last period, all should be sent to France...[as] prisoners if they have acted ill. Then has come the moment to assure the colony to France forever. On that same day, at every point in the country, you will arrest all suspects in office whatever their color, and at the same moment embark all the black generals no matter what their conduct, patriotism, or past services, giving them, however, their rank and assuring them of good treatment in France.

In other words, destroy local leadership, so that only Frenchmen will be obeyed.

Leclerc stayed on schedule for a time, paying little attention to his wife, Napoleon's frivolous sister Pauline, who is said to have quickly started her usual sexual revels with officers and planters. Within ten days, he held all the main coastal positions, then moved toward the interior. There he encountered Toussaint's most effective general, the brutal Jean-Jacques Dessalines, and suffered some losses. But those were overcome, and he soon appeared to be in control of the island. Toussaint and his generals—whether sincerely or treacherously—submitted their surrenders, and Toussaint retired to his estate. But at this point, Leclerc, seemingly obeying one of Napoleon's prescriptions, committed a shameful act of treachery. Possibly suspecting that the surrender had been a trick, he sent

Toussaint an invitation to come to dinner "to discuss important matters that cannot be explained by letter." The black leader, not suspecting that a gentleman would so abuse his dinner guest, came, was seized, and was shipped to France.

Leclerc's version of the event was reprinted in *Le Moniteur de la Louisiane* on June 11, 1802:

> From the General in Chief to the Citizens of St. Domingue:
>
> General Toussaint did not wish to profit from the amnesty that had been granted to him. He continued to conspire, he was going to re-ignite the civil war. I had to have him arrested. The proofs of his bad conduct after the amnesty will be repeatedly published. This measure, which assures peace in the Colony, should in no way disturb those who have turned in their arms and submitted to the good faith of the Republic.

Napoleon imprisoned Toussaint in the Fortress of Joux, and Toussaint died within months from the harsh effects of the freezing cold.

In mitigation of this sorry incident, it should be noted that the French generally showed higher ethics and more humanity on the subject of race and slavery than did either the British or the Dutch. In the words of historian W. Adolphe Roberts, "Frenchmen were never able to swallow the convenient doctrine that Negroes were a sub-human species."

As far back as 1672, Governor General Jean-Charles de Baas had written from Martinique to the powerful Chief Minister Jean-Baptiste Colbert, in Paris:

The slaves are forced to work twenty out of every twenty-four hours. If, then, these miserable wretches do not have beef to eat, how is it possible for them to endure so much work by eating only potatoes, yams and cassava bread? If Irish beef is not imported, it is certain that they will not be fed on French beef.... I confess, Monseigneur, that I exhibit a great deal of weakness in the matter of carrying out your orders, for slaves are human beings, and human beings should not be reduced to a state which is worse than that of cattle.

This daring letter was written to challenge the rule that Martinique could only import its needs from France and to plead for the right to import the less costly Irish beef. It was rare for anyone to win a dispute with Colbert, but de Baas eventually got his way. The ban on importation of Irish salt beef was lifted soon after the letter arrived.

Half a century later, in his *Chronicles of Louisiana*, Le Page du Pratz wrote similarly sensitive lines:

As we know from experience that most men of low extraction, and without education, are given to thieving for their necessities, it is not at all surprising to see Negroes thieve, when they are in want of everything, as I have seen many badly fed, badly clothed, and having nothing to lie upon but the ground. I shall make but one reflection. If they are slaves, it is also true that they are men, and capable of becoming Christians. Besides, it is your intention to draw advantage from them. Is it not therefore reasonable to take all the care of them that you can?

Thoughts of exactly this kind had led to the decree by Louis XIV in 1685 of the Code Noir, a charter for the protection of slaves. While the very existence of slavery and the need for such a code was abominable, this edict did contain some provisions of a higher order than anything decreed by the northern slave nations. Whereas, "The English slave code was cruel in the extreme, giving the master almost unlimited power, and sanctioning some of the most horrid enormities ever tolerated by law," as a Jamaican historian wrote, the Code Noir decreed that old and sick slaves must be properly cared for, or if abandoned, they were to be taken to the nearest hospital and maintained at their owner's expense. Masters were prohibited from torturing or mutilating their slaves "under any pretext," even that of obtaining evidence of a heinous crime. Slaves had the right to appeal to the proper officials against their masters, and the courts are known to have acted liberally on many occasions. All serious charges had to be brought before a magistrate, so that the only punishment a master was allowed to inflict, based on his own judgment, was a whipping with a light stick or a piece of rope. Moreover, the rules for emancipation were much more liberal than in other slave-owning countries. A similar document was adopted for Louisiana in 1724. But the United States of America—even a hundred years later—lacked most such protections.

The fact that Napoleon started permitting slavery to be restored in the Caribbean islands in 1802 was more a sign that he was allowing a former policy to prevail than that he actively favored slavery. He had rejected the French Revolution's principle of assimilating the colonies to France, making them into overseas departments. Instead, he said they should have laws suitable to their special problems. But there he had been less definite than usual and failed to specify either the laws or the purposes.

Rather than a true belief in the institution of slavery, he had made an ill-timed move of desperation in the attempt to keep alive the dying dream of an empire in the Americas. It was a bad one, for even the blacks who had been passive became inflamed into fanatic action, causing the desperate Leclerc to write accusingly to his powerful brother-in-law: "I begged you, Citizen Consul, to do nothing to make these people fear for their liberty till the moment when I should be prepared....The moral force I had acquired here is destroyed." He predicted a catastrophe unless he quickly received more money and troops from France, and he was right, but not for these practical reasons.

The May rains brought yellow fever with special fury that year, and the ones it struck hardest were the newcomers who had not acquired the slightest immunity to it; the black natives were hardly affected. Three thousand French soldiers were dead in a month, and then the pace worsened. One regiment that had landed with 1,395 men had only 190 left alive, and 107 of those were hospitalized. Nearly every unit had similar statistics. Leclerc, who had been weakened by malaria, was hit by the Yellow Jack as well and quickly expired.

Command of the French forces passed to General Donatien Rochambeau. Napoleon had not yet abandoned his American dream. Still audacious, he sent more troops.

Chapter Four

ONE SPOT
ON THE GLOBE

While Leclerc was being sucked into the quicksands of Saint Domingue, the follow-up operation for the colonization of Louisiana went on with every appearance of seriousness. In a back-up effort, the strikingly handsome General Jean-Baptiste Bernadotte, who was alternately derided or spoken of as the second-most important man in France, was assembling ten thousand troops and a large group of hopeful colonists in the Netherlands. This meant that their arrival in New Orleans—and perhaps other points—would be a massive challenge to whatever defenses the United States might mount. Moreover, it was believed that Bernadotte would be dampening the opposition of any westerners who might be inclined to contest his arrival, for he would come with a guarantee that U.S. rights under the agreement with Spain would be fully respected, so that navigation of the Mississippi was in no danger. With no threat of blockage and little or no demand for payment, Americans would have all the rights they had ever enjoyed. What issue would they want to fight about?

Thomas Jefferson, however, was not about to consider this guarantee from a man like Napoleon Bonaparte. A leader who could capture title to Louisiana in secret could just as easily rescind any new promise about rights to the river. Without waiting for the arrival of the troops, the colonists, or the message they might be carrying, Jefferson felt he had to send a message of his own that the French dictator would not mistake. It could not be directed personally to Napoleon, for that would make it an ultimatum, possibly leading to war before America was ready for it. It would have to go through the American minister in Paris, where, unfortunately, Jefferson and Madison had a man they didn't trust in this supremely important and delicate post.

Madison, as noted earlier, had already written to Robert Livingston about a warning to Napoleon, albeit in a most ineffectual way. But Jefferson sought a direct way to communicate his displeasure. He read with dismay a letter of Livingston's to Madison, giving a colorful thumbnail sketch of what Napoleon was being told that whetted the First Consul's appetite for the Louisiana territory: "That it was one of the most fertile countries in the world…that the French had better relations with the Indians than any other people…and that once the French had New Orleans, they would command the trade of America's entire western country…all of which made it a darling object with the First Consul."

Livingston's wordiness and dainty language were a special irritant to Madison, the lover of conciseness, but this was, in fact, quite a shrewd assessment of the fantasy world that sometimes circled around Napoleon. The notion of special ties between the French and Native Americans had some small truthful basis, but it became so overblown in Paris that a Frenchman named Tatergem, a self-promoter from the days of the old Directorate, had contrived to convince Napoleon of his very close relations with the Creek nations, who were said to be ready to raise twenty thousand warriors to follow him. Now Napoleon had elevated him to General of Division, indicating that he would be given substantial funds and troops to organize the Creeks. Livingston's assessment was "I believe him to be a mere adventurer," but the information about him had to be taken seriously, because the belief in France's special relationship with Native Americans was another factor convincing Napoleon that his occupation of Louisiana might work brilliantly.

Just as he did when he moved troops into Spain and later when he marched into Russia, Napoleon now appeared to be tempted by any hopeful sign from New Orleans and ready to ignore the indications that men, money, and energies might be mired down for years.

Now, in the spring of 1802, Jefferson was determined to mount a far harsher campaign to discourage Napoleon than the Madison letter had suggested; no more gentle thoughts about how to treat prospective neighbors. The French were not wanted as neighbors, and that had to be made clear. As elegant as his written lines could often be, the president was now feeling almost bombastic, and he had in mind a collection of threats that were sure to make Napoleon think again before instituting a New Orleans adventure. They were brilliant writings, for even vitriol took on a certain beauty when it came from Jefferson's pen. He knew exactly what he would like to say if he could address the First Consul himself. Writing it in a way that would turn Robert Livingston into a messenger of doom was the real challenge.

Stirred by "the fever into which the western mind is thrown by the affair at N. Orleans," as he once put it, Jefferson penned a letter to Robert Livingston on April 18, 1802, that is surely one of the most emotional letters ever written by an American president. It was an intentional exhortation to make this supposedly mild diplomat strongly warn the French of their perilous course, and no one can doubt Jefferson's intensity as he wrote it. The letter began:

The cession of Louisiana and the Floridas by Spain to France works most sorely on the United States. This subject the Secretary of State has written to you fully, yet I cannot forbear recurring to it personally, so deep is the impression it makes on my mind. It completely reverses all the political relations of the United States, and will form a new epoch in our political course. Of all nations of any consideration, France is the one which, hitherto, has offered the fewest points on which we could have any conflict of right, and the most points of a communion of interests....Her growth, therefore, we viewed as our own, her misfortunes ours. There is on the globe one single spot, the possessor of which is our natural and habitual enemy. It is New Orleans, through which the produce of three-eighths of our territory must pass to market, and from its fertility it will ere long yield more than half of our whole produce and contain more than half of our inhabitants. France, placing herself in that door, assumes to us the attitude of defiance. Spain might have retained it quietly for years....Not so can it ever be in the hands of France: The impetuosity of her temper, the energy and restlessness of her character, placed in a point of eternal friction with us...

Jefferson's letter went on with the same white heat to a much-quoted passage about "the day that France takes possession of New Orleans." Not only did he say that day would be a low point in France's history, for it would seal America's marriage with the British fleet and nation, but he added, astonishingly, that it would start a massive shipbuilding program: "We must turn all our attention to a maritime force, for which our resources place us on very high ground." The new Anglo-American alliance, he declared, would make it impossible for France to reinforce her settlements in the Americas. The alliance would also destroy any existing European agreements, and hold both continents of the American hemisphere for the common use "of the United British and American nations." Jefferson's unprecedented act of independence and defense was done to safeguard one single place that the United States did not even own or have any claim to.

New Orleans was every bit as special as Jefferson insisted—special not only to the United States, but also to all the other lively trading nations of the world. It is rare that a specific place captures the attention of almost every capital. Just as in the affairs of men, there is a tide in the affairs of cities or geographical locations that suddenly elevates this or that one to prominence, sometimes for only a passing hour, but often as a lasting concern. Gibraltar, the Dardanelles, the English Channel, the Suez—these have all commanded world attention because they signified both money and power, not only to the nations that contested for control in each case, but also to all the spectator states that would gain or lose from the outcome. So it was with New Orleans of 1802. It had the potential to spell another shameful Spanish retreat from power, another Napoleonic *coup d'eclat,* or a first great American victory. The outcome would also be pivotal for the continental Europeans who depended on Napoleon's rule and for those who hoped to see it decline. It was even more clearly meaningful to Britain, which longed to seize New Orleans for itself and schemed to arrange for a reunion with its American offspring, not as a full partner, but as a powerful weight against the French.

New Orleans was a glittering focal point for the early 1800s, composed of low-lying islands that made it seem like a water-based Venice, and so positioned that it was the absolute guardian over access to the majestic Mississippi River. As a city, New Orleans was dramatic—exciting in itself, with a remarkable outreach that engaged the world's attention. Its seamy side seemed to sing throatily of Marseilles, of Shanghai, of places that were regarded as being deliciously low, for it had been created not only by French and Spanish priests and adventurers, but also gradually enlivened by Italians, Filipinos, Slavs, Dalmatians, Portuguese, blacks from a great variety of origins, plus a few Jews and Chinese. Here, as on the Caribbean islands, it came to be a mark of status to be called a Creole, which originally implied French or Spanish heritage and local birth, because many Creoles had made themselves successful enough to hire tutors for their children or to have them educated in France or the United States. Because it was a backwater as far as public education was concerned, with only a few hundred persons having become literate through the school system, this gave many educated Creoles a great practical advantage as well as prestige.

Much of the city's flavor and vigor also derived from the Cajuns, as they are colloquially known, many of them living outside the city proper. These were long spoken of as mysterious people, with their unique foods and oddly accented French dialect. But they are actually Acadians, descendants of a stubborn French group who had been virtually expelled from northeastern Canada for being on the wrong side politically. Living in the Canadian maritime province of Acadie, they detested English rule, and the feeling was mutual. The rulers broke up their settlements and confiscated their farms. The victims moved first to New England, but kept an eye on more agreeable climates where they might recreate a French life. Even the French West Indies beckoned as a possibility. But early in 1765, about 650 of them moved to Louisiana, and sent back such good reports about the climate and conditions for growing crops that 2,500 more came in the next few years. A few went farther south to

Guiana, but most stayed in the area around New Orleans where their penchant for insisting on their own ways and projecting the flavor of France has persisted to this day.

Small as the numbers of all these groups were in the eighteenth century, they tended to form into separate hamlets. Called quarters (from the French *quartiers*), they were still quite tiny. Little discipline was exerted by any single authority over the activities in any quarter. So prostitution, music, cuisine, and, regrettably, health standards were all more free-flowing than in almost any other city on the continent.

For the dozen years leading up to 1802, New Orleans had received a flood of refugees from Saint Domingue, due to the violence there. These arrivals were included in the term "Creole," the word for island-born French Colonials, which was applied to white New Orleanians of Latin blood. Coming from the Spanish word *criolla*, meaning "indigenous," it was never meant to imply a mixed race. Some of these *émigrés* were penniless, while others came with hoards of gold, valuables, and slaves who had elected to stay with them. The city was a magnet for the beautiful people, the handsomest *émigré* being General Jean Robert Humbert, who had been in Leclerc's forces and then served as an escort for Leclerc's widow, the former Pauline Bonaparte, when she returned to France. Because Napoleon suspected that Humbert was one more of Pauline's innumerable lovers, he made his disgust clear, and the general left for New Orleans and remained there for life.

A more industrious refugee named Louis Duclot founded a French weekly newspaper, *Le Moniteur de la Louisiane,* which was welcomed, as most newcomers were, and survived for twenty years. But the most "American" in spirit, although many would have denied it, were those Creoles who had come as working-class persons, then climbed the economic ladder. Descendants of such families who resided in New Orleans in the years when several nations were about to lay claim to it reveal how this exotic place retained its variety, yet was ready to adopt American ways quickly when the opportunity presented itself.

A telling case history—because it shows a Creole and a famous American forming an unlikely bond—started with the arrival of a family named Plauché from Seine-sur-Mer, France, in 1762. They were shipwrights by trade, and they thought they were coming to a French colony, knowing that there should be plenty of work in their line in this seaport that was virtually floating on the water. However, they had not known that France was, in that very year, ceding the whole Louisiana territory to Spain. So they left for a French colony and wound up in a Spanish one. The shift in government would be kept secret until 1764, but then life went on without much change. A Spanish governor ruled, instead of an official from France. Edicts were printed in both languages. There was some resentment, but not enough to create protests. Many New Orleanians felt that being close to the United States would one day bring the best fortune of all.

The Plauchés worked hard at ship repairing, put aside a little capital, and their younger generation diversified into the business world. In addition, one young family member named Jean Baptiste found time to moonlight—to do a little cotton trading. Following the invention of the cotton gin, cotton had become a big-money crop. Young Jean Baptiste Plauché had a "Yankee's" flair for buying low and selling high in the cotton market, and he began building more capital as he traded. He was notably honest, a straight shooter, and other men took notice of him. When it appeared that fighting over the possession of New Orleans might develop, some of his new acquaintances suggested that he should join a volunteer force, in order to be prepared with an officer's rank if fighting should break out.

Plauché was a junior officer, probably a lieutenant, when he first met the renowned American general Andrew Jackson, but it was not on a military occasion. General Jackson was an eager businessman who grew cotton on his Nashville farm, and he encountered Plauché in a cotton-trading session. The general, who was destined to become one of America's most unusual presidents, was like Plauché in his reputation for total honesty. Their entwined destinies played a curious part in the nation's life a dozen years later.

The city had a curious blend of freedom and harshness. For instance, the Code Napoléon prevailed as the legal code, even after Louisiana became a U.S. state, and there was a Code Noir whereby free blacks were allowed to own slaves, and free blacks were also allowed to enlist as slaves to either white or black masters. But not even the easy liberality of New Orleans tolerated the spread of the voodoo cult brought by arriving slaves. The practice was considered so menacing that the city banned any more blacks from Saint Domingue. The Catholic leaders succeeded in promoting a law banning Jews as immigrants that remained in effect until after American rule took over in 1803. Yet, the same Catholic leaders arranged to send over great numbers of Ursuline nuns from France, who for two centuries ran the Charity Hospital and made it into a model for the nation.

Knowing what reactions to expect from such a population in case of war was a great challenge. Since the French language had continued to dominate, even after almost forty years of Spanish ownership, the probability that Napoleon's troops would be welcomed joyously had to be considered. But reasons could be found to argue that a great many New Orleanians believed in the eventual victory of British sea power, while still others thought America was the wave of the future and were anxious to sail on it.

If such a blazing comet of a city, the one focal point of the whole negotiation, was as complex as this, it is little wonder the massive tail called the Louisiana Territory that went with it was unknown and unknowable.

The sprinkling of facts on record about the interior came mostly from intrepid Jesuits who had risked their lives to venture into areas inhabited by unfriendly Native Americans, or from early French explorers who had established somewhat better relations with the Native Americans than the early British settlers were able to. But estimates of the continent's overall size and shape remained a mystery, partly because little curiosity existed in what lay beyond the Mississippi, as though the river put an end to the interesting part of the world. Until now, the world had usually paid more attention whenever Asia was mentioned, for Europeans generally still believed that the rest of the American continent was quite small and was intended to serve mainly as a passage to China. But awareness of a much greater continental expanse was growing among Americans. The leaders in Washington could only guess how westerners would react if confronted with a foreign presence in the Louisiana Territory that threatened their future.

Jefferson's high state of excitement over New Orleans was no doubt partly assumed for strategic reasons, but it also clearly echoed the popular concern that had arisen over the cherished city. Since Americans later went through isolationist periods when they paid scant attention to world affairs, it might be thought that these 1802 happenings were of interest only to a few officials in the new capital of Washington, D.C. But that was far from the case, for leading newspapers were full of stories on the subject. Many of these accounts appeared, and many letters to the editors were well reasoned and temperate in contrast to some comments in Congress. Even the English-language *Louisiana Gazette*, which regularly carried a report on the Congress on the front page, took care to give the most prominence to members' remarks that appeared significant, rather than overwrought.

Rumors of the threat spread surprisingly fast, causing excited reactions in most of America's growing number of states, especially in the western areas (a term that was then applied to anything more than fifty miles inland from the Atlantic coast). Most people knew little about Napoleon's personal status, as he used the ambiguous title of First Consul to rule as a dictator, and they were perpetually confused about whether to think of New Orleans as French or Spanish at any given moment. But they did know that the Mississippi, having been threatened with closure before, might be facing a much more serious threat this time. And they were letting their representatives in the Congress know that they wanted their government to take a firm stand.

Jefferson suffered a shock in mid-December of 1802, when he was criticized for seeming insufficiently disturbed about the danger to the great river. In contrast to the excitement he put into his written words, he always tried to maintain the look and sound of great composure when he spoke in public, which made him a surprisingly ineffective speaker. But he may have had a strategic reason for sounding especially low-key on one visit to Congress. The legislators in both houses had been talking so excitedly that Jefferson, fearful of being pushed into a war for which America was unprepared, may have wanted to be sure to avoid stirring up emotions. Whatever the cause, he said, limply, "The cession of Louisiana to France will, if carried into effect, make a change in the aspect of our foreign relations."

The understatement received such bad press that Jefferson returned a week later and turned up the temperature of his remarks a little. It was still a lackluster performance, proclaiming his awareness "of the obligation to maintain in all cases the rights of the nation, and to employ for that purpose those just and honorable means which must belong to the character of the United States." The House was so dissatisfied with Jefferson's response that it sent a message to the president saying that the members "must express their unalterable determination to maintain the boundaries and the rights of navigation and commerce through the river Mississippi as established by existing treaties."

Jefferson's outward reserve was a pose, intended to project a lordly manner that was the way he liked to think of himself. But the bottled-up feelings often spilled out when he held a pen. So the president's letter to Livingston had been of such grandiloquent scope that Napoleon himself might have respected its flashes of fury. But the First Consul did not get to experience the emotion it contained, for Robert Livingston had a softer way of presenting himself and his country's business. Livingston had done very little to carry out the warning spirit of Madison's directionless letter of the previous September, thinking it more important to maintain his own good standing with Napoleon and his top ministers. The State Department in Washington could not be sure just how he was presenting the case, but what little feedback was available made it seem that very little of the first barely audible warning from Madison had been conveyed. Now his decision to handle Jefferson's much more powerful and insistent letter in his own soft way was far more questionable.

Livingston held back from using the president's strongest phraseology. Exactly how many of the Jeffersonian thoughts he tried out on Talleyrand, or perhaps another of Napoleon's ministers, is not documented. He undoubtedly gave one or more of them the gist of the president's message, but in a softened tone, implying that these unpleasantries could surely be avoided. There were times, in fact, when Livingston implied that he personally, far from favoring an Anglo-American marriage, hoped to see America wedded economically to

France. This view, rather than his president's, was a shocking departure from correct ambassadorial behavior. But his disobedience was part of a pattern that participants on both the French and American sides would engage in during the entire Louisiana negotiation. Far beyond democracy in action, it was more like administrative anarchy.

Livingston's notion of propriety is best illustrated by a letter he had written to Talleyrand in 1802, upon first learning that the Treaty of San Ildefonso had been secretly concluded sixteen months earlier:

Paris, February 20, 1802
To the Minister of External Relations

The undersigned, Minister Plenipotentiary of the United States, has seen, with some concern, the reserve of the French Government with respect to the cession they have received from Spain of Louisiana.

He had hoped that they would have found a propriety in making such frank and open communications to him as would have enabled him to satisfy the Government of the United States that neither their boundary nor the navigation of the Mississippi, secured by their treaties with Spain, would be, in any way, affected by the measure. It would also have been very satisfactory to him to have taken such arrangements with the Minister of External Relations as would have had a tendency to dissipate the alarms the people of the Western territory of the United States will not fail to feel on the arrival of a large body of French troops in their vicinity; alarms which will probably be increased by the exertions of those Powers that are interested in keeping the two Republics from cementing their connection....

The letter goes on to ask for certain points of information, all said to be directed toward making the most practicable arrangements and removing causes of discontent. The whole of it reads as if Livingston is lecturing the fabled diplomat, saying, in effect, *Here we are, the friendliest of governments, and anxious not to be separated from you by the British, who never cease to intrigue for just such a purpose. Why in heaven would you not tell us about your treaty? Why risk having some of our western people be startled when your troops eventually arrive and perhaps fall prey to the British troublemaking? Now, please answer a few questions, and let's be sure we keep our communications straight, so we can go on being friends.*

It must have startled the suave Talleyrand to read how hurt Livingston claimed to feel at the thought that France had taken Louisiana from Spain without letting him know about it. Livingston silkily referred to the secrecy that the French had practiced against the United States as France's "reserve," the politest possible euphemism for "stealth." Here Livingston, referring to himself in the third person, showed clearly why he and Jefferson could both have valid thoughts and stylistic merit, yet be destined to disdain each other's approach. The good fortune that has characterized America's history was never needed more than when the future of the United States depended on the cooperation of these two unlikely colleagues.

In contrast to Jefferson's message, Livingston seems to accept France's occupation of New Orleans, while Jefferson's flatly rejects it. But it should be carefully noted that neither Jefferson's direst warnings—the substance of which reached Napoleon from several sources— nor Livingston's subtleties deterred the dictator from making moves to occupy the coveted city. France had proceeded to despatch troops, and the vessels bearing them into the Caribbean had, indeed, been originally destined for New Orleans, and only the black uprising raging in Saint Domingue had prevented this plan from being carried out.

Now, however, as French soldiers were dying by the thousands, and General Leclerc himself was among the casualties, tending to this catastrophe became Napoleon's first order of business, for Saint Domingue was the center and focal point of France's operations in the New World. If that were lost, every other nearby action would be pointless. While the new reinforcements made their way to Saint Domingue, the New Orleans venture was put on hold, although General Bernadotte continued to prepare his separate mission of troops and colonists who were to sail to Louisiana from Holland. Another piece of good fortune that benefited the United States was that Bernadotte fell behind schedule and was frozen in by winter.

The struggle on Saint Domingue created another French-American dispute because Leclerc had accused the United States of trading peaceably with the black rebels while making it difficult for him to obtain desperately needed supplies. The United States was mainly concerned with the protection of American ships that were trying to carry on normal trade with the island, but innumerable instances occurred where the distinctions between cargoes that were normal supplies and those that were contraband placed Madison in a very difficult position with the French embassy in Washington. As a slave-owning nation, the United States feared that the example of a successful rebellion would create echoing effects in the southern states, yet it wanted to respect international law by recognizing the rights of the revolutionary black government on the island. The situation was further complicated by the unspoken fact that France's problems on Saint Domingue were, in fact, a godsend to the administration that would otherwise have been facing French landings in New Orleans.

At the time, it appeared that there had been no more than a temporary reprieve from Napoleon's threat to New Orleans. Thomas

Jefferson thought of it as only a fortunate moment before the attempt to land troops in New Orleans would resume. Because slave rebellions had almost never gained permanent success, and no one realized what a truly great leader Toussaint had been, most observers continued to believe that France would finally control the island and that the threat to New Orleans would materialize. The fateful clash of French troops with western Americans was prevented only by the unforeseeable events on that chaotic and disease-ridden island. In a sense, although yellow fever played a major role and Toussaint's life ended tragically, his rebellion can be said to have played a significant part in preserving America's future in the continent.

In any event, when Livingston read Jefferson's letter while in Paris, he knew the president wanted his official representative to goad Napoleon with what he considered intemperate saber-rattling. Livingston thought it would provoke equal or greater excesses on the First Consul's part. And while that storm raged, he could imagine how little luck he would have getting anywhere near Napoleon after that. He had worked too hard and come too far in prodding these people to the point of talking seriously about some amicable arrangement for New Orleans. He honestly felt that some of the French talked to him as a person, apart from his status as the American minister, putting them almost at the point of confiding things they would not say officially. That was certainly true of Marbois, although within strict limits. One could never be quite sure with Talleyrand. And he knew it was unthinkable that Napoleon should utter a confidence, but he thought the impulse to do it was in all their minds. Not only was this attitude pleasantly flattering, but Livingston believed the impulse alone was worth something in the delicate job of diplomatic compromise.

He would put war talk aside for now and present the American case with his customary logic and dignity. The State Department might, in case it intercepted and read French messages, suspect this insubordination, but they could never prove that he had failed to deliver Jefferson's warning verbally. In any case, he saw no reason to feel guilty. If his own reliance on civility proved effective, he would be serving his country well—and the Virginians would claim the credit for it anyway.

Chapter Five

THE
MISTRUSTED ENVOY

A s 1802 moved along, Robert Livingston began to feel an inner
excitement that had a pleasurable side, but also a disquieting
one. He had been in Paris long enough to know a great many people, and he was seeing both Talleyrand and Marbois often enough to
know their verbal patterns and to realize that an ongoing decline in
France's cash position might be altering Napoleon's posture on the
subject of Louisiana.

Added to this information came appalling news from Saint
Domingue. The formerly lush, profit-producing possession had
become an island of yellow fever and death. Livingston could detect
the hidden anxiety that hung in the air when leading Frenchmen
talked with each other. His knowledge of spoken French was inex-
act and his hearing was less than normal, but his sensitivity was
acute, and it was clear when certain sentences broke off short of
completion. It was as if he had learned another foreign language—
not merely French, but now the language of Napoleonic government: troop movements, shifts in personnel, the First Consul's

whereabouts. The men around Napoleon followed his movements minute by minute. "He is leaving his desk. He is going into the reception. Now he is talking with the Spanish Ambassador. No, that was broken off very quickly. He is approaching the ladies, telling them a story. He is smiling...." Every such report was thought to hold a meaning.

Talleyrand, of course, was somewhat different. He was attentive to Napoleon, but not entirely subservient. And as he listened to the reports of the leader's movements, he wore the self-assured expression of one who usually understands what each change of mood means.

Livingston had known Talleyrand only by reputation, and while he knew that the man was destined to be a major historical figure, he was impervious to this type of fame. Livingston had been surrounded by powerful men since childhood, knew that he was going to become the head of a great landholding New York family, and was not easily impressed by a person whose acceptance of lavish bribes was better known than his clever diplomacy. That might seem normal to the Europeans, but to an American, a bribe-taker seemed like little more than a well-dressed beggar. François Marbois was entirely another matter. Livingston had known him quite well when Marbois was a young French diplomat in Philadelphia. Meeting again in this totally different situation, the two men were drawn to each other, and there were times when they found it hard to remember that they were on opposite sides of an intense negotiation. Marbois was very much inclined to see things from America's point of view, and Livingston, as a patrician, was even more disposed to talk to Marbois as if he genuinely wanted to pass along some good advice for French consideration. Marbois often found the advice very sound—*bien sérieux et tout à fait normal.*

The sense that a change of direction was in the wind both excited Livingston and made him apprehensive, for he felt that the change might rob him of a great opportunity that he was beginning to envision. In a way, the French ambience was beginning to feel more like home to him than the America with which his correspondence produced such contradictory responses. The sensations he gathered as he talked with so many highly placed people—French, English, German, Dutch, Belgian, Swiss—made renewed war in Europe seem likely. That, in turn, would alter the First Consul's thoughts about the New World. It might push them into the future, or it could open the way for some new arrangement in which Robert Livingston would have a leading role.

He was proud of having been chancellor of New York State, and he liked being addressed by that title, as he often was. He was proud, too, of having administered the oath of office to George Washington when the first president was inaugurated in New York City. But he knew that these distinctions had resulted from family connections. Except for his advanced farming and animal husbandry, he had accomplished little on his own. Now, for the first time in a comfortable life, he might become the central figure in a great affair, not just one of a successful group. Most everything written about Livingston (except for a splendid biography by George Dangerfield) has pictured him as a smug and totally self-satisfied New York aristocrat, which is very superficial, if one considers his past.

When the colonies were on the brink of war in 1775, Robert Livingston had been plunged into revolutionary politics as one of New York's delegates to the Second Continental Congress. He had seemed to have a young man's sense of daring at first, writing that "the coercive aspect of Parliament seems odious to me," and saying that "If the King is determined to subdue us by force, it will be far from an easy matter. If America falls, it will fall like a strong man."

But his father, a highly respected judge, kept reminding him of the arguments for moderation. By June 1776, after his father's death, he was siding with those who wanted caution and delay. It has been said that "He was important enough to be a leader, but a leader for postponement." When, on June 11, he was appointed to a committee of five who would draw up a declaration of independence, he found himself in the company of Thomas Jefferson, John Adams, Benjamin Franklin, and Roger Sherman. When it was asked what Livingston was doing in such a group, it was said either that he was there to represent the minority or, at best, that he was supposed to get New York committed to the declaration. He never alluded to his labors there. His own biographer wrote, "To have sat in silence among the immortals is a memory from which few men would extract any gratification. And Livingston certainly did not do so."

When most of the signers performed that act in Philadelphia on August 2, 1776, Robert Livingston was immersed in local defense matters back in New York, and it was Philip Livingston, a cousin, who signed for the family. These inglorious memories would appear to throw a different light on the American minister's hopes for the Louisiana negotiations and his exceptional distress when the opportunity dissolved.

Livingston was far from the cipher that Jefferson and Madison considered him to be. He had gone to Paris full of determination to make his mark as a diplomat, even sensing as he did that his superiors did not fully believe in him in the way that matched their trust in some others—and particularly their endless faith in fellow Virginians. As a new American minister, the chancellor had begun his Parisian stay by devising some clever stratagems for becoming closely connected with leaders that were difficult to approach. But the distrust of his superiors brought out the worst in him. This is where the usual description of the man as a smug aristocrat seems to go astray. Wanting to impress, he sent Madison too many reports with too many words that were obviously meant to show how cleverly he was handling affairs. Far from being smug, he was begging for approval. Madison—with a positive genius for clear, concise, and minimal communication—answered few of these missives, and only did so in the most dismissive way.

This odd relationship would be a feature of the negotiation until the very last day. Livingston's ideas often interested Napoleon, and that fact alone was enough to make Talleyrand or Marbois more respectful of him. They sensed that he was not well regarded in Washington, and so they wondered what kind of game was being played by such clever and capable men as the French knew the U.S. leaders to be. Why had they sent a poorly regarded person to the key Paris post? The French even wondered whether it might be some kind of ruse—was Livingston a skilled investigator who fooled people by his simple ways?

When Livingston failed in—or at least long delayed in—delivering President Jefferson's pungent warning to the French, he was to some extent motivated by a hopeless bitterness of his own. The Virginians who now ruled in Washington just barely tolerated Livingston, and he knew it. Jefferson and Madison thought him windy and slow-witted, and they may have harbored a poor memory of the days in 1776 when he had been such an indecisive young man. Whatever the cause, they would not normally have considered him for the delicate Paris post. Their first and second choices had reasons for turning down the offer, and the pressures of party politics had forced them to call on Livingston. The same political pressures that had put Livingston in line for the job had prevented Jefferson from replacing him as his confidence waned. Besides, to change envoys after a very short tenure would have signalled the French that the Americans were in disarray, so Livingston was left in Paris to soldier on. But not once had Jefferson or Madison given him the feeling that they really valued his observations. And he was not at all the only northerner who had experienced this sense of exclusion.

The group of superior Virginians that destiny had bestowed on the new nation operated like an "old boys' club." They supported each other through successes and reverses, cleverly arranged political ploys that usually carried the day, and carefully nurtured the younger Virginians, such as James Monroe, who struck them as being the right sort. This one state, it has been said, had so many illustrious men that Socrates himself would pass unnoticed and forgotten in Virginia if he were not a public figure and some of his speeches were preserved in a newspaper. George Mason, Peyton Randolph, Dabney Carr, and several others could easily have held their own in intellect or debate with the better-known figures like Washington, Jefferson, and Madison, if they had had a mind to do so. Even when they disagreed among themselves, these larger-than-life leaders shared a trust that was seldom extended to anyone from the north. Surely it was not extended to Livingston, the New Yorker.

Despite his rather slow and effete manner, Livingston was more analytical than they knew, and he was all too aware of their low regard for him. He thought they had let him stay on as a token northerner because they had not realized how delicate the French relationship would become. But even now, their responses to his letters showed little interest in hearing how the atmosphere had altered since Jefferson's days in Paris, and what it was like to deal with devious officials who were themselves unsure of how their headstrong First Consul might change his views from one day to the next.

How much more confidence the administration had in its other envoys than it did in Livingston is shown by a letter that Madison wrote to Charles Pinckney in Madrid on May 11, 1802. This is a quite voluble and broadly explanatory letter, such as Madison hardly ever troubled to send Livingston. He told Pinckney that the French refusal of any explanations seemed to admit that the cession had taken place, adding, "Still there are chances of obtaining a reversal of this transaction." At this point the secretary of state clearly gave Pinckney full powers to negotiate a variety of possible deals with the Spanish government if vital territories could be secured that way: "Should Spain retain New Orleans and the Floridas, I repeat to you the wish of the President, that every effort and address be employed to obtain the arrangement by which the territory on the east side of the Mississippi, including New Orleans, may be ceded to the United States..." And a few lines farther along, he added, "I am charged by the President now to add, that you may not only receive and transmit a proposition, but may make the proposition yourself, in the forms required by our constitution. You may infer from the enlargement of your authority, how much importance is attached to the object in question."

The downgrading of Livingston by American leaders had become obvious to others, and some apparently referred to it openly. It can well be imagined how far the slurs may have gone in personal conversations, considering the offensive remarks that were actually committed to paper. These eruptions sank to the level of farce. Rufus King, for example, was a New Englander with strong anti-slavery feelings and close ties to New York, having married a New Yorker. He would normally be expected to have been at least tolerably well-disposed toward Robert Livingston, and, being a leading Federalist, not intimately connected with the Virginia Republican Madison. Yet, when he was American minister in London, he found occasions to make derogatory remarks to the secretary of state about his colleague in Paris.

One letter of King's to Madison in March 1801 actually implied that it might be quite easy to arrange the Louisiana matter if the

Americans only had a competent minister in Paris who could explain things clearly. These remarks about a colleague are breathtakingly insulting, considering that this was an official communication that might possibly be seen by the intelligence services of both England and France. It ended: "What effect a plain and judicious representation upon this subject, made to the French Government by a minister of talents and entitled to confidence, would be likely to have, is quite beyond any means of judging which I possess; but on this account, as well as others of importance, it is a subject of regret that we have not such a character at Paris at this time."

Despite this lowly standing he had among colleagues, a grand hidden ambition stirred Livingston's thoughts—the idea of seeking the vice presidency of the United States. It would have been a foolish dream, except for the very practical fact that the Paris post had introduced him to a group of wealthy supporters, headed by one hard-driving individual, a speculator named James Swan, who promised to promote his candidacy. He would do this in return for Livingston's efforts to win some large sums from France for losses these supporters had sustained when their ships and cargoes had been captured and their crews mistreated. It would all be very proper. Livingston would be doing his job on behalf of some American citizens, and they might naturally show their appreciation and their conviction that this was a public servant who merited an even higher role. Now, if some great coup in securing New Orleans and rights to the Mississippi should also shine a spotlight on Robert Livingston, the road to a great national office would be widened and smoothed.

There was apprehension in this happy scenario because his correspondence with Washington—especially with Secretary Madison, but also occasionally with the president himself—was oddly unsatisfactory. It made him wonder if the blow of being recalled, just as a triumph might be looming, was going to tumble out of some day's mail packet. The more Livingston sent them evidence of his tremendous efforts in Paris, even signs that he was making a considerable impression on the French leaders, the cooler and more distant his superiors at home seemed to become. He wondered if they could have an inkling of his vice-presidential hopes, which might make them want to suppress his chances of success.

Livingston was actually a part of the Jeffersonian party at this time—after having made some dramatic moves between that group and the rival Federalists. Yet Jefferson and Madison might well prefer to see some protégé of theirs glorified with a Louisiana triumph, rather than letting it fall into Livingston's hands. But with such a great national issue as Louisiana in the balance, would these lofty leaders have let mere partisan politics influence their dealings with their own envoy? The answer is almost certainly yes. It has become apparent that they knew of Livingston's political ambitions and arranged to keep him out of the election; so it is credible that they might have been willing to jeopardize the success of his vital Paris mission rather than risk handing him a public and political triumph. If it is hard to picture two men of such stature as Jefferson and Madison in this light, it should be noted that they later discussed Livingston's political hopes with James Monroe, and they agreed with the latter's suggestion that he be detained in Paris after the negotiations had ended in order to be sure of eliminating his electoral chances.

A more mysterious form of evasive behavior on Madison's part could have had greater consequences. The secretary of state pointedly and repeatedly refused to answer one of Livingston's key questions that was tied to the nation's destiny. It concerned the possibility that the United States might have an opportunity to buy some piece of property that would guarantee navigation rights of the

Mississippi forever. Ownership would be more secure than renting or leasing rights, and Livingston had heard hints that made such an arrangement seem a distinct possibility. There was no question that Napoleon needed cash, and his need would be greater if renewed war with England broke out. Since only a limited area, such as New Orleans and part of Florida, was thought to be involved, he could easily have sold some rights to the United States without foreclosing his dream of an American empire. So Livingston had written to Madison, very specifically asking what sort of money he would be authorized to offer in case such a buying opportunity suddenly presented itself. Livingston then repeated the question a second and a third time and received neither a response nor even an acknowledgment that the subject had been raised.

It is easy to see why such a secretary of state was irritated by the wordiness and the style of his envoy in Paris. But it is harder to see why his assessment of Robert Livingston was unfavorable enough to cause such negative behavior. One possible reason could have been a fear that Livingston would almost certainly bungle any such negotiation; but it will be shown that Madison was capable of writing detailed instructions for step-by-step diplomatic negotiations, and he could not have doubted his ability to manage a property purchase at a distance. So the likelier explanation is that, here again, the secretary of state was determined to avoid any possibility of a transaction that might bring glory to the New Yorker.

Often a fountain of bright ideas, Livingston was possessed by neurotic fears and misgivings that must have seemed a tiresome waste of energy to Madison. That does not, however, fully explain Madison's curious maltreatment of his envoy. What at first may seem to have been a simple lack of attention becomes a purposeful refusal to answer some of Livingston's legitimate questions, virtually making it impossible for the envoy to operate effectively. Madison's lack of support had been in evidence from the start of Livingston's mission to Paris, but as the year 1802 passed, it began to appear to be a policy of total rejection. The United States was facing the most threatening situation it had ever known: France was now known to "own" Louisiana as an absentee landlord, to be trying to hide its plans for taking possession, and apparently preparing to move in with great force at some point.

The small American diplomatic corps would certainly have been expected to work together as closely as possible. Yet it was clear from the written correspondence that the secretary of state who headed this beleaguered group unaccountably withheld key facts from his man in Paris, making it impossible for him to take advantage of a great opportunity.

There had been earlier signs that Livingston was asking for guidance about how much he might be authorized to offer for certain key concessions from the French. But it became a glaring issue in July 1802. In a letter to the secretary of state, Livingston clearly describes a series of conversations he had contrived to have with the Spanish ambassador and a number of other diplomats based in Paris. From these talks, he understood that France considered the two Floridas to be part of the territory it had taken back from Spain. He also mentioned his own belief that France's expedition to New Orleans would be postponed, which proved to be correct. Toward the end of the letter, he wrote about the possibility that he would receive an offer from France to sell West Florida and New Orleans to the United States. He told Madison of meetings in which Talleyrand talked to him in a very personal way, and he implied that a genuine deal might well be proposed to him, adding, "I am sorry that you have not communicated to me what are precisely the utmost limits of the sum I may venture to offer in cash...."

On August 10, although it was too soon for that plea to have been answered, he correctly anticipated that no answer would be forthcoming, and he reinforced his request, adding, "I am very much, however, at a loss as to what terms you would consider it as allowable to offer, if they can be brought to a sale of the Floridas either with or without New Orleans...." But nothing came of that either.

Whatever Madison's purpose was, there can be no question that Jefferson was well aware of the failure to answer, for the two men were clearly in a constant discussion. They jointly avoided giving Livingston the orders he asked for until—in the following year—they could finally tell him that they had fully briefed James Monroe on these points and he would explain it all on his arrival in Paris.

Technically and formally, the explanation was said to be that Monroe, when he would just be coming from Washington, would have the advantage of face-to-face briefings. That might have been a valid point if Livingston's question had been asked very near the time of Monroe's departure. But the envoy's queries had begun before there was even any talk of Monroe's coming to Paris. Part of the explanation for Madison's curious behavior may have been his irritation with the elaborate proposals Livingston was preparing almost weekly for the eyes of Talleyrand and Napoleon. They were actually quite impressive, with shrewd assessments of the military and trade possibilities that drew Napoleon's interest, but they had implications for U.S. policy that Livingston had no right to suggest. The American minister in Paris should have been set straight on the inappropriateness of his writings for an official French audience, and this creates another mystery: Madison failed to write a word of rebuke or correction to Livingston, which would have been his duty.

Jefferson and Madison's lack of respect for their envoy in Paris went deeper than dislike. The philosophical differences between

Livingston on the one hand, and the Jefferson-Madison team on the other, may have been the basic reason for their distrust. Both Jefferson and Madison were superlative politicians, instinctively seeking the "workable" and the "possible" on any issue; Livingston seemed to feel above politics, more inclined to search for what was "fair" and "right." Livingston's sensitivity and fair-mindedness had failed to win him great esteem and his reactions were often seen as unusual, rather than politically correct.

An example from his earlier career is quite revealing. Livingston had been a member of the House of Representatives when, in 1798, a spy scandal erupted in which certain persons were accused of being pro-French agents seeking—among other things—to give Louisiana to France. One of these was a historian named Volney and another was the "Citizen" Genêt who had once been a popular French envoy to America, later became the center of a great dispute, but then had settled quietly as a naturalized American citizen. The 1798 charges were ridiculous, but when the Federalists had whipped up such emotions that few dared to preach moderation, Livingston had the courage to demand facts in place of vague suspicions. "No evidence having been produced," he told the House one day, "we have a right to say that none exists." He could have been admired for his fairness, but instead there were those who called him "hard to understand."

He had a most interesting mind and a unique way of attacking intricate problems that he had never dealt with before. But because his approach was often an unusual one, once again, it tended to be regarded as odd rather than creative. This certainly applied to his performance in the Paris post. While his own superiors apparently found him tiresome or worse, it is noteworthy that all of the French officials involved studied Livingston's writings with great interest—and also a little wonderment. They didn't know what to make of a minister who, when discussing an issue, might suddenly begin looking at it from the French point of view, rather than his own country's—actually making suggestions on what France might do, even if they seemed at odds with American wishes.

He once wrote a quite improbable note concerning France's obligations to American claimants whose ships had been seized. Livingston slyly commiserated that perhaps the French Treasury could not afford to make payment. Both Napoleon and Talleyrand suffered such pricks to their pride that Napoleon instructed his foreign minister to write that French finances were not at all a problem and that payment could certainly be made if the claims were verified. Livingston repeatedly had conversations with Talleyrand and Napoleon that were unlike those of any other country's representative, causing them to come forth with thought-provoking remarks about Louisiana. It occasionally seemed that they had said more than they meant to say, as men may do when they are dealing with a person whose nonthreatening manner lowers their guard.

Some accounts have reported that such a spontaneous exchange occurred when Talleyrand, as early as 1802, astonished Livingston as they talked about Louisiana by suddenly asking, "Do you want to buy it?" Livingston is said to have been quick-minded enough to say, "No, but I think France should want to sell it." Talleyrand then said he had only asked that question on his own, that it was not an idea the First Consul had ever mentioned, and he begged Livingston not to repeat it. But there is no strong evidence that this exchange actually took place. A more serious and deliberate query of this kind would occur, but only in April of the following year, at the climax of the negotiation.

Among Livingston's failings was a tendency to pursue any ideas of his own that seemed good, without carefully examining them for flaws and pitfalls. He had tried, for example, to rouse the British minister in Paris to see what a danger to Britain's interests these Louisiana developments posed, for he felt that England might try to discourage Napoleon and lessen the need for action on America's part. He had also asked Rufus King, the American minister in London, to press the subject there. In either case, it had the appearance of a likely initiative, but not if one has considered that Britain coveted New Orleans and might very well regard this suggestion as an invitation to occupy that key city "in order to protect it from a possible French takeover." Seen in that light, it was an amateur blunder. Such a move would have been far more disastrous for the United States than any French action, for the much greater British naval force could not have been displaced. War against the country that provided most of America's trade earnings was far less thinkable than hostilities against France. Livingston had put himself on a very dangerous track without taking the time to assess it.

For his part, having had no previous experience in diplomacy, Livingston was proud of the way he had handled his delicate assignment. And—until he marred the whole experience with his bad behavior after the deal was done—his self-judgment seems to have been reasonably justified. As the scion of one of the country's great families and the longtime chancellor of New York state, he felt affronted at having to make himself into a social climber in order to start a form of relationship with Napoleon. Talleyrand had duly presented him one day as a matter of course, but then had minimized the chance of further contacts.

Livingston, however, had found a way to encounter Napoleon on his own. He had ingratiated himself with the British ambassador and was often invited to the other embassy for receptions when the great man was to be present. This served the purposes of both envoys, for the English wanted to keep Napoleon reminded that the former colonies were the closest of trade partners and might team up as military allies, if necessary. Livingston had had several personal talks with Napoleon, who surprisingly sensed and respected the aristocratic strain in the New Yorker's makeup. The First Consul seemed to take a special interest in him, probably because a person who was in a high position, yet apparently not highly regarded by his own countrymen, might hold the clue to some weakness in the U.S. posture. Or, the brilliant Napoleon must also have wondered, might there not be a slim chance that Livingston's strangely French-oriented ideas were actually an alternate policy that the Americans were considering and testing in a most unusual way? But apart from these practical possibilities, Napoleon apparently felt an affinity for the underestimated American. He had even quickly noticed that Livingston was hard of hearing, and he showed a rare consideration by enunciating his staccato comments a little more clearly when addressing the courteous New Yorker.

⚬

Among the small points of pride that Livingston cherished from his experience in high diplomacy was the fact that he had actually come very close to bribing the great Talleyrand. Although he looked down on bribery, he seemed delighted with himself for having nearly done business with a debauched person of such distinction, like a simple man who is thrilled to have actually discussed terms with a famous courtesan. Even though the number of persons who could claim this experience was remarkably large, Livingston felt that they were all established diplomats, men who might be seen meeting with Metternich, the ultimate diplomatist. So when Livingston had first noticed Talleyrand's disinclination to bring him into Napoleon's orbit, he imagined that the foreign minister's subtle reasons for wanting to keep the relationship in his own hands probably included the hope of earning a bribe for himself if any deal were concluded, as Talleyrand had done in so many previous negotiations.

At a later stage, Livingston rather surprisingly managed to concoct a plan for bribing Talleyrand, and he did it well enough to make the foreign minister take it seriously. The incident showed how far the U.S. had moved from its earlier abhorrence of bribery. Livingston clearly had Madison's approval, for it is boldly stated in their correspondence, which gives an interesting picture of what the founding fathers were ready to consider when the nation's top priorities were at stake. The term "personal interest" was the euphemism for a bribe, and our infant State Department not only had the expression in its vocabulary, but also had a numerical code number to express it in the very simple cipher that U.S. diplomats were taught to employ. In one of his messages to Madison after learning that he would be joined by Monroe, Livingston declared it to be a pity that Monroe would need a long time to get onto the same terms he had established with Talleyrand on what regards "540.1675.1460.1541," which decodes to "personal interest."

Livingston liked to forget, when he belabored this point in his later complaints, that his bribe was far outstripped by a massive one that the British proposed to Talleyrand and Joseph Bonaparte, brother of Napoleon, if they would convince Napoleon to abide by a former peace treaty and let Britain retain Malta without going to war. This arrangement would have allowed Napoleon to hold on to New Orleans and take over the Floridas—in effect keeping his dream of a New World empire alive. It had so many attractions for Napoleon—and for Talleyrand, who went to work on it aggressively—that it might have prevailed, except for the surprisingly effective warning dispatches from the French legation in Washington. By warning that the Americans might fight very hard against a French troop landing in New Orleans, Louis-André Pichon was living up to his foreign minister's expectations—telling the truth even if it was not what Talleyrand himself hoped to hear.

If Livingston was rather pleased at having learned to hold his own on this demanding scene, the low esteem of his American superiors saddled him with a steady resentment and fear that they would somehow undercut his chance for greatness. Apart from his long service to New York in roles up to the chancellorship, he felt he should have been considered one of his nation's founding fathers. Even if he had not been a great contributor to the committee that worked on the Declaration of Independence, he had surely done nothing to oppose any of Jefferson's ideas. How could it be, he wondered, that their approaches to vital problems were now so different?

Chapter Six

NAPOLEON'S
ODD COUPLE

A politely conducted but important clash between two of Napoleon's closest confidants was under way at this time. Independent-minded as he was, the First Consul had a great need to hear others comment on his plans. He might respond brusquely or appear to ignore the words, but stating an idea and hearing a reaction seemed to steady Napoleon, much as one looks into a mirror for orientation or reassurance, then walks on.

Talleyrand, the foreign minister, would normally have been the First Consul's closest confidant in an international negotiation, but it is significant that Napoleon was elbowing him aside in the case of Louisiana. For one thing, the French pretended, at the outset, that there was nothing to negotiate. They had already worked out an arrangement with the Spanish in 1800, making Louisiana legally their own, even though they had chosen not to let the world know and then had been unready to take possession. Napoleon gave a firm order that Talleyrand, who wanted to see France retain and expand the colony, must be kept informed of any moves, but he depended increasingly on François Marbois, his treasury minister, as a go-between with the Americans. This can surely be taken as a sign that the idea of selling Louisiana was already in the ruler's mind, but no one seems to have noticed it at that time. And this minister's strong views in favor of selling the colony were as opposite to Talleyrand's as the two men were in every other way.

François Marbois, later the Marquis de Barbé-Marbois, had come to the United States in 1779, at age thirty-four, as secretary of the French Legation, then located in the temporary capital of Philadelphia. He remained until 1785. There can seldom have been a more popular visitor who showed such an appreciation of the new country's good qualities.

When he found himself aboard ship with John Adams, who was returning from a stay as American minister to Paris, he had the courage to use his rudimentary English (and some of Adams's serviceable French) to engage the crusty great man in prolonged conversations, from which they emerged lifelong friends. And he did so despite the fact that Adams was considered to be strongly anti-French in his Federalist policies. On that voyage, the youthful Marbois also spent long hours with Adams's son, John Quincy, learning American slang from him, and later putting it to good use when he met, wooed, and married a wealthy and beautiful Philadelphia girl.

But even before that, Marbois had been so taken with America that his memoirs and letters from that visit were made into a volume with the title *Our Revolutionary Forefathers* (meaning that the American Revolution was the forerunner of the French Revolution). The volume delighted Americans because its observations were reminders of how exceptional their country could look to a friendly visitor. At the start of the second chapter, titled "Boston 1779," he wrote: "We are now in Boston. When I see these regions which were once savage and almost deserted, and today are peopled, fertile, and covered with orchards, I cannot tire of admiring the progress of civilization, which has made more advance here in a hundred years than Europe has made in ten centuries."

His descriptions of Cambridge are memorable—its beauty as the site of a great university, and the very impressive center of learning that he found Harvard University to be. But he was far from a sycophant, for a few pages later he said, "We shall not have a word to say to you about Titian, or Raphael, or Correggio, or Poussin. I do not believe that there is a single good picture in the entire United States....There will be no examples of architecture worthy of attracting our attention for a moment, and not a single remarkable bridge...."

He wrote admiringly about the simple American qualities that "these same men who open doors for themselves and buy their own food, are those who have brought about this Revolution, and who, when it is necessary, raise a musket to their shoulders and march on the enemy. And between ourselves, I am not sure that people who have porters, stewards, butlers, and covered carriages with springs, would have offered the same resistance to despotism."

This estimable young man had gone on to have the kind of roller-coaster career that many Frenchmen experienced during that revolutionary epoch, enjoying high titles at some moments and arrest and near execution at others. Now, these twenty-two years later, Marbois was Napoleon's treasury minister. The only critical comment that has been made about Marbois was his lack of imagination. He was certainly intelligent, and in the days of his stay in America, the youthful charm of a friendly Frenchman made him appear to be accomplished. But in the company of Napoleon and Talleyrand, his want of brilliance was apparent.

He had lived through some horrifying times, especially when the radical French Directory exiled him to a convict colony in French Guiana, even though no wrongdoing was proved against him.

Having lived five years as governor of Saint Domingue, he knew how to survive the tropical heat that killed most prisoners. He was freed by Napoleon, who had heard reports about his good character. From then on, he advanced to ever-higher offices, for Napoleon was always wise enough to know the rarity and immense value of a truly honest public servant.

As much as Napoleon detested the contractors who made fortunes by overcharging for every item they sold the army and the scurrilous types who tried for high office with no thought of really accomplishing anything, he felt that he must put up with the occasional rare schemer, like the incomparable Talleyrand or the unique police chief Fouché, men whose brilliance in a specialized field was indispensable, even if he could not know to what extent he could trust them. But even while admiring the most talented, albeit contemptible, advisors, he respected and cherished the rare person of real integrity and loyalty. He felt that he had one in Marbois, and he totally entrusted the treasury to him.

Not even total confidence, however, prevented Napoleon from inspecting and auditing his work with a flood of suggestions. Napoleon wrote Marbois from camp on one occasion that he had reviewed some reports on the previous night, "and I see that among the holders of terminal annuities, you are paying one person born in 1701, two in 1702, and more than 2,600 persons from before 1720. This means that among the terminal annuitants, there are 2,600 persons more than eighty-five years old. An account of those 2,600 persons must be printed and of all the annuitants up to 1725; their accounts must be sent round to the prefects to verify the existence of these individuals and to assure that they are the same persons to whom the annuity was credited."

Marbois told that story with delight, and he probably was not nearly as distressed about being taken to task by Napoleon as the sensitive Livingston imagined. The fifty-eight-year-old American minister's great empathy caused him actual pain when he thought of the hurt pride that Marbois, of the same age, must have felt to be working for the thirty-two-year-old Napoleon. He felt it was offensive to see one who was so esteemed by Americans ordered about by the young dictator. It was not that Napoleon was normally as rude or explosive as people imagined; he simply talked as if France were his house or farm and he was telling servants what to do in a few short monosyllables. In the words of one nineteenth-century observer, "He does, it is true, consult two ministers of state, but he turns abruptly away from the advice of one of them, and to the other he gives directions as positive and arbitrary as if he were directing a broker to sell a cargo."

But while Livingston especially felt the similarity of their ages as a bond, other factors played an even stronger role in Marbois's relationship with Livingston. Marbois must have found him to be one more American with a remarkable view of affairs, one who was not an ordinary or even a professional diplomat, but instead someone who invented his own solutions to an issue. For example, Livingston had prepared a document of more than a dozen pages, suggesting to the First Consul himself a whole new approach to running the French economy. Forget about colonies, Livingston had said—not because we Americans don't want you in our area, but because colonies make no sense for France. Colonies are for countries that have an excess population and insufficient ability to produce fine goods that can be exported to others. You are in exactly the opposite position. Your wonderful craftsmen and makers of fine wines and foods have great products that the world is waiting to buy. With America as the friendly ally that it has always been, some of the huge profits that England now makes from trade with America could be your profits. Instead of spending millions of francs to support colonies, you could take in all that gold in exchange for your goods—and so on.

There were Americans who found these pages overlong and windy. Monroe said so outright. Madison received copies, and seems never to have commented on the effort. But Marbois and Talleyrand had both read the memorandum with great interest and suggested it to Napoleon—usually a risky business, since the First Consul was not pleased if the subject turned out to be boring. In this case, he read the pages with some seriousness. Clearly, he would not have considered the overall plan for making export profits rather than war as a general policy. But he may have thought that the risk-versus-reward picture, as it applied to Louisiana, was worth rethinking.

A number of such incidents during these past two years had brought Marbois into contact with Livingston. Like all his colleagues, Marbois wondered about the oddity of the man's high position, yet apparent lack of standing with Washington. Even his title was not as elevated as the State Department could have made it. Why not? Was the administration in Washington trying to send some kind of diplomatic message—perhaps a sign of displeasure with the Napoleonic regime?

Whatever the case, Marbois liked and respected Livingston personally, and he hoped—for both countries' sake—that his mission would succeed. In this view, he was again very different from his colleague Talleyrand, for the latter had dangled a global plan before Napoleon, one that relied on eventually taking over New Orleans, spreading colonists out into the Territory, creating a new empire in America, and then continuing westward along the allegedly short route to China—where an Asian empire might be considered.

Even with his limited role in this negotiation, Talleyrand's presence was reflected in almost every turn of events. His character and influence can be better understood by ignoring the corruption that has dogged his memory. The French foreign minister was one of the most creative of all political strategists. He had already made himself famous before he played a major part in making Napoleon the dictator of France. Among many of the ideas he offered to the First Consul was his original proposal of a broad plan to create more strong French colonies, which had inflamed Napoleon's imagination and led to his interest in Louisiana. Yet his astonishing ability to keep observing things afresh enabled him to review ongoing developments as dispassionately as though he was seeing them for the first time.

The frequent emphasis on Napoleon's disdain for this diplomat is based on just a few flippant comments the conqueror made and on recollections late in Napoleon's life. In between—and definitely during the start of the nineteenth century—the First Consul admired Talleyrand's intellect, liked talking to him for hours, and counted on his advice—though in the unique Napoleonic way that could sometimes shut him out of a subject for weeks at a time. Through much of this negotiation, Napoleon was disregarding Talleyrand because he knew the minister was opposed to any sale of the Louisiana property, and this was the direction in which Napoleon eventually began to proceed. But with Talleyrand, to be shunned was immaterial. He managed to be in the right rooms and part of the right conversations often enough to know what was happening and to interject incisive remarks or reminders.

A few impressionistic recollections of Talleyrand help to explain his greatness. Charles-Maurice de Talleyrand-Périgord was born in 1754. His father had been a lieutenant general, related to the greatest houses of France, but was rather poor because he was a second son. Distinguished lineage was supposed to be more important than wealth, but little Charles-Maurice seems to have suffered enough in his early years to have concluded just the opposite.

His uncaring parents had farmed him out to a woman who was paid to raise him safely. He seemed unexceptional, but it was discovered when he was small that he was somewhat lame, which contributed to a low estimation of his prospects in life. So his parents decided that the priesthood was his best chance to make something of himself. He was bitterly opposed to taking his vows, but no sign of his iron will or vivid personality had emerged at that time, so he spoke of having "felt too weak to say no to his mother."

As a young abbé, he began to behave in a rather dissolute fashion and to be seen with questionable companions. On his deathbed, his father apologized to him for having forced him into the religious life for which he was so clearly unsuited. His father's notion of making up for this wrong was to ask the king to make his little son Bishop of Autun, and the king signed that order two days before the father's death.

At the ceremony elevating him to this office, Talleyrand, barely thirty years old, stumbled over the liturgy as badly as his crippled leg stumbled over his vestments. But his love of good food, wine, and fine conversation made the reception that followed a huge success.

From then on, the dinners he gave at the Bishop's Palace were great affairs, and he was almost like a politician on campaign in his wooing of the public in his diocese. Soon he stunned his own people and attracted national attention when he proposed a program of economic and social reform that was daringly liberal for its day. Among other things, he said that freedom of speech and of the press were essential, education must be available to all citizens, and trial by jury and habeas corpus should be guaranteed. His program, so clearly ahead of his time, led to his election as a delegate to a convention that Louis XVI had been forced to call because all levels of the population had become restive and the economy was in shambles. The hope was that reforms might be introduced that would give France a constitution and a revived spirit. Talleyrand's role proved to be so great that when he left Autun in 1789 to go to the Estates General meeting in Paris, he would never return to his diocese again.

While Talleyrand was sincere in believing that the people deserved all the privileges he had proposed, he was horrified at the idea of their claiming or demanding these rights. He felt that it was the role of the upper class to bestow the rights. Popular demand, he thought, was akin to snatching away the rights. He would always love order and hate extremism or violence.

When the Assembly passed the famous Declaration of the Rights of Man (which gained added fame when Thomas Paine published his classic English translation of it), it became known that Talleyrand had authored the sixth of the twenty-two articles. The article pretended to deal with the finances of the state, but it actually went far beyond economics. It said that all persons are equal in the sight of the law, equally eligible to all honors, places, and employments, according to their different abilities. In other words, no accident of birth should give one man a special place and deprive another of the position for which he has a natural talent. That in itself had made him an exceptional figure. Then, when he asked permission to speak to the Assembly on October 10, 1789, he unleashed a real thunderbolt.

The finances of the state were exhausted, he said, and the people could not be taxed any further. According to the Bishop of Autun, there was only one source of revenue left to be tapped. Said Talleyrand, "This source, it seems to me, is the property of the church."

The church owned about a fifth of the nation's property. The bishop proposed that it be nationalized and all the expenses of the clergy and relief to the poor be paid from the proceeds. Then he quietly sat down and made a move that became a Talleyrand trademark—he took no part in the debate that raged for nearly a month. Having set things in motion, he was never seen to fight. While others argued heatedly for and against the measure, he never again rose to speak. When it was passed by a large majority, he became the most famous and popular man in France.

In his memoirs, his obsession with good taste led him to understate the many things he proposed and actually accomplished during a five-month period that followed, including the founding of a national bank, reduction of interest on the national debt, voting rights for Jews, and police regulations for Paris. He was proudest of his *Report on Public Education*, which affected schools all over Europe, made the French system highly admired, and had an effect for well over a century, with its insistence on a carefully structured plan of schooling for all young persons.

He explained all these accomplishments by saying he had followed the advice of his greatest patron, the Duc de Choiseul, who did nothing himself that he could delegate to others, "so that one day's work has more than twenty-four hours." He was physically lazy but unusually mentally active—which he recognized, discussed, and considered the perfect combination for the conduct of diplomacy.

Even when discussing the most urgent political issues, Talleyrand is described by one biographer, Jack F. Bernard, as "lounging nonchalantly on a sofa, with his face mobile, undecipherable under his powdered wig, saying little, occasionally interjecting a subtle or telling phrase, and then lapsing into his posture of distinguished lassitude and indifference." Nearly everyone, including women, found him charming despite the childhood limp that he never overcame.

Talleyrand's passion for dissipation was almost as great a part of his reputation as his talent for earning bribes. As in all such subjects, like the remarks about how Talleyrand's illegitimate children could be found like chestnuts all over Paris, both truth and exaggeration were mingled. That a less-than-handsome person with a limp was such a ladies man was due more to his skill with words than to any other talent that has been recorded. The brilliant Germaine de Staël put it best when she said, "If Talleyrand's conversation could be purchased, I would gladly go into bankruptcy."

As the most famous person of the moment, admired and applauded wherever he went, he was elected president of the Assembly for a fortnight. This was a time when the mobs were getting out of hand. The king and royal family were seized. It is doubtful whether Talleyrand could have used his popularity to save them and the monarchy, but he didn't lift a finger to try. He had said he would never again "raise any obstacle between opportunity and myself," and it seems that he considered the king more an obstacle than an opportunity.

Like his colleague Barbé-Marbois, Talleyrand had "undergone" a stay in America, and the two men showed the difference between them with such immoderate disagreement in their opinion of the New World. Marbois never ceased praising how much the Americans had accomplished in so short a time. Talleyrand could hardly wait to leave. He had left France because his head was threatened by the Terror, and he had felt such relief to be out on the open water—even when hit by seasickness—that he never forgot the exaltation of being on the sea. This was so strong a feeling that he nearly transferred to a ship bound for Calcutta just to have several more months of total insulation from the need to set foot on land. But there was no room on that other ship, so instead, he said, "I submitted to being taken to Philadelphia."

He had been disinterested in any of the sights that others might admire, but he did want to meet some of the persons who had created the United States. One was Alexander Hamilton, then secretary of the treasury, with whom he formed a lasting friendship. But when he saw Hamilton about a year later, he was totally puzzled to find that he had resigned from government and opened a law office. Hamilton's explanation of his financial plight and the need to earn a private income made no sense at all to Talleyrand, because in France, rich men were supposed to become even richer in office. How could this not be so in America, where money was worshiped even more? To a French friend then living in the United States, Madame La Tour du Pin, Talleyrand talked at length about how silly it was for persons of talent to be forced to leave government, where they could serve the whole nation, in order to seek employment that would benefit only a few.

All his life, that same principle made him feel that gifts accepted by officials were not only normal (as most Europeans considered them) but also sound economics—money exchanged for a service rendered—so long as the service also redounded to the benefit of one's own country. For that, one had to count on the good sense and honor of the public servant. If he lacked those attributes, then it was not the bribe that was the problem, it was the fact that he should not have held that position at all.

Talleyrand's expectation, and even demands, for payment when he was able to provide some benefit was no different from the usual practice in France and in most of Europe, but the amounts he took in were greater because the results bought by the bribery were so remarkable. (When he failed to deliver what was wanted, he often returned the gift. Once he was paid eight million francs for an arrangement that a Polish group wanted from Napoleon, but Talleyrand failed to get the desired result. He promptly repaid the entire eight million.) During one two-year period when he was foreign minister, he is believed to have taken in between twelve million and fifteen million francs (about two-and-one-half to three million dollars).

Life as he viewed it in this dull and somewhat misguided country was so little to his liking that he wrote to his great friend and lover Germaine de Staël, summing up most of his notions of the place, "If I have to stay here for another year, I shall surely die." When it was finally deemed safe for him to return to Paris in July 1796, he was determined to watch and wait, rather than plunge into the murky politics of the day, "since I perceived no element of order, no guarantee of stability in the various political factions whose struggles I witnessed." Instead, he brought himself to the attention of the public as an academician by reading thoughtful papers at important meetings. One of them was coolly anti-American because it showed how the English language kept America totally English in character and customs. This meant, he said, that only England could derive advantages from America. The English could see their former colony grow with the energy and rapidity of a nation while being entirely devoted to English interests—and trade.

A second paper expanded the subject of colonization to show the advantages that France could gain by establishing more colonies, putting French citizens into new lands, and opening great new markets to French enterprise. It will be immediately obvious that this was exactly opposite to the argument that Livingston made just a few years later, showing why colonies were not the best policy for France. Typically, Talleyrand would not quarrel when that time came, but merely observe what the First Consul's reaction would be and try to form his own policy around it.

The most important of the ideas he advanced on several occasions was his incredible but sincere desire for a very close relationship between France and England. It was astonishing because he was fated to spend most of his career as a trusted adviser of men whose thoughts ran in the opposite direction. No more surprising or surreptitious policy has ever dwelt hidden for so long a period. It remained, probably stronger than ever, when the ex-bishop went on to be the confidant and strategist of Napoleon Bonaparte, who lived to make war on England.

But Talleyrand meant what he had said years earlier: "Two neighboring nations, the prosperity of one being founded on commerce and of the other on agriculture, are compelled by the very nature of things to reach a mutual understanding and to reap a mutual profit." He preached this subtly to Napoleon, to the Bourbon kings of the first restoration, and to the second restoration, or July Monarchy. France, he tried to tell them all, would never really be secure in Europe unless it was bound to Great Britain by the closest ties. Having grown up in the school of Voltaire, he genuinely believed that peace was the only natural state of man. War was not victory for one nation and defeat for another, it was irrationality and loss for both.

If Talleyrand considered these public readings to be a form of abstention from politics, he soon found that the liveliness of his ideas contrasted so sharply with the dullness of the Directory that they were making him an important force again.

In the summer of 1797, the five-man Directory government had chosen Talleyrand to be its foreign minister because he had ingratiated himself with Paul de Barras, the Directory's leader. Within a week, Talleyrand made one of his brilliant moves. Deciding that the Directory was "a corpse waiting to be buried," and that General Bonaparte, then in Italy fighting lightning battles, was likeliest to become France's future leader, he wrote Napoleon a letter promising to keep him informed of important developments and proposing a regular correspondence between them. Napoleon answered very favorably, creating a political partnership that was unknown to anyone else.

When Napoleon returned to Paris, after having redrawn the map of Europe in his dazzling campaigns, Talleyrand chose a time when he thought it appropriate for the "corpse" to be buried. He was sure the Directory was headed for extinction, so he sought to take advantage of it as a way of giving France a more stable government. He wanted the five-man Directory to have fewer numbers—one, in fact: Napoleon. It happened that General Bonaparte was in Egypt at that time, having just invaded and effortlessly conquered it with fifty thousand men. But most inconveniently, a major part of the French fleet, anchored at Aboukir at the disposal of the victorious general, was surprised and destroyed by Britain's Admiral Nelson. Napoleon found one small vessel to take him daringly away from this sandy prison, left his deputy to shift for himself without even meeting him in person, and returned to French territory, landing at Fréjus. He lost not a day in publicizing his return, and his skill in describing disasters as glowingly as victories made the nation rise to acclaim him.

While a few careful observers noted that Napoleon's Egyptian campaign was actually a failure, Talleyrand ignored the charges and became the principal architect of a coup that brought Napoleon to power. He decided that the Directory was to be dissolved and replaced by a Consulate, with Napoleon as First Consul. There were two other Consuls, with roles so small that Napoleon would be a virtual dictator. Talleyrand also took on the key role of informing the Vicomte Paul de Barras, head of the Directory, that his rule was over. Typically, a large amount of money was to change hands, but this time Talleyrand was not on the receiving end. He understood Barras well enough to know what would make him step down without causing trouble. A banker named Gabriel Ouvrard was advancing three million francs in the form of a letter of credit, and Talleyrand, calling Barras "the greatest patriot in France," handed him an elegantly worded letter of resignation to sign, while also handing over the letter of credit.

When an arrangement of this kind was safely completed, Talleyrand liked nothing better than to spend an agreeable evening with friends. On this occasion, dinner was at the home of a Belgian banker whose wife had been a famous actress and, until just the day before, had played a dual role as the mistress of Barras.

One of Napoleon's first official acts, as soon as he had settled into the Luxembourg Palace, was to call in Talleyrand and reinstate him as minister of foreign affairs.

One of his last official acts, years later, when he was thoroughly beaten but still technically emperor, was to beg Talleyrand to return as minister of foreign affairs. Talleyrand, already determined to restore the Bourbon monarchy, refused. Napoleon screamed furiously, "You are planning to betray me!"

"No, sire. I cannot assume office because in my opinion your policies are contrary to my own conception of the glory and happiness of my country," Talleyrand countered. There was probably some sincerity in these words, for Talleyrand thought of himself as a dedicated patriot, even though most of his years of service to Napoleon were spent submerging his own deepest beliefs: that France's only hope of good government was to install a two-chamber system similar to the British Parliament, and that the best hope of happiness and tranquillity for its people was a close commercial, political, and even royal relationship with England. He preached this view in the waning days of Louis XVI and in the days of the two Bourbons that he restored to the throne, and he tried as hard as he dared to preach it to Napoleon Bonaparte by insinuating subtle suggestions into all his words of advice. But Napoleon seemed hardly to notice, because tranquillity was the last thing he wanted to hear. War with England was his lodestar.

The one thing that is always quoted about Napoleon's image of his foreign minister—"a silk stocking full of *merde*"—is misleading.

He said it, and he meant it, but in a way that combined some truth with humor. The insult is meaningless without knowing how much Napoleon admired Talleyrand, and found him charismatic and endlessly stimulating. He did not trust him, but that did not get in the way of his essentially favorable reaction to the personality. Bearing in mind how much Napoleon worshiped the concept of daring—*l'audace, encore de l'audace, toujours l'audace* (audacity, more audacity, always audacity)—it is clear how exciting he found this man's audacious way of first making himself a national figure by being the churchman who proposed what all churchmen feared most. Only months removed from having been an unknown abbé, the scoundrel had accomplished what only King Henry VIII of England had previously tried: expropriating the properties of the church. To Napoleon, the fact that he had even thought of it was wondrous; that he had dared to stand and say it was sublime. And Napoleon found that an hour with Talleyrand seldom failed to bring fascinating ideas that were similarly new and deliciously daring.

During much of 1802 and 1803, the First Consul paid less attention than usual to this favorite adviser. Napoleon was, in fact, in an unaccustomed, un-Napoleonic situation. Often before, he had been the one to strike unexpectedly. But this time, even his advance move of taking title to Louisiana from Spain had been suspected by Jefferson. Napoleon had done the unexpected by taking that title secretly and keeping America in doubt for a year and a half, but he had still been forced to act against his usual instincts in making long, slow preparations to assemble a striking force and colonists before making an overt move. This period of careful planning after he took Louisiana from Spain had given the United States time to anticipate a French landing and to adopt a fighting attitude, even if it lacked a coherent force. Now Napoleon was facing an adversary who was clearly on the watch for his move. There was no way for him to take New Orleans by coming from another direction or by striking somewhere else in his usual diversionary way.

He had been harried, too, by the drain of men and money caused by the ongoing disaster of Saint Domingue. He had to spend money he couldn't well afford in trying to deal with this side issue across the ocean, when he really longed to use the cash to get ready for a new war against the English. He had been handicapped by the fact that Talleyrand, the adviser he looked to for his best ideas, was a great advocate of colonies and therefore tried in subtle ways to prevent the abandonment of Louisiana and to head off war in Europe. Even as late as 1802, Talleyrand hoped to share in a huge bribe that the British had offered to him and to Napoleon's brother Joseph if they could arrange for England to retain Malta without fighting a war. This offer produced a famous and furious Bonaparte family quarrel in Napoleon's bathroom, with his brothers Joseph and Lucien shouting that the First Consul was being a fool to throw away a colony for mere money. Rising angrily in his tub to denounce Joseph, Napoleon hurled his jewelled snuff box in anger, but slipped and fell, while his valet fainted dead away. Such distractions had not been big factors in his decision, for Napoleon was too independent-minded to let anyone else's opinion sway him. But Talleyrand's steady pressure against giving up the Territory caused Napoleon to shorten the time he spent with his foreign minister.

Consequently, the First Consul's usual method for considering a variety of approaches before settling on a course of action had been distorted in these two years. Normally, it was in character for him, when surrounded by officers or ministers who were his experts on specific subjects, to throw out a number of daring ideas, often bringing forth cautionary comments from one of the others, which were frequently brushed aside. In most cases, he opted for more risk than anyone around him had proposed or imagined. In this period, however, the First Consul more often made remarks of a conservative nature—that is, featuring ideas that avoided major action. And the more he heard, the more risk-averse he became. As his mind turned more toward a sale rather than a landing in New Orleans, he seemed to tilt the playing field in that direction by giving very brief instructions, little more than hints, to Ministers Talleyrand and Barbé-Marbois, and even those lacked his usual conciseness. The instructions were vague, and the ministers took them as generalities rather than specifics. Their interpretations of his words, naturally based on their own preferences, led the two men to move in opposite directions—Talleyrand trying to slow the sale idea, Marbois much more definitely pressing it forward.

Reports on the American president's immoderate attitude were playing their intended part in the contest for the First Consul's mind, as well. The French ruler had never been known to steer clear of a determined antagonist, but in this case, Jefferson's stand simply added weight to the risk factors that went with this troublesome colonial activity.

In hindsight, it may have been as early as 1801 that obtaining a large sum of money for a war against England began to seem more attractive to the First Consul than the prospect of diverting ships and troops to an inhospitable New World. He knew that Talleyrand leaned the other way. If Saint Domingue had stabilized and started producing profits again, rather than disease and death, the clever Talleyrand might have guided Napoleon's thoughts toward the Caribbean and Louisiana. As it was, this became one of the times when the foreign minister had to play a quiet, and somewhat devious, waiting game, while Napoleon preferred to let his treasury minister, Marbois, conduct most of the business.

Chapter Seven

CONFUSING BONAPARTE

W hile Thomas Jefferson deliberately schooled himself to seem emotional and even unreasonable on the Louisiana issue in order to unsettle the French, his opposite number, Napoleon, needed no special effort to appear inconsistent. Napoleon was given to wide mood swings and had a penchant for snap judgments that were often brilliant but occasionally deplorable. Although Napoleon certainly had a mind of exceptional speed and power, it is instructive to learn that even in these prime years of his youth, he had baffling moments. And the Louisiana negotiations brought on more than the usual confusion.

Napoleon could work eighteen hours at a stretch, turn from subject to subject with total recall, and remember the whole face of France well enough to move regiments and approximate their stock of arms and their supply of ammunition. It might seem like mere boasting when he said of himself, "Last night, at 2 o'clock, I got up to examine the field reports sent in by the Minister of War. I found twenty mistakes." But such feats could be attested to by many subordinates who had felt the sting of his reproofs. He was his own inspector general and minister of the whole. Nothing was small enough to escape his attention.

Perhaps the most astonishing aspect of his multifaceted personality is that he was not restricted simply to facts and figures. He thought in personal and psychological terms as well. His conversation and endless accumulation of written messages proved that he pictured and understood the feelings of peasants and of the small bourgeosie in deeply human ways, and realized equally the feelings of men who had served in the Revolutionary armies and of those who ached to escape the stigma of having once joined Radical clubs. He hated, but understood, each of the thousands of speculators who had made fortunes from army contracts.

Coming from a bright but contentious and often sordid family, Napoleon's natural instinct for military brilliance is less astonishing than his towering accomplishments as a civilian ruler. Bertrand de Molleville, who had been a minister under Louis XVI, told of his amazement when he heard the First Consul discoursing. "Where in the devil did he learn all that?" he asked himself. And no one has ever come close to answering that question. Where did he acquire such a clear realization of the many things that were wrong in society, government, and education? When did he find time to understand the details and to develop the methods for improving the way so many things were done? And the final question, perhaps, might be: How could anyone with so fine an understanding have made the truly mindless blunders that shattered an unparalleled career? Still, long after his death, it remains true that, as a fine biography by Robert Asprey has shown:

> Almost all the institutions that are revered by the French elite
> were created by Napoleon. He established the prefectural

corps, the Légion d'Honneur, and the Civil Code, a legal system that still governs the lives of people all over the world and that was drafted under Napoleon's aegis after the battle of Marengo. Perhaps his most significant single legacy for France was the reconstitution of the École Polytechnique, originally set up as an artillery school and now responsible for the high quality of French engineering. It is literally true that long after he was gone, many nations were still governed by Napoleon's mind.

Yet the First Consul had moments of confusion and weakness that one would not expect. His instant decision-making was often faulty, and his surprise at finding himself wrong could lead to utter confusion. Sometimes—and the Louisiana affair is very much a case in point—he did things haphazardly. But like anyone in a leadership role, his good days and bad days depended largely on how the people he had chosen were performing. And his personnel choices were well above average.

In this case of the Louisiana question, Napoleon threw out a variety of ideas that baffled his underlings, sent off two ministers to do the same task, almost as competitors rather than colleagues, and tossed out random numbers as potential sales prices, then appeared to have forgotten what he had said. But in the final analysis, these aides were competent to carry off the situation well enough to allow Napoleon—with some justification—to claim the result as a victory.

Napoleon can be credited with having chosen Talleyrand and Marbois, but a fourth member of the French team that managed the Louisiana negotiation was a young man whom the foreign minister had personally plucked from obscurity and placed in charge of the

French Legation in Washington. Louis-André Pichon, the lowest-ranked player on either side of the affair, was an able and clear-headed twenty-nine-year-old who had already had nearly ten years of diplomatic experience and more knowledge of American affairs than any of his predecessors in the post. His excellent English was another advantage. He had been a mere assistant chief of the Foreign Ministry's Southern Division, and was a surprise appointment to be the *chargé d'affaires* in Washington during the autumn of 1801, even though his youth and rather modest previous duties made many feel that the job was far above his proper level.

The detractors were wrong, because the man who knew best—Talleyrand himself—had been keeping an eye on Pichon since the young man had taken the initiative and gone far beyond his limited assignment in Holland two years earlier. As a lower-level embassy employee in the Netherlands—although one who may have been encouraged by Talleyrand to act boldly—he had opened indirect communications with U.S. President John Adams through William Vans Murray, American minister to the Netherlands. He had the delicate task of persuading Adams that France wanted peace with the United States, convincing Talleyrand that Adams was not so warlike as he appeared, and urging all parties to try a new negotiation. The French took a chance on Pichon's view, proposed a reopening of relations, and were rewarded with Adams's surprise acceptance in the face of heavy political opposition at home. Only a few insiders realized that such a minor functionary as Pichon, by taking responsibility beyond his station, had actually prevented a needless Franco-American war. Now, no one else understood why a person so young was put in charge of the major mission in Washington. But the astute Talleyrand—with that well-known ability to be constantly serving his own interests while also doing what was best for France—thought Pichon could be trusted not only to report what he saw in America, but also to give honest opinions without trying to say what his superiors would like to hear.

Again, as in the case of Livingston, Pichon began by being underestimated on both sides of the Atlantic. In Livingston's case, his superiors thought less of him as time went on, while the opponents valued his work more highly. Pichon's superiors, on the other hand, paid increasing attention to his views, and let him know of their approval. The adversaries who dealt with him in Washington agreed with that higher assessment, but they took advantage of it to channel more disinformation through him, making this an example of how reliant even the greatest figures often are on the characters and abilities of the information gatherers and message bearers who serve them.

Repeatedly, Pichon was the person who gathered and transmitted the ideas that Napoleon and Talleyrand had to work with on the Louisiana issue. When he picked up gossip about some remark of Jefferson's or Madison's or a prominent senator's and found what appeared to be warlike sounds, it was Pichon's duty to transmit them to Paris. As he had done when writing from Holland, the feisty young man made it his business to add some of his own interpretations, and, in time, it turned out that Napoleon and his ministers were listening for the Pichon comments—not always accepting them in full, but seldom disregarding them. They got not only facts, but subtleties as well. Pichon clearly conveyed his respect for Madison, which helped to give his superiors in Paris a sense of the caliber of men they were dealing with. He said of the secretary of state, "His name and reputation are respected by both parties. He is always dignified. And if he has adopted some favorable leaning, he hides it under an austere impartiality which, however, does not prevent him from being both communicative and pleasant company."

So the balance of forces between the two sides of this negotiation included the odd fact that the French were relying more and more on analyses received from "Napoleon's Man in Washington," while the Americans were operating as if they hardly had a man in Paris at all.

It is another of the oddities of this unique negotiation—much like its ability to surmount the inattention to orders—that the French side got the worst of the information exchange. For although Pichon did a fine job in many delicate situations and could hardly have played any better with the cards he was dealt, the "Jefferson-Madison Theatrical Society" took disinformation to a new level, and the presence of a good minister in Washington whose reports were carefully studied served as an open channel for misinforming Napoleon. (No written word exchanged between the president and the secretary of state proves the existence of such a strategy, but there were too many successful repetitions of it—all conveying the exact message that was appropriate to the moment—to leave room for doubt.) It is possible that an exceedingly suspicious person in Pichon's place might have had a qualm or two about the remarks and attitudes he was reporting to Paris. But it should be kept in mind that when Talleyrand read every word of these reports and found the news not to his liking, he never doubted that the facts and the reasoning were correct.

Pichon happened to be a partisan who opposed a French adventure in Louisiana; but even when he tried being an accurate reporter, Pichon could not have been expected to see through the veil of deception woven by Jefferson and Madison. And it was made totally undetectable by the fact that they were hardly ever in the room together when their carefully orchestrated remarks were made. Jefferson would have been presiding over his dinner table in the White House; two weeks later, Pichon would be sitting in the secretary of state's office and hearing a different tune. How could he help but conclude that one of them was being more frank than the other—or more pro-French?

Pichon was given the impression of total realism by the fact that the good and bad cops sometimes changed roles, as human beings often do. There was the time, for example, when Pichon had come to see the secretary of state about finding a way to procure supplies for Leclerc's troops in the Caribbean. Since Leclerc had arrived with insufficient provisions for the unexpectedly long stay on Saint Domingue, he was desperate for supplies, could not get credit from the New York dealers who were approached, and raged at Pichon for not doing more to help through his Washington contacts.

Now the French *chargé*, who usually got such a fine welcome at the State Department, was stunned by a flurry of aggressive questions from Madison: Why had so large an expedition been sent? Why had the U.S. not been given advance notice? Was the expedition ultimately expected to take over Louisiana? After managing to fend off all those challenges, Pichon asked for a loan that would help with the procurement of supplies. Don't even speak of it, said Madison. Considering France's mistreatment of American shipping and then refusal to pay the claims, any cash advances to that country would cause cries of rage. But when the persistent Pichon took his loan request to Jefferson, he was able to report, "The President spoke to me with the language of sincerity…and even said he would consider what could be done." In fact, nothing was done.

While every such nuance was read and analyzed in Paris, meaning that the voices of Jefferson and Madison were able to send clever misimpressions across the ocean, nothing of that sort happened in the other direction. Napoleon and Talleyrand could say nothing to Livingston that might have had this kind of effect in Washington. It wasn't clear whether Madison even read most of Livingston's letters, although an example of one he did read was revealed later in a conversation with Pichon.

The amount of time that the secretary of state gave to this one foreign diplomat was most unusual, and of course it was a very worthwhile investment. It must be kept clearly in mind that France had never made the fateful move of trying to occupy New Orleans. Its "ownership" was written into a treaty, but nothing more. So the Jefferson administration had two main objectives always in mind: to discourage and deter any such physical occupation, and also to set up a situation in Napoleon's mind that would encourage him to offer a deal favorable to American interests. Madison's talks with Pichon were wide-ranging, but usually slanted toward those goals. The sessions did not always confide information, but were often highly critical. One of Pichon's analytical reports to Paris told of Madison's complaint that French coldness and unfriendliness was playing into the hands of the Federalist party, which was strongly pro-British. France, he said, should prepare itself for the fact that if this opposing party won, it would steer the United States into an alliance with England, very likely aimed at making war against France.

On one visit in the summer of 1802, Pichon found Madison very angry about an article in *La Gazette de France* that said the United States was heading toward domination of the New World, to the detriment of Europe. And the role of France in Louisiana, it added, was to arrest that destiny. Madison's "very stern lecture" insisted that France's bad faith and dissimulation seemed to justify American fears of the change of ownership. The French possession, he said, "would unite Americans, and one has to argue that France can not long hold Louisiana against the will of the United States." On several of these occasions, Pichon added that Madison had spoken "with much calmness and deliberateness," which clearly added to his respect.

Sharp sessions of this kind found their mark, as Pichon inevitably brought them to the urgent attention of his superiors in Paris. One of them was Madison's sudden crisp query: "Is it not singular, Mr. Pichon, that Mr. Livingston had not been able to obtain, at the date of his last letter from Paris, a word of response to the inquiries he has made on the subject of our interests and our rights upon the Mississippi? Certainly if people behaved thus toward you, you would regard this silence as a sort of declaration of war."

Pichon's reports often had to take the form of strict warnings, designed to prevent serious miscalculations. For example, Talleyrand passed some of Pichon's warnings along to Admiral Dénis Décrès, Minister of Marine, who had a major role in preparing for a possible landing in New Orleans. The admiral was cautioned, "You will not count on the cooperation of the United States...and you must be able to disguise these measures so that the Americans will not know of them." As is usually the case, the bearer of unwelcome messages is blamed, rather than thanked. So although the incredibly open-minded Talleyrand reacted gratefully to Pichon's important warnings, they turned Décrès into a serious enemy who thought Pichon was poisoning the First Consul's mind.

The tumult on Saint Domingue, which was to prove a decisive factor in the fate of Louisiana, was a most delicate challenge for Pichon in advising Paris what to expect of American policy. Many in the French government believed that America was secretly supportive of Toussaint's rebellion, since it was reducing the chances of a French expansion in the Caribbean and onto the mainland. Others tended to accept the quiet American assurances that the United States did not support the violent overthrow of existing governments. Madison had said that America would gladly help to restore France's rights on the island if it could be done in accordance with international law; but especially if France was to be at war with England, there was no legal way to arrange this. Behind the whole subject, of course, lay the question of how seriously the Americans were concerned that the example of a successful black rebellion might bring on similar uprisings in the southern states.

Pichon's word to Paris was that Jefferson and Madison apparently differed on the whole subject, though both were handling it in the quiet way that every dispute between them was managed. Pichon thought Jefferson inwardly feared that a black government so nearby would act to stir slave revolts in the U.S., while Madison had no such fear and was "very reserved on the matter," appearing to have no notion that American slaves might try to copy what the island people had done. It was a clever interpretation, but Pichon had clearly been taken in—and not for the only time—by the secretary's deceptive manner. Apparently, Madison's soft voice and nonemphatic way of talking on subjects that roused most others to excited statements convinced Pichon, time after time, that Madison's stated views—though sometimes so improbable—were exactly the way he saw matters.

Whenever the key subject of Louisiana came up, Madison was in his best thespian form. Early in Pichon's period as *chargé,* after one of their most significant conversations, Pichon reported to Paris that he had asked the secretary of state why he was concerned about the possibility of seeing France in Louisiana. "Does the U.S. wish to go beyond the Mississippi?" he had suggested.

"The idea is a chimera," Madison replied.

"But surely," Pichon said, "the U.S. would not make it a crime for France to recover lost territory? Since France's principles are more enlightened than Spain's, why couldn't France offer an agreement covering all points that could cause disputes?"

Madison simply repeated that if there were any such transfer (of New Orleans to France), there would be no way to avoid a collision. Because this exchange had come early in Pichon's period as *chargé,* he felt the need to apologize to his superiors in Paris for having ventured into such a serious debate without instructions.

Clearly it was Pichon's job to interpret and assign some level of validity to the remarks, the scuttlebutt, and occasionally the direct quotations he gathered. He might have done better in that area, for much of what he heard was precisely intended to influence Napoleon in a certain direction. But he knew that to err on the side of downplaying the threats could have led Napoleon to move troops and colonists into a fatal trap, so Pichon cannot be greatly faulted if he was often an alarmist. A more mature person might have turned greater suspicion on the American administration's remarks, which exaggerated the nation's military prowess. But even that is questionable, for Pichon did pick up what appeared to be confirming information from other sources. For example, he was conscientious about covering Congress more than most diplomats did, and some of the legislators went even farther than the executive branch in talking of stiff resistance on the New Orleans issue. Their remarks were often exaggerations based on the slightest information, but there were no good sources of governmental facts available in print at the time, so the congressional chatter had to be taken into account, if not entirely believed. Pichon could not, in good conscience, have refrained from transmitting the warnings back to Paris.

There were times when the young French diplomat felt the need—and did not hesitate—to lecture his seniors and even the greatest figures that he worked for. He tried time and again to let the leaders in Paris, including Napoleon, understand that when Leclerc and his officers made raging public statements against American attitudes, it made no difference whether they were right or wrong. They stirred up press campaigns against France, and then—even if the American government had wanted to help Leclerc—public opinion would have made it impossible. It seems that not even Napoleon understood this logic, for one account has him saying that, after all, the American newspapers had carried very bad words about the French, so why should the French officers not speak their minds in return? Nor is it known whether Talleyrand, after having scolded Pichon for talking to members of the American Congress about France's need for a loan, saw the merit of the *chargé d'affaires*' characteristically straight and instructive answer: "I give full weight and justice to your observations on this subject. But by the nature of this government, all is known to the members of the legislature, and it is impossible to avoid the inconvenience of publicity."

The times when Pichon's very careful analyses went pardonably astray occurred when he swallowed what appears to have been a neatly planned scenario played by Jefferson and Madison with the hope that the envoy would promptly transmit it to Paris. This was the case when Pichon was forced to send word that Madison had told him vigorously of his own fears about Jefferson's plan to "marry the British fleet," while Pichon himself had "observed at table that he [Jefferson] redoubles his kindnesses and attention to the British *chargé d'affaires*." Probably both Madison and Jefferson were play-acting according to a previous arrangement, but the strange result was that it nullified Livingston's cover-up of the powerful warnings that Jefferson had asked him to convey to the French. Whatever Livingston failed to pass on to the First Consul, the latter heard from his source in America. And coming through their own man in Washington, it must have seemed more convincing to Talleyrand and Napoleon that perhaps the Americans really were ready to fight for New Orleans—and in league with the British, if need be. Even if they suspected that what Pichon witnessed was a set piece that Jefferson and Madison performed for his benefit, this must have seemed most unlikely to them and certainly nothing to be relied on as a certainty, so the threat Jefferson wanted to impart would have had to be taken into account.

The great campaign of truth-twisting that Jefferson and Madison were running took other inventive forms. There were, for example, repeated announcements of large population increases in the western areas—partly truthful, but considerably inflated—implying that many of these people would swell the number of volunteers willing to fight in any struggle over New Orleans. Jefferson had often said, "Population is power." Now Madison, as if talking to Pichon on an unrelated subject, would mention some spurious new figures, throwing in a brief reminder of the president's words.

The truth was that, even without exaggerations, America's growth was astonishing. Pichon simply sent a summary of the American census of 1800, showing a population increase of two and one half million, indicating a doubling every twenty-two years, which outstripped even Benjamin Franklin's largest prediction. "These developments boggle the imagination," he told Talleyrand. And on the following day, he sent word of the first American victory in the naval war against the Barbary pirates, which Pichon noted was, "very flattering to the pride of a new people."

At one critical juncture, however, while Livingston was covering Madison's desktop with reports of his attempts to set up a bribe for Talleyrand, it appeared that Jefferson and Madison began to give Pichon an impression exactly opposite to what they had wanted to convey earlier. The young Frenchman sent word to Paris that, despite the bursting excitement of the pro-western Americans, the Jefferson administration had a peaceful attitude. When he sent word that Monroe was being posted to Paris again, Pichon implied that this was only to appease the westerners' demand for action (because of Monroe's reputation for being pro-western). Monroe's role was to help buy time, he said, because the United States actually felt it could act more effectively on the Mississippi after having ten more years of growth. Right now, it feared that the costs of war would hurt the government's popularity. This seemed opposite to the message Jefferson wanted to send Paris, so it may appear hard to fathom why the administration gave Pichon such an impression.

But it was apparently part of a plan, a sign that an important turning point had been reached. Just six days later, on March 28, Pichon confirmed this view with a similar message: he had dined with the president on January 12 and had been told that because Monroe was known as a friend of the western people, they would be reassured that their interests were being well guarded just by knowing that Monroe was taking part in the Paris talks—thus preventing unfortunate incidents. A secondary conclusion to be drawn from this is that the two men wanted Paris to believe that the westerners themselves were taking the lead in urging action, that the American people—and not only their government—were determined to fight any landing by the French. And they may have wanted to play down the notion that the Monroe visit was aimed at concluding an agreement, so as to depress French hopes that American eagerness might produce a very large price.

This would seem to be supported by Pichon's report of a remarkable briefing in Madison's office. In veiled terms, Madison had pleaded that France should not provoke the forcible expansion of the United States beyond the Mississippi River. It was not in the interest of either country, he said, "for these emigrations tended to weaken the state and slacken the concentrations of its forces. It would surely give birth to a second American state, certain to clash with the Eastern part of the country. The relations of one or both of these with England would be as critical to France as to the American people."

Madison, of course, did not at all believe that the United States was in danger of splitting into two nations; he believed just the opposite. The philosophical tone of his language shows him to have been choosing words that would appeal to the nuanced French mind. It certainly seems to have made an impact on the authorities in Paris, for

Napoleon soon included some of Madison's misleading thoughts in his own comments. And he mentioned with relish the possibility that he would renounce Louisiana "in order to let the Americans grow and teach the English a lesson."

ᴄ⨪

This change in the atmosphere happened to come at a time when Madison's words to Pichon were reinforced by a bizarre incident that must be counted as a major turning point in the negotiations. A Spanish official at New Orleans known as Intendant Juan Ventura Morales abruptly closed the port in November 1802, cancelling the right of Americans to store their goods while awaiting export to the outside world. Since an intendant was a manager, not a policymaker, the usual interpretation of this action—that it was one individual's abrupt move that did not reflect any government policy—is not credible. It seems much more likely that Manuel de Godoy had actually inspired it in order to stir the waters and perhaps attempt to retract Spain's cession of Louisiana to France. The arrogant and unfeeling statement closing the port could not have originated with an unknown functionary, who was of so little account that most history books have not troubled to find his first name, and refer to him simply as "Morales." It began, "As long as it was necessary to tolerate the commerce of neutrals, which is now abolished..." and went on to say, "The privilege which the Americans had...shall be interdicted...and in order that nobody may allege ignorance, I order it to be published." In any case, until the edict was reversed, the uproar that the event produced in the United States was bound to give Napoleon another reason for believing that the American people were united in opposition to foreign interference.

The first effect was shock in many capital cities, consternation in the State Department, and then a comment by Secretary of State Madison that this must have been an unauthorized act. The Spanish minister in Washington echoed this view, insisting that his government in Madrid had nothing to do with it. Both those remarks were, of course, *pro forma*. But it was the reaction of the American public that was most important. As if the people were determined to be indignant and to disregard the calming words, a storm of public protests broke out. There were boisterous street demonstrations, and angry signs appeared in the windows of many homes. Large newspaper headlines were little used at the time, but letters to the editors were many and strong. They were closely studied by members of the Congress. The fury might have been expected of the westerners, but even eastern Americans, usually thought to be interested only in their own shipments from Atlantic Ocean ports, were infuriated. Apparently, after years of hearing about British and French attacks on U.S. shipping and mistreatment of American sailors, both East and West were just waiting for one incident that could unite them. While officials in every capital kept insisting that this was surely a mistake, the American public roared on—and the Congress was quick to board the bandwagon. "We must reopen the Mississippi by force," read one letter. Another said, "Congress must warn that we mean to go to war." Congress did just that, but the secretary of state worked hard to resist the pressure.

Despite the losses that American farmers and shippers were suffering as their goods rotted, the governments that had called this port closing an "accident" bumbled along for months without reopening New Orleans. Meanwhile, the Federalists, usually the party of the North and East, saw a chance to broaden their base by appealing to the frustrated westerners. As Jefferson wrote at the time, "The opposition caught it as a plank in a shipwreck." They kept up a drumbeat of demands for action to reopen New Orleans by force, if necessary.

By March 1803, Senator James Ross of Pennsylvania was roused to introduce legislation giving the president the power to enlist fifty thousand men and use $5,000,000 to take New Orleans. His speech was supposed to be in the privacy of the Senate Chamber, but Ross then repeated it to Pichon himself outside the chamber. Pichon was so stirred by this confirmation of Madison's statement, "The Federalists move heaven and earth for war," that he took a direct action that was probably beyond his authority. He published a letter to the Spanish governor of New Orleans saying that France disapproved of the closing of the port. This showed what confusion there was over the status of New Orleans. France "owned" New Orleans, but had chosen not to take formal control of it. Yet when a French envoy in another capital commented on a Louisiana subject, no one felt confident enough to rebuke him for the curious action. The total effect of the whole incident worked in the direction that Jefferson and Madison were hoping for: a demonstration of the apparent groundswell for American control of New Orleans.

Pichon never ceased being concerned every time he saw Jefferson appearing friendly to the British *chargé,* that "necessity might be forcing Mr. Jefferson to give up his scruples against an English alliance." He may or may not have known that Monroe would be going to France with a letter in his pocket from Edward Thornton, the British *chargé* in Washington, to Lord Whitworth, the British ambassador in Paris, which showed that he had full power to act for the United States, therefore implying the right to arrange an alliance between the United States and Great Britain. But Pichon alerted Talleyrand to the fact that Monroe had complete freedom to decide for himself on a possible detour while he was abroad: if things went badly in Paris, Monroe was authorized to go directly to London, presumably to conclude an alliance on terms that Jefferson and his cabinet had determined.

Monroe did, in fact, have such authority, but the president may have given him verbal instructions modifying this course of action, so it is not proof positive that Jefferson was truly willing to bind the U.S. to Britain as an ally in war. The fact that Pichon was able to alert Talleyrand about any part of Monroe's instructions shows that he was buying something that purported to be inside information—perhaps even from a State Department employee who was planted as a double agent and regularly informed Pichon of "facts" that Madison wanted to have passed to the French. So Monroe's "complete freedom" to form an alliance with Britain may very well have been an imaginary arrangement, set up with the deliberate wish for it to be learned by the French through a Washington source.

Apart from that, Pichon may have been taking Jefferson's sympathy for the British too strongly. The president's real intention was to appear as impartial as possible between the two rival powers, in order to avoid seeming to be "in either country's pocket." That was the carefully planned policy that Jefferson and Madison gave as a briefing to Monroe, one that he would take with him to Paris. It has been noted that there was a certain amount of truth in at least two of the excuses they had made to Livingston for sending Monroe as a coworker. They said they did so to placate the westerners, who felt confidence in Monroe. Jefferson and Madison also wanted to send to Paris for the endgame someone whom they had been able to talk with at great length. The appearance of impartiality in the treatment of France and England was a very definite part of the instructions they had given to Monroe.

As it happened, Pichon's warnings were suddenly and dramatically supported by the arrival of newspaper clippings from the *New York Morning Chronicle*, telling of the motion by Senator Ross to vote such a large fund and at the same time raise so many troops for the seizure of New Orleans. It came just at a critical moment, when Napoleon was still showing strong signs of wanting to hold on to his American empire and Talleyrand was falsely telling him that

Monroe's coming might be delayed, partly to further his own hope of a bribe for a separate scheme he had spawned.

Soon after that, Livingston sent Talleyrand the clipping from the *New York Morning Chronicle* giving the text of Senator Ross's bill. Napoleon had already read the *Chronicle*, which he received with remarkable speed from London. The First Consul, who could command a huge intelligence operation, became inordinately cocky whenever he was the first to learn a political fact, and the speedy delivery of a newspaper distributed by the British often afforded him this simple pleasure. In this case, moreover, there was a practical effect: Napoleon saw the story as a confirmation of what he had been hearing from Pichon, and he was almost at the point of giving up all interest in retaining Louisiana.

Despite France's long-standing and superior intelligence operations, it is likely that the constitutional relations between Congress and the executive branch of the U.S. government were not well understood. Louis Pichon doubtless knew that a senator's motion might die without ever becoming effective, but even he was probably unaware of how poorly informed the legislators were because they had no constitutional right to insist on information from the president if he deemed such a revelation contrary to the public good. The noisy demands for such details in modern times may be misleading, but the Constitution contains nothing that obligates the president to furnish diplomatic or military information to Congress if he judges that the subject is best kept secret. This remains as true today as it was in 1792, when George Washington's cabinet unanimously concluded that a demand of this kind from Congress could be turned down or deferred until the president judged that it could be safely met.

A House committee conducting the first congressional inquiry wanted to know the circumstances that had resulted in a Native

American victory over Major General Arthur St. Clair and his men in the Northwest Territory. The committee had asked Secretary of War Henry Knox for pertinent correspondence. Knox asked President Washington if he was supposed to comply, and a cabinet meeting was called. It was Thomas Jefferson, then secretary of state, who reported the cabinet's decision to the House in 1792, saying that "the Chief Executive should comply if the public good would permit it and ought to refuse those requests which would endanger the public." In that instance, the president saw no reason for secrecy, and he ordered Knox to comply with the committee's request.

Four years later, however, Washington refused a House committee's request for correspondence relative to the intensely controversial Jay Treaty with Great Britain. Although Senate ratification was being held up, the House was debating a bill to implement portions of the treaty. But in this case, George Washington felt that the request might lead to a further inflammation of the issue, and Congress amended its resolution, making it into a request for the president to provide the information whenever, in his judgment, it could safely be made public. The House eventually passed the bill, but without seeing the correspondence.

Numerous other tests of this point have occurred in U.S. history, and they have always ended by confirming that the framers of the Constitution clearly believed it was impossible for a body as large as the Congress to keep a secret, so the chief executive could withhold information on matters of national security. Not knowing this fine detail, Napoleon and his extremely able advisers were, in a technical sense, overly impressed by the congressional proceedings. It is an interesting example of how democratic institutions, often thought to be slow and inefficient compared to the raw power of a dictatorship, can sometimes have a unique impact of their own. Nothing the administration might have threatened could have worked so powerfully on Napoleon's mind as the evidence that a chamber composed of the people's representatives was apparently preparing to raise money and troops against him.

Chapter Eight

THE DU PONT WAY

A ll during 1802, the ministers and envoys were testing each other with hypothetical questions and delicately exchanging tentative proposals. Some of these seemed aimless but were intended to elicit responses that might lead to a substantial issue. They often complained that a few principal subjects dominated their talks as they met for evening entertainments with European friends, especially when the men separated from the ladies. From the letters that Robert Livingston, Rufus King, and Charles Pinckney wrote to their friends back in America, it is possible to summon up conversations that recurred almost nightly:

—"Where do you suppose those ships that Bernadotte is assembling will be headed? Louisiana or the Floridas?"

—"Ah, but has Spain given the Floridas to France? I have heard that they deny it."

—Or, "Has it occurred to you that when the French Government sends America a large body of people from France, it will add to them all the most agitated and discontented blacks of their West India colonies?"

Livingston was particularly active in these endeavors, often astonishing Talleyrand or Marbois with direct questions, such as: "Would it be advantageous for France to take possession of Louisiana, do you think? The question presents itself from two points of view. As it affects commerce, and as it affects her positive or relative strength."

While such verbal testing was slowly building toward the talk of specific areas and possible prices that would emerge near the end of that year, President Jefferson was running a separate operation—a nongovernment effort—that bypassed and sometimes threatened Livingston's work in Paris. In his unusual way of doing things, President Jefferson enlisted private persons—including two members of the du Pont family—as helpers, and there is every reason to believe that one of them may have made a significant difference in the outcome of the Louisiana affair.

The du Ponts had become prominent American figures without ceasing to be a part of France, and they had total access to anyone they wished to see in either country. As is often true of families who achieve distinction over generations, the du Ponts, whether in France or in America, were strong-minded individuals who frequently disagreed among themselves and with other people. And they were quite capable of disagreeing even with presidents and autocrats.

The originator of the family's greatness was not, as is generally supposed, a maker of gunpowder. He was not even a business success. Pierre Samuel du Pont, based in New York by then, but crossing the

Atlantic often, was a brilliant multi-aptitude intellectual who had been forced to learn watchmaking because it was his father's trade. He became highly skilled in the work, but it bored him. To prove his point, he made a fine creation that embodied everything he had learned, left it as a gift to his father, and broke away from home to examine and fix something more complex than timepieces. It was mainly the economy of France that he wanted to restructure, and when he was barely twenty he published some monologues with economic theories that captured the acclaim of the multifaceted Voltaire and famed economists François Quesnay and Anne-Robert-Jacques Turgot. His writings had a major impact on French policy, and it was during this period in the late eighteenth century that he became a friend of Thomas Jefferson, who was then American minister in Paris. Because Pierre Samuel du Pont's patrons had been reformers and his own works were essentially liberal, they led to his arrest in the era when the guillotine ruled Paris.

After narrowly escaping execution, he moved to the United States and founded an underfinanced investment company that tried to raise funds in France for investment in America. He proved to be less brilliant in handling real money than he was as a theoretical thinker. The firm survived, but with only minimal success, although nothing ever dampened Pierre Samuel du Pont's optimism and enthusiasm. He and his son Victor were much alike—free spirits who always had many projects afoot. Between the two of them, they were trying to raise funds in France for seven major projects in America, and the results were all unsatisfactory to the French investors.

Fortunately, another of Pierre's sons, Eleuthère Irénée, though rather diffident and considered not too promising, got the idea for project No. 8, the production of gunpowder. Being patient, meticulous, and well organized, the quiet young man founded a company that eventually became a great success, although he was never out of debt in his lifetime because his father and siblings were a serious drain on his resources.

Jefferson knew that Victor, who had once been French consul general in New York, had sent off a long report to Talleyrand in 1798, when he feared that the U.S. and France were rushing toward war on the old issue of France's assaults on American shipping. Victor had acknowledged to Talleyrand that President John Adams (who happened to be an old personal enemy of Victor's) had shown unfriendliness to France, but he argued that this did not excuse "the acts of violence, of brigandage, of piracy committed by French cruisers…against American commerce." And he warned that this French blundering might cause war, costing America its liberty, weakening France, and benefiting only the British. Historian Samuel Eliot Morison considered this message so powerful that he credited Victor du Pont with the avoidance of a Franco-American war. There were other factors and other claimants for this credit (the role played by Louis Pichon while serving in the French Embassy in the Netherlands has already been mentioned in an earlier chapter), but Victor du Pont may well have contributed to peace, as it is clear that American sailors were released and attacks on the high seas stopped just after his intervention.

Three years later, in 1801, Jefferson sounded like a warlike leader when he called on Victor du Pont for help in the Louisiana matter. He heard that Victor was about to leave on a trip to France. He asked Victor to approach Talleyrand to explain the serious consequences for France if it moved to take New Orleans. Du Pont did what he was asked to do, and pointed out to Talleyrand the obvious reasons for France to avoid creating an American backlash, but did not really seem to have engaged the foreign minister's interest. It would appear that Victor probably made a rather flat presentation of the facts, not the kind of impassioned talk that Jefferson was, rather unsuccessfully, exhorting all of his contacts to stage.

Meanwhile, Victor's father, old Pierre Samuel du Pont, had been trying to position the family he headed to benefit from any trend in American politics. In the presidential race of 1800, he had clearly favored his old friend Jefferson, but he also engaged Alexander Hamilton, head of the Federalist party, as a lawyer for his company. Jefferson had shown no sign of resentment, and as president he had continued to send Pierre du Pont long personal letters of warmth and openness that are rare between a chief executive and a private citizen.

The president was asking the elder du Pont, just as he had made the request to Victor, to spread the word to Napoleon or his aides that the U.S. was preparing for a fight over New Orleans. Jefferson had even suggested that he put out some exaggerated numbers about how many troops were being readied for this showdown. Du Pont began by expressing doubts about this warlike approach, then plainly derided it. He insisted on thinking of himself as a businessman, and he thought it might be much better to talk money with the French.

President Jefferson did not argue with him, but continued to threaten an armed conflict. In the spring of 1802, with the pace of Louisiana discussions in Paris accelerating, he heard that Pierre Samuel du Pont himself was about to leave on a business trip to France. Here, he thought, is one man who can get Napoleon's ear and be sure the whole message is understood. The president probably didn't know that Napoleon had once ridiculed du Pont for being an impractical philosopher who had rewritten the Lord's Prayer in stodgy French for the benefit of congregations called "Theophilanthropists." This was a deistic society established in Paris during the Directory aiming to institute a new religion in place of Christianity, offering belief in the existence of God, in the immortality of the soul, and in virtue. Napoleon had said, "Philosophers have no conception of religion as a popular force. If I had to make a religion for philosophers, it would be very different from what I would supply for the credulous."

In any case, Jefferson invited the elder du Pont to Washington and gave him a two-hour presentation—insisting that only his own pacifism made him determined to convince the French of his warlike intentions. In short, he was urging du Pont to threaten Napoleon with war as a means of preserving the peace. Although it is not clear how du Pont responded, Jefferson must have realized that his message was again meeting with resistance, for he soon wrote du Pont a heated letter, in which he warned: "Our circumstances are so imperious as to admit of no delay....Whatever power...holds the country east of the Mississippi becomes our natural enemy." He also gave du Pont an assortment of memoranda and letters that were aimed at making Talleyrand, and perhaps even Napoleon himself, see the great danger in letting differences over New Orleans and the Mississippi traffic fester and destroy the once admirable relationship between France and America.

Jefferson was determined to convince du Pont, a private citizen, to carry out a mission that he was uniquely qualified to perform. In a letter he wrote to du Pont on April 25, 1802, he made a great point of saying, "You will perceive the unlimited confidence I repose in your good faith and in your cordial dispositions to serve both countries when you observe that I leave both letters for Chancellor Livingston open for your perusal." (He even referred to some passages that were in cipher, which he told du Pont to simply ignore, as they were for Livingston's eyes alone.) He went on to warn him of the dire consequences that would befall France if Napoleon should gain control of New Orleans, the great port of the Mississippi. There was the flat assertion that there would be "a war which would annihilate France on the ocean and place it under the despotism of two nations, which I am not reconciled to the more because my own would be one of them."

With the kind of blunt honesty that the president had not been getting from anyone else, Pierre Samuel du Pont now expressed his alarm at such a threatening approach. "To say, 'Give up that city or we shall take it from you' is not at all persuasive," he told Jefferson. He then explored several approaches that might be considered, including a promise to help France win back Canada, but they all seemed too aggressive. Afterwards, he wrote this piece of solid advice:

> What then are your means of acquiring and persuading France to an amicable cession of her property? Alas, Mr. President…it is payment in money. Consider what the most successful war with France and Spain would cost you. And contract for a part—a half, let us say. The two countries will have made a good bargain. You will have Louisiana and probably the Floridas for the least expenditure possible; and this conquest will be neither envenomed by hatreds, nor sullied by human blood.…But offer enough to bring her to a decision, if it can be done, before she takes possession.

The president's reply is not known, for he asked du Pont to destroy it. But apparently Jefferson did not reject the idea of a cash purchase, for when du Pont wrote again, just before sailing, he thanked Jefferson for his letter, saying that he had duly burned it. He renewed his urging for a cash purchase, even proposing ways of financing it if the full purchase price were not available.

♋

Du Pont's inventive mind played with other commercially oriented ideas as well. At one point, in late February 1803, he wrote a note to a French Consul Le Brun, in which he clearly tried to portray himself as a dedicated Frenchman, making a proposal that was entirely for the good of France. In this plan, he would have had both France and Spain sharing the use of New Orleans with the United States, and also benefiting from a promise that those two countries alone would be exempted from any and all duties on their merchandise entering American territory by way of the Mississippi. England's products, on the contrary, would only be admitted by land and would pay 12 or 15 percent duties. He wrote to the French official:

> In this manner, we shall have conquered for the benefit of our manufactures, our silks, ironmongery, and glass of every description, and for the consumption of our wines, vinegar, oil, and dried fruits, all the commerce of the five states of the West, as well as of the new states, which, in this country, multiply so rapidly....This will give us the assurance that the interior of America, from the Allegheny on the one side to the elevated mountains beyond the lakes on the other, will only be populated and supplied by means of the manufacturing industry, the agricultural prosperity, and the commercial riches of France.

On the Paris end, Livingston had been uneasy about du Pont's intervention at first, and he certainly would have been distressed by the totally pro-French nature of the letter to Le Brun, for it could have raised expectations of American trade favoritism for France that Jefferson could not have considered. Livingston must have been thinking exactly that, and also been eager to show Madison his dislike of having his work cluttered by the efforts of others, when he wrote very correctly, "I fear du Pont de Nemours has given them, with the best intentions, ideas that we shall find it hard to eradicate, and impossible to yield to." But later he was pleased with the turn this intervention took, for the businessman's dislike of Jefferson's warlike approach made him into an ally of Livingston's. In fact, there is evidence that du Pont actually suggested to Livingston that he avoid hurling Jefferson's challenge at the French, but play a waiting game instead. Whether or not this is so, Livingston clearly needed no urging in that direction. So here, in a sense, two rebels against Jefferson's wishes were joining forces.

Most interestingly, Madison also seemed—in these early months of 1803—to urge Robert Livingston to show greater caution, suggesting that he not appear too bellicose to the French. This was new and exactly opposite to Jefferson's previous pleas, but it is not likely that Madison was openly differing from the president at that point. There had been an earlier time when Madison had appeared uncomfortable with Jefferson's warlike approach, and other times when the Jefferson-Madison team had employed the conscious strategy of making the president appear unreasonable in order to soften the opposition. At this point, however, there is a difference. Now it would seem that this pair had sensed a turn in the wind, one that might be bringing a moment of opportunity. If both sides were envisioning a way to come together, each side must be allowed to appear as something of a winner. It did not seem to call for threatening language.

Pierre Samuel du Pont must have been puzzled to find in Jefferson's curious and turbulent letter two places where the American president referred to the possibility that du Pont would meet with an accident while on this trip. In one case, Jefferson asks him to seal the open letters with wafers that would guard against their being seen by others "if any accident should happen to you." Later in the letter, Jefferson tells of his confidence that the letter would, in any case, be safe if it were delivered by Mrs. du Pont with her own hands "if any accident happen to you."

The grim tone could not have helped bring du Pont to the president's point of view as he read that Jefferson still wanted him to use words that pressured the French leader, rather than suggestions for a businesslike arrangement. That idea certainly did not appeal to him in the least. His business-oriented mind—coupled with what he knew about Napoleon—told him that warnings were not the weapon of choice for this situation. And so Pierre Samuel du Pont turned out to be one more player in this game who consciously turned away from what he had been asked to do. He did get to see Napoleon personally, avoided the elaborate formulas that Livingston had been trying on Talleyrand, and plainly proposed a simple bargaining approach. Napoleon must have been surprised to hear a philosopher talking so clearly. Like a good honest broker, du Pont said the same thing in Paris as he had in Washington: Didn't the whole Mississippi affair really boil down to setting a fair price for a piece of valuable real estate? Napoleon responded only with a sly look—noncommittal, but not entirely negative. It could very well be that du Pont, a private citizen, was the person who remade this affair into a negotiation, with both sides engaged.

With his thoughts naturally turning to the gunpowder on which his son's company was based, du Pont said that by his own calculations, New Orleans could probably be bought for less money than the cost of ammunition needed to fight a war. What point was there in going to such expense—not to mention the casualties and the always-uncertain outcome of any conflict—when perhaps the Americans would be willing to pay several million dollars for a firm agreement on the city's future and permanent rights to use the river?

There was no on-the-spot conclusion, but it is likely that this one businesslike discussion played a major role in fixing the idea of a monetary deal in Napoleon's mind. The First Consul did not need a reminder from du Pont to realize that the struggle against England depended heavily on the ability to spend, and the French exchequer was low in funds. But the repeated admonition would have been one more factor for Napoleon to consider, just as he undoubtedly bore in mind the bizarre reports about Jefferson's rash attitude. An impassioned enemy, even if he was unwise in the practical sense, was a dangerous foe, for he might rouse his people in ways that were incalculable. A good cash offer might seem more attractive to Napoleon when compared with the war-like posture of an opponent who appeared to have become demented. And rather than just "several million dollars for rights to use the river," Napoleon might have thought, why not offer the whole territory, which was all but lost anyway, and demand a great many millions?

How seriously Jefferson took du Pont's role—even when this intermediary appeared to be opposing the presidential strategy—is confirmed by the fact that he made sure to keep du Pont in the picture at every turn, and one letter to him arrived as the negotiations were coming to a head. In this one, incidentally, there was no warning about du Pont's suffering a possible accident. Instead, Jefferson's note of dubious cheer on this occasion reminded him that a kinder death by natural causes might intervene, saying, "You and I are now at the time of life when our call to another state of being cannot be distant and may be near." That slight upgrade in the personal prospects he held out to his friend was dimmed, however, when Jefferson let him know how he regarded the government of du Pont's native land, for he added, "Besides, your government is in the habit of seizing papers without notice. These letters might thus get into hands which, like the hornet, extracts poison from the same flower that yields honey to the bee...."

Chapter Nine

AN EXTRAORDINARY MINISTER

In Paris, the blow that an apprehensive Livingston had expected to receive reached him during January 1803. His worst fears were not quite realized, for he was not being recalled. So the possibility still existed that he would be a participant if some historic event materialized. Moreover, he might yet be able to announce success in winning payment of many millions of dollars for the Americans who were claiming losses from French capture of their ships. Then promoter James Swan could put his political skill to work, and the happy and admiring recipients would have the chance to show their appreciation by pressing for the successful minister's consideration as a worthy vice-presidential candidate in the forthcoming national election.

But the insult, the indignity, that he would meanwhile have to endure seemed too much to bear. Letters from both the president and secretary of state told him that he was shortly to be joined by yet another minister, James Monroe, fifteen years younger than himself, who would be coming with what Livingston considered a higher rank than his own. Madison had finally written to Livingston at some length on January 18, 1803, but that was probably because he could cheerfully tell Livingston all about the dispatch of Mr. Monroe, "who will be the bearer of the instructions under which you are jointly to negotiate." At last, after Livingston's pleading for some idea of how much the U.S. might offer for certain properties, Madison deigned to tell him that the information could soon be had by consulting his new colleague. Added to his discomfort was the fact that Monroe had been American minister in Paris nine years earlier in 1794, had made a blunder, and had gone home almost in disgrace. But his was the classic example—as Livingston saw it—of how much favor a Virginian and a protégé could enjoy in the eyes of Jefferson and Madison.

Livingston knew Monroe to be a good, solid man whose sole indiscretion in Paris had occurred because the instructions he received from home were misunderstood—a subject on which Livingston could be empathetic. Those who drew confidence from Monroe's placid personality noticed that he always thought in terms of doing the right thing, rather than of winning approval.

This kind of conduct had generally kept his life on a steady course. Even those who disagreed with him on political grounds were respectful of his motives. But the one glaring exception to that—which had occurred in Paris—must have been terrible to live with. Livingston's unusual mind thought how searing that memory must be to Monroe, and how strange was the fate that was now pulling him back to this same city.

Monroe's first appointment as minister to France in 1794 was considered a great opportunity for a young man of thirty-seven years. The towering successes of both Benjamin Franklin and Thomas Jefferson in the sensitive position of American minister to Paris had made it an even greater test for any successor, with more attention focused on it. It was a tortuous time in French-American relations because the

United States, having been a revolutionary government itself, was expected to be especially understanding of France's way of dealing with royalty. President Washington and Vice President John Adams had not wanted to express admiration for the butchery that went on in Paris at that time. Adams, writing to a friend in England, had said, "Mankind will in time discover that unbridled majorities are as tyrannical and cruel as unlimited despots."

Jefferson, however, had been quite stubbornly determined to consider the 1789 disorders and demonstrations against the king as evidence of democracy at work. He had sailed for home that year, offhandedly blaming Queen Marie Antoinette for the country's woes. He had not been in France during the worst of the Terror. And as he increasingly became a political opportunist, Jefferson actually hailed the execution of Louis XVI in a letter to a New York newspaper, saying, "Mankind is now enlightened. They can discover that kings are like other men....Monarchy and aristocracy must be annihilated, and the rights of the people firmly established."

With the worst excesses of the Terror over, when a new minister had to be named to the unfilled post and several candidates had personal reasons for being unable to take the position, James Monroe, a much younger protégé of Jefferson's, had been selected. Though Monroe became a balanced and successful president twenty years later, his judgment at the start of his first Paris stay proved to be badly flawed. True, he had been considered young for the job, but being thirty-seven years old does not explain how he could have created such embarrassment for his government.

Monroe's 1794 mission to France had been mainly about American shipping on the high seas, which the French constantly threatened in their effort to blockade England. American shipping on the Mississippi was also involved in his assignment, although the French did not admit any connection with it, for Louisiana belonged to

Spain at that time. It was before the advent of Napoleon, so France had not yet regained an all-around aggressive attitude. But its bullying ways on the high seas kept the U.S. wary of what the French were going to be like when they had a settled government at home. Monroe had been instructed to use every possible connection and every bit of guile he could summon up to detect any such dangerous change, especially as it might affect Mississippi traffic.

Monroe had been a surprise choice to take on the harrowing Paris job. Harrowing it was because France and England were at war, both threatening American ships and detaining them at times. The new American minister was supposed to walk a fine line that would show basic friendship and respect for France, but he was instructed not to be so friendly as to jeopardize America's shaky dignity, as the French had only recently stopped their merciless guillotining. Also, he was to avoid offending either the pro-French or pro-British parties back home.

Everyone agreed that Monroe was wise, modest, upright, and "much too kind to have a sense of humor." But clearly, a sense of humor was what he would need most. With all those conflicting factions to satisfy, Secretary of State John Randolph had handed Monroe one more when he gave him his formal instructions a month later: "You will show our confidence in the French Republic without betraying the most remote mark of undue complaisance." He added, with uncanny foresight, "Among the great events with which the world is now teeming, there may be an opening for France to become instrumental in securing to us the free navigation of the Mississippi. Spain may perhaps negotiate a peace with France, separate from Great Britain. If she does, the Mississippi may be acquired through this channel...."

Monroe's first arrival in Paris had been in mid-summer 1794, just after the fall of Robespierre and the Terror. The prescription for failure that he had been handed went to work within days. The way he tried to explain it, after he was openly derided and finally recalled, was this: since no other civilized nation had a recognized representative in France at that time, and the minister from Geneva had been waiting more than six weeks to be received, "I was fearful I might remain as long, and perhaps much longer, in the same situation." He therefore addressed a letter to the president of the Convention (a body that represented the entire nation), and it was a remarkably successful pitch, for a decree was passed at once that the minister of the United States "be introduced into the bosom of the Convention tomorrow at two P.M." It was as if a Protestant asked to visit the Vatican and was told that the entire College of Cardinals would promptly convene to receive him. And no wonder, for with his request, Monroe had enclosed a copy of the speech he planned to give. It went a tad over the fine line of strictly limited friendliness that he had been ordered to walk.

After telling the delighted French that his admission into the assembly filled him "with a degree of sensibility which I cannot express," he had spoken of the regard that the French nation had always shown to its ally (forgetting about the American ships that were detained in French ports), and continued for ten minutes with such sentiments as these:

> Republics should approach near to each other. In many respects they all have the same interest; but this is more especially the case with the American and French republics. Their governments are similar; they both cherish the same principles and have the same basis. [All this in spite of the fact that France was not a republic at all and had no such democratic basis.] I speak the sentiments of my own country...and if I can succeed in such manner as to merit the approbation of both republics, I shall deem it the happiest event of my life.

The French leaders, knowing themselves to be pariahs to most of the world, were overjoyed to be praised by the young nation that was admired by so many. To show their gratitude, the French leaders not only recognized Monroe as the accredited minister of the United States, but ordered that his speech be printed in "French and American," carefully leaving out any reference to English, in order to credit the friendly new country with having a language of its own.

Secretary of State John Randolph had not entered into this joyous partnership that Monroe had embarked on. He wrote his man in Paris that, "We all supposed that your reception as minister would take place in the private chamber of some committee....We should have supposed that finding yourself in the Hall of the Convention would have brought to mind these ideas: The United States are neutral. The allied powers are jealous. With England we are now in treaty. By England we have been impeached for breaches of faith in favor of France....We do not perceive that your instructions have imposed upon you the extreme glow of some parts of your address...." Clearly, he would have liked to recall Monroe at once, but that would have created an incident of a different kind. Monroe, fuming over the criticism, was allowed to stay on for just two years, a minimal time, until August 1796.

But foreign affairs are even less predictable than most human events. John Randolph had first sent Monroe to France with hopes of winning only the right to navigate freely a Mississippi River that would continue to be owned by some larger nation. No one would have believed that this nearly disgraced James Monroe would be back in Paris seven years later with the power to sign or turn down the outright purchase of that whole river and nearly a million square miles of land lying beyond it.

Every player in this affair—whether American or French—has been shown to have certain questionable traits of character and very considerable countervailing talents. James Monroe would have been an exception to that rule, had it not been for his major blunder on the first assignment to France. Other than that, he was a paragon.

One great qualification would work for him from the moment of his return to Paris: he spoke excellent French, his whole family having learned it during his first tour of duty there. It was no ordinary schoolroom French, and not at all like that of the previous American envoys. Benjamin Franklin had parlayed a few clever phrases and strategic silences into an undeserved reputation for fluency. Thomas Jefferson had made himself understood, with an excessively American accent. Only the conscientious John Adams had managed a workman-like ability to converse effectively. But Monroe, as early as 1796, had been able to dispense with an interpreter, even for the most difficult official interviews that required very precise word choice.

A deeper way of gauging this man Monroe is to note his exceptional resistance to capital punishment while he was governor of Virginia. He openly condemned the passion for vengeance, even when it earned him strong protests from many citizens. And he worked to install practical preventive measures that would lessen the number of executions, especially of slaves, whose confessions seemed to him to be fear-induced and of doubtful value.

His first tour of duty in Paris had also provided another way of probing Monroe's character, for it featured one more trait that not even the great men around him could measure up to. Against every notion of what was politically correct or even socially acceptable, Monroe had devoted himself to helping Thomas Paine, whose flaming words are thought by some to have saved the American Revolution during a time of despair. Paine had alienated nearly all the founding fathers by remaining a firebrand after they comfortably became part of the victorious new establishment, and they preferred not to be seen even talking with him. Disgusted, Paine moved to

France, and there continued his inflammatory behavior, landing in prison as a result. Monroe, only thirty-seven years old at the time, ignored what his superiors might consider correct behavior, and wrote and informed the State Department that he had not only devoted much time to getting Paine released from jail, but then befriended him in this astonishingly kindly way.

Monroe wrote his superiors:

September 15, 1795

Mr. Paine has lived in my house for about ten months past. He was, upon my arrival, confined in the Luxembourg, and released on my application; after which, being sick, he has remained with me....The symptoms have become worse, and the prospect now is that he will not be able to hold out more than a month or two at the farthest. I shall certainly pay the utmost attention to this gentleman, as he is one of those whose merits in our Revolution were most distinguished."

[signed] James Monroe

Although still in the formative stage of his career, and already on poor terms with the administration in Washington, Monroe had not been deterred by the likely disapproval of his older mentors—nor had he even cared if they felt that his attention to Paine was a rebuke to them. He did what he judged to be right and did not dissemble in telling about it.

This was the new colleague who would be joining Livingston in a matter of weeks. The United States would now have two men with very unusual minds in Paris.

Chapter Ten

WAITING FOR MONROE

Would this tense half-life go on for another few months or a year or five years? No one could have known as the early months of 1803 came. With hindsight, more than one historian wrote that the Louisiana issue was pretty well decided in 1802 and that Monroe's trip to Paris the following year was no more than a formality. The principals who were in suspense, especially those in Washington, would have been glad to learn this; there was no such feeling at all until virtually the final moment of signing—and even after that, the dangling questions about the validity of the deal and the possibility of a turndown by the Congress were so worrisome that Jefferson and Madison would have a serious difference of opinion about how to address them.

The pressures were so great in early 1803 that time itself seemed to have taken on an altered meaning, and the passing of days had varying effects in different capitals. While the outcome of the Louisiana issue had come to seem as important as life itself to the Americans, it was of secondary significance to the French. At any moment, they might be at war in Europe—their real world—and against Great Britain, their classic enemy. Money for the war was scarce, and a cash sale of Louisiana would help, but it was not an imperative, as New Orleans was to the United States. Paris cared about the New World as a matter of deep interest for the long term, but the dream of creating an empire there might have to be left unfinished for years, as some of the First Consul's advisers saw it.

These men around Napoleon were divided on the issue of Louisiana. He would sometimes call in retired ministers, tell them of some plan he had, then ask them to be totally frank in critiquing it. He could be so hypnotic at times that they would take him at his word and tell him straightaway if they found something with which they disagreed. In such cases, he would sit silent for a few minutes, then—with no direct comment on what others had said—announce a decision, often one that came as a surprise. But not so on Louisiana. Several such critics told him to hold on to Louisiana at all costs; others said he should defend Saint Domingue, but forget New Orleans until he had defeated the British—the real threat to France's future. On this subject, he often broke off the meeting without a conclusion.

Napoleon was experiencing some confusion because he had lately become more aware of the power and importance of money. Probably because of the clarity of Marbois's explanations, he realized that Britain was able to dominate the oceans because its massive income from trade enabled it to build and equip a huge fleet of ships.

It was largely because of her colonies that the British had such enormous trade earnings, and now his most level-headed advisers were telling him to raise money by getting rid of France's most promising colonies. His favorite source of bright ideas, Talleyrand, understood the logical conflict, but would not discuss it with

Napoleon, thinking the First Consul would be bored by the subject of finances.

In Washington, tension mounted because the fury over New Orleans was not about to abate. The Jefferson administration—apart from its genuine national concerns—worried that a popular desire to see action might create a political tide against the administration. The Federalist party, usually strongest in the Northeast, saw this situation as an opportunity to build its popularity in the West, so it tried to outdo the Republicans in calling for war—against either the French or the Spanish—to assure America's control of Louisiana. To hear easterners taking the lead in calling for the support of westerners was a new turn, indeed, a political ploy that had a unifying effect on the nation.

In January 1803, Jefferson began to take the steps of actually forming an alliance with England. He scheduled dates for cabinet meetings in which the terms and projected timing of a possible alliance with the British would be discussed, but it is not known whether this was a genuine possibility or a continuation of the long-running act he staged to frighten France into making a deal. One of the principle questions planned for such a meeting was whether to let the British take New Orleans or to reserve that city for American action. When it was discussed by the cabinet, opinion was firmly against allowing the British to act in that area. It is noteworthy that as talk of a possible alliance with England increased, it brought out even more American suspicion and fear of Britain as a partner.

Also notable as a clue to the administration's true attitude toward alliance with England is the fact that Madison, at this point, tried to cool Congress's furor, while watching the calendar to track Monroe's probable whereabouts. He tried to imagine the day of Monroe's arrival in Paris and how soon he would be presented to the government, making him eligible to start talking business with the

French. If he and Jefferson had genuinely favored the alliance and a possible war with France, their administration would have welcomed the supportive war spirit in Congress. But Madison, more clearly than anyone else, saw that if the matter could be arranged by a treaty and a purchase, this port-closing episode, although it could be considered a tempest in a teapot, would be a major historical event because it showed that the American people were willing to fight as one, putting an end to the East-West rivalry and joining America's eastern and western interests in a matter of weeks. Americans who talked, demonstrated, and sometimes fought each other about the beckoning emptiness to the West were increasingly settlers rather than explorers.

While most eyes were on the calendar, the passing dates had a different meaning for Robert Livingston. After learning in January 1803 that Monroe would join him in Paris, thus putting in doubt Livingston's hope of personal glory, he had been told that a good many weeks might pass before the Monroes would be ready to leave. After that, it would be close to another month, at the very least, before he would arrive. Livingston's hope for some great happening that might benefit him within that time had dwindled as the French seemed to believe that serious discussions would wait for Monroe's arrival. The weeks had become unbearably tense for him as time began to run out.

Livingston's bitterness was palpable. As it appeared increasingly likely that France would offer America an opportunity to buy and own its future as no other nation had ever done, Livingston hammered at the question that Madison kept refusing to respond to: How much are we willing to offer for this or that piece of property, be it New Orleans, Florida, or any part of it? He had begun months before literally to beg for an answer. In July 1802, he complained, "I am sorry that you have not communicated to me what are precisely the utmost limits of the sum I may venture to offer in cash...." On December 20, 1802, he wrote, "Pray be explicit in the amount of what I may offer....I would wish, in case favorable circumstances should arise, to know how to act." On February 18, 1803, he said, "I have never yet had any specific instructions from you how to act or what to offer [in case the First Consul should indicate a willingness to sell the United States land]" and soon after that begged, "I pray you again to give me some instructions, for I may be acting contrary to your intentions."

At no time were any of these requests answered. Even if Madison felt disinclined to include specific sums in dispatches he would mail, he might at least have been expected to make reference to the questions and to give a hint of why an answer could not be given.

Livingston's problem of trying to decipher his own foreign minister's meanings seemed especially difficult to him, and it was certainly bizarre, but every player in this game had problems on his own side of the field, as well as in confronting the opposition.

If one were looking into the offices of the two foreign ministers, Talleyrand and Madison, the scenes would not be what one would normally have expected in either Paris or Washington. American leaders usually worked at desks, where they often conducted talks, like the transplanted Englishmen most of them were. In business or in law offices, some even used "partners' desks," large furniture with seven drawers on each side, or they might pull up a chair to another man's desk and turn the visit into a small meeting, with ideas freely exchanged and rebutted. A French minister would leave his papers on a delicate desk of Louis XV or Louis XVI design and know that when he went into the next room, people would rise and become attentive to his thoughts, rather than offering their own. If it was a commercial office, the desk would be of coarser design, but either way, others would stand when a superior appeared, and if their rank was lower than his, they would listen and nod as he spoke. It was more a lecture than a meeting, and many of the leader's ideas were unspoken.

These distinctions would not have been applicable if one had been a secret observer of the two foreign ministers, Talleyrand and Madison. Both these men talked only enough, it seemed, to elicit words from others. They were less interested in telling people things than in waiting to be told. Talleyrand was a great conversationalist on social occasions, but any aide who was expecting him to hold the floor and explain his policies would be in for a very short session. A person who had a new thought to express would find the minister more interested in listening than in speaking. Like a manufacturer who needs raw materials to work with, Talleyrand was an avid collector of facts and particularly liked to combine several unrelated facts in ways that created enhanced wealth or power. That he preferred watching and listening soon became apparent. He kept drawing information from others, only rarely saying aloud what he made of it all. That was the secret of how he endlessly created new strategies to be tried. While these were often self-serving, they usually proved useful to others as well, which is why his services were always in demand.

On the surface, Madison's manner was quite different: he was softer-voiced, almost retiring, and he gave less evidence that he was listening for facts. But that was really a pose. He seemed quite content to let a conversation dawdle. He used these silences as a way to get others to introduce subjects. People who knew him well thought Madison said only a small fraction of what was in his mind. But such remarks as he made usually sounded as if they concealed a vast amount of knowledge.

Any close observation of Madison's actions and methods gives the feeling of a man who plays with his cards unusually close to the vest. Some persons who can be so described seem unpleasantly devious.

Madison was quite the opposite. In his brevity, he seemed to be saying all that was needed. And everything from the softness of his voice
to the quietness of his facial expression gave the impression of total
candor.

If Madison's methods were difficult for Livingston to deal with,
imagine how they put Louis Pichon at a disadvantage. As bright as
Pichon was, he seems never to have suspected that the secretary of
state who begged France "not to force the United States to become
involved in anything on the far side of the Mississippi River" was a
dedicated expansionist who wanted the whole continent for America.
Madison's words, as we have seen, were so beautifully chosen that they
set every suspicion to rest. It is tempting to imagine a direct conversation between Madison and Talleyrand. Perhaps neither of them
would have believed a word the other said. But in that case, they
would have been doing themselves a disservice, for they both spoke
wisely much of the time—and even truthfully, on occasion.

Talleyrand's reputation for serving France well, even while
enriching himself, was fully deserved. It has been shown that his
choice of personnel for important posts in France's diplomatic
corps, as in the case of Louis Pichon, was normally intended to put
high-quality individuals in place, not simply men who would
inform and serve his interests. Often he devoted extra time to
achieving both ends, in contrast to most people who settle for the
first workable solution that presents itself. He was painstaking
enough to sift endlessly through every situation and every possible
appointment until he could make a decision that would work for
the dual purpose of serving both himself and France.

Again, in this mental trait Talleyrand and Madison were much
alike. As far as is known, Madison had no trace of the venality that
ruled Talleyrand, but their mental energy was the same. Endless

effort to be fully informed and perfectly prepared was the only way Madison knew of dealing with any subject.

When he became secretary of state, this trait grew more pronounced and there were frequent brief intimations of privileged information that could only have come from espionage. He had, in fact, taken that subject up seriously after lagging in attention to it when he first inherited the State Department.

The clear evidence of how much espionage Madison made use of and how much he must have encouraged his diplomats to put into action can be gathered from phrases in which the secretary and some of America's envoys referred to facts they quoted from unnamed persons. The revealing mentions—indicated by added italics—usually took forms like the following remarks, which are on a variety of subjects:

—Madison to Pinckney, Minister to Spain (on how he had learned of the port closing in New Orleans): "*A letter from a confidential citizen* at New Orleans has just informed us that the Intendant, at that place…had prohibited the deposit of American effects…and that the river was also shut against the external commerce of the United States…."

—Madison to Livingston (on the same subject): "*Private accounts render it probable* that the Governor of the province openly dissented from that act."

—Livingston, from France, to Madison (on a deal Napoleon was making with Spain): "In addition to my last, *I have obtained accurate information* of the offer to Spain. It is either to sell them Parma for forty-eight millions of livres, or to exchange it for Florida. I fear Spain will accede to their proposition."

Sometimes even President Jefferson referred to something he learned from a person unknown, though more likely a distinguished visitor than a paid informant:

> —Jefferson to Livingston (apparently shocked to have learned of unfriendly French feelings toward America—possibly told to him by Pierre Samuel du Pont): "It is well to be able to inform you *through a safe channel* that we stand completely corrected of the error that either the government or the nation of France has any remains of friendship for us. On the contrary, it appears evident, that an unfriendly spirit prevails in the most important individuals of the government, toward us."

Just as there is sometimes a lull in a war, giving the impression that perhaps nothing decisive will ever happen, these low-key exchanges went on for the first few months of 1803. Even the leading players appeared to undergo a sort of mood shift during these months, as though people on both sides were focusing more on what had previously seemed to be minor points. The big, broad outlines of the rivalry had drawn most of the attention when the French and Americans first appeared to be preparing for a showdown. Now personal irritations were coming into prominence, and as the crucial days of decision approached, there was the danger that these trifles would blur the larger design. The pettiness on the part of men charged with the future of nations was monumental, if such a massive adjective can be married to such a weasel of a noun.

Apparently despairing of anything that was going to save him from accepting second place, Livingston became increasingly contentious. The superficial respect he had normally shown Madison seemed to evaporate. He soon began to complain about his rank and stature in a way that he had never addressed a superior before. For example, he wrote the secretary of state, "I am not satisfied, from examining my instructions and commission, that I am empowered to do anything but the common routine of business....I find that I have no precise diplomatic character, not even an envoy ordinary or extraordinary, though it had been usual for the United States to grant this latter grade to gentlemen of less standing than myself." He added at this point that one of Napoleon's envoys was actually forced to go to the U.S. at a lower grade than he expected because his status was not allowed to exceed the standing of the lowly American minister in Paris.

By March 24, more whining of this kind was mingled with serious business. Livingston was writing Madison with news that the troops and colonists assembled in Holland and destined for Louisiana were "stopped for the present, in consequence of the state of things here." And at the same time, he included a wordy passage that was clearly meant to show how the administration's decision to send Monroe to Paris had spoiled a very promising arrangement he had almost concluded with the French. As he put it, "Unfortunately, dispatches arrived at that moment from Mr. Pichon, informing them that the appointment of Mr. Monroe had tranquilized everything." Even though it was perhaps poor judgment for Livingston to complain in this way, it must be acknowledged that his point seems to be confirmed by a letter he received from Talleyrand: "I see with pleasure...that the excitement which had been raised on the subject of Louisiana has been allayed by the wisdom of your Government, and the just confidence which it inspires...."

This letter was meant to praise the wisdom of sending Monroe to Paris. Yet, without waiting for Monroe to reach Paris, although he had already landed in France, Talleyrand would invite Livingston to his office on April 11. And there he would offer a whole new idea to the startled American minister. For the first time, the thought of

America's buying Louisiana was broached, although Talleyrand pretended to have said it as his own random notion.

In fact, as Talleyrand very well knew, a great many things had happened, all converging to an imminent moment of decision. On April 10, Easter Sunday, Napoleon had been meeting at Saint Cloud with two ministers who had opposing views on whether he should hold on to or sell Louisiana. Marbois was urging him to let Louisiana go to the Americans, who "could conquer it easily anyway." Admiral Dénis Décrès, a distinguished and outspoken naval man, was telling the leader that without colonies, France would soon have no navy and would become a minor power. The former minister of marine gave reasoning that now appears truly inspired. According to the memoirs of Marbois, Décrès first explained why the combination of colonies and a powerful navy was necessary to France's security and greatness. Then he added:

> Louisiana can indemnify us for all our losses. There does not exist on the globe a single port susceptible of becoming as important as New Orleans....The navigation around the Cape of Good Hope to the Indies has changed the course of trade from Europe. What will be its direction if at the isthmus of Panama a simple canal should be opened to connect the one ocean with the other? Louisiana will be on this new route, and it will then be acknowledged that this possession is of inestimable value.

The First Consul may well have seen the merit of this reasoning, but he seemed determined to make the sale—partly for his stated reason of keeping Louisiana out of England's reach, but also as a way of getting the cash he needed to make war. Talleyrand would have liked to see the opposite decision, for he considered peace better for the country, and it could also mean another big payday for him personally. Lord Whitworth, the British Ambassador, had offered Talleyrand and Joseph Bonaparte, the First Consul's brother, 100,000 pounds—and perhaps double that sum—if they could convince Napoleon to let them keep the island of Malta without going to war. In that case he would not have been inclined to sell Louisiana. Napoleon kept the two advisers at Saint Cloud overnight, with the future of the United States hanging on the First Consul's decision.

In fact, as Marbois later wrote, he felt that the decision was already made. That was probably because he had always known that Louisiana could not prosper as a French colony unless France also controlled a prosperous Saint Domingue. And that island was proving to be Napoleon's worst disaster to date. The First Consul, even knowing all the uncertainties of the Caribbean and especially the diseases that wiped out far more troops than any human enemy, had continued to cling to the thought of a new dominion if he could maintain control of wonderfully lush Saint Domingue. But even the twenty-five thousand fresh troops he had sent there under General Rochambeau after the Leclerc debacle, as Marbois knew, were clinging to only a few towns on a shattered island that was clearly headed toward black independence.

On Monday morning, April 11, at dawn, Napoleon told Marbois, "I renounce Louisiana. It is not only New Orleans that I mean to cede; it is the whole colony, reserving none of it." Among other things, the First Consul had read London newspapers of April 7, reporting that the U.S. Senate had voted to build fifteen gunboats to patrol the Mississippi River. This information followed the Ross resolution calling for fifty thousand troops and Senator Samuel Smith's remark that he considered the country on the eve of a war.

No one on the European side of the Atlantic could have known yet that on April 8, Jefferson had actually called the long-awaited cabinet meeting to consider the conditions of an alliance with England if one should prove necessary. By a vote of three to two, the cabinet agreed that the United States might bind itself to a mutual pledge of no separate peace. So Jefferson's threat to "marry the British nation and fleet" had not been entirely hollow, although he did delay this meeting until a deal making it unnecessary seemed near. (In fact, word came on the very next day, April 9, that Spain had ordered the American "right of deposit" to be restored in New Orleans. This meant that American goods could again be safely stored at reasonable cost while awaiting shipment to the outside world—a big blow to those who were promoting war.) And even now, the cabinet that pretended to be ready for an alliance with England still voted unanimously against allowing the British "partner" to take Louisiana. Acquisition of that special property was to be reserved exclusively for Americans. Even so, the cabinet decision, added to the several congressional actions under way, made it clear that Napoleon's readiness to sell what was virtually lost was the only sane course. The executive and legislative branches of the government in Washington have seldom worked so effectively together.

Marbois himself later said in his memoirs that he and Napoleon were alone when the First Consul told him that he was to negotiate the sale without telling anyone except Talleyrand. Napoleon had sketched a draft treaty calling for one hundred million francs (a little less than twenty million dollars), plus an American assumption of war claims. Marbois told him that was more than the Americans could possibly raise, whereupon Napoleon said, "Make it fifty million then (about nine and one-third million dollars) but nothing less. I must get real money for the war with England."

Another version of this moment of decision was said to have occurred when Talleyrand was in the room and Napoleon turned to Marbois and said, "You are the treasury minister. You sell it to them." The piqued foreign minister, seeing himself left out of it, supposedly said not a word. This version was preferred by the Parisian gossips because it would make room for a popular witticism, rather typical of Talleyrand, in which he later derided Napoleon's drastic price change by saying, "That was the fastest decline in property values in the history of the world."

Chapter Eleven

AGONIZING MOMENTS

On that same Easter Sunday night in 1803 when Napoleon was toying with two ministers while already quite resolved on what he wanted to do, Robert Livingston—conflicted and out-raged—sat at his desk to write a brief letter. He had just learned that Monroe had arrived in Le Havre. It was not unexpected news, but it was soul-searing.

The future had arrived, and Livingston's memory bank broke open. The thoughts that spilled out onto the pages of complaining letters to presumably sympathetic friends and even to the notably unsympathetic James Madison form a complete dossier of dissatis-faction. He even told his sorrows to an embassy employee, who passed the words along to Monroe. After more than two years as American minister in Paris, groaned Livingston, tilting with the well-lubricated windmills of French bureaucracy, probing the minds of such dissimilar types as Talleyrand and Marbois, trying occasion-ally to see Napoleon Bonaparte himself and having to show grati-tude for the favor; after Livingston had suffered all that and more,

President Jefferson's friend and protégé, Mr. James Monroe, was within hours of arriving in Paris as Livingston's superior.

The president's letter had not been worded so starkly. Nobody could deny that Jefferson had one of the age's smoothest pens. Monroe was coming to help him—as a "special envoy" who was to be called extraordinary and plenipotentiary—an emissary who had been specially briefed to act with the authority of his chief of state. But then Monroe was a Virginian, and a close friend of Jefferson and Secretary of State James Madison to boot. His old Virginia mentors had total faith in his honesty and judgment, even after Monroe's indiscretions seven years earlier had caused his recall from this same post as minister to Paris. His lavish praise of the French Revolution, his friendships with new government leaders who were only months removed from the taint of the guillotine era, had been an embarrassment to the U.S. just a few years earlier. Yet this man fifteen years his junior was coming back to Paris as a senior in rank. How must that make Livingston look to the French? And how, he wondered at this moment, could states as different as New York and Virginia, or any other state and Virginia, for that matter, hope for a fair future in such an unequal union?

Livingston had said virtually as much in previous notes to friends and would do so again. On this night, he pushed himself away from those time-wasting thoughts, for a letter had to be composed promptly because a man was waiting to take it to Le Havre: a careful, friendly letter of welcome. It would not do to show pique, for Monroe would surely report to Secretary Madison on the kind of reception he found in Paris. Despite that reminder to himself, the little letter he penned was not the smooth prose of an elegantly reared New Yorker. Abrupt and disconnected, it read:

> I congratulate you on your safe arrival. We have long and
> anxiously waited for you. God grant that your mission

may answer your and the public expectation. War may do something for us; nothing else would. I have paved the way for you, and if you could add to my memoirs an assurance that we were now in possession of New Orleans, we should do well; but I detain Mr. Bentalou [an embassy messenger], who is impatient to fly to the arms of his wife. I have apprised the minister of your arrival, and told him you would be here on Tuesday or Wednesday.

Like everything he was doing in these hideous days, the few words betrayed Livingston's agitation. They ended abruptly on the flimsy pretext that the waiting messenger was his concern, and proclaimed a mind that was dangerously lost to careful judgment. The fourth sentence, "War may do something for us; nothing else would," was an unprofessional remark that would come back to haunt him within months.

The next day was both better and worse. As if designed by fate to create the greatest anguish for Livingston, Talleyrand invited him to his office on April 11 and exploded the bombshell. It happened in the middle of an apparently casual talk that Talleyrand, obviously pressing to introduce the subject, asked, "Would you Americans wish to have the whole of Louisiana?" The whole of Louisiana? No American mind had seriously thought in such a dimension. The conversation can be heard verbatim in Livingston's own words from a letter he wrote to Madison later that day.

"No, our wishes extend only to New Orleans and the Floridas," Livingston managed to respond, while attempting to catch his breath, "although, as I showed in a note which was sent to you, the policy of France should dictate giving us the country above the river Arkansas, in order to place a barrier between yourselves and Canada."

"But if we gave New Orleans, the rest would be of little value," Talleyrand countered. "I should like to know what you would give for the whole."

Livingston, saying he had not thought about the subject, said he supposed that it might be about twenty million francs, or a little less than four million dollars. Talleyrand said that was too low an offer, asked him to think about it, and then ended by saying that he did not speak from authority. "The idea merely struck me," he had said. It was not unusual for Talleyrand to introduce a subject, then withdraw it in this way, but it seems a rather surprising habit for anyone of such experience and sophistication. He must have realized that others did not at all believe that the idea "merely struck him." That was just why he did it—to show that he had this new interest, but then to make it "off the record." In fact, Talleyrand was risking the First Consul's wrath by trying to inject himself into a deal that Napoleon had clearly assigned to his colleague, Marbois. That he was willing to take this chance could well indicate that the brilliant foreign minister had arrived at one of the numerous moments when he so disapproved of Napoleon's course that he sensed disaster ahead and was willing to risk his position as foreign minister.

Whether consciously or not, Livingston quickly proceeded to employ a similar technique of slipping into a deal without authorization, for he thought he might gain credit for having brought about this great historic coup without the risk of actually signing anything. Clearly, he could not conclude a transaction, for he had no authority and had never been given the estimated figures he asked for. But if he had Talleyrand's word that he had offered the whole of Louisiana to Robert Livingston, he thought, it would be hard for anyone to deny that he was the hero of the whole affair.

With very bad judgment, because there was not the slightest chance that Talleyrand would write such a note, he begged the

French foreign minister in writing on the very next day for "Something in the form of a note or letter on your part, couched in generous terms. You could express the friendship of the First Consul for the United States, his desire to give them striking indication of it in ceding the whole of Louisiana to them....We could work to mature the treaty even before the formal reception of Mr. Monroe...." He had put his whole self-absorbed motive on paper for Talleyrand to see and doubtless smile over. And then, in the same style as his recipient, he added, "Please, Sir, regard this as unofficial."

It was Livingston's great misfortune that these new vistas of possibilities that made his heart pound were opening up at a moment that was otherwise so bleak. The curious mixture sapped his judgment and drove him to the brink of recklessness. Livingston found himself with the exciting, yet terrifying notion that he might be on the verge of some great event that he had no authority to consummate. Along with a barely suppressed panic, there was fury. Those two men in Washington had left him here in Paris—two full months away from any possible exchange of correspondence—with no idea of what price he was authorized to pay for each of the various deals that might suddenly be suggested. Time and again, he had asked—almost begged—Madison to tell him a range of possibilities. Now he was enraged at that man's cruel silence. Had he been intentionally left to fail in the face of some historic opportunity, or left to be the sacrificial lamb who would risk making a bargain that might be scorned by the Congress and disowned by the president? How could he have fixed a price without the deliberations of many expert minds? What coals might be heaped on a New Yorker who dared even to begin negotiating on such a new concept? So he would be left again as the man who had been silent until others made the great decisions. Now Monroe would soon arrive—with the power and the knowledge that whatever he did would be supported by the powerful men at home.

The churning in his head made it almost impossible to think clearly. In the back of this mind was the one subject far removed from Louisiana that could bring a smile to his lips—the thought of returning home in the fall of 1803 to make a run for the U.S. vice presidency. His friend James Swan, a very active foreign trader and speculator who had major cash claims against France, was still talking of being his campaign manager, backed by a group of other claimants who would all show their gratitude to Livingston if he succeeding in getting France to pay their claims. Now Livingston had good reports on that subject, and in his haste to keep his supporters happy he had let Swan know about his hopes that the claims might soon be approved. He knew he might be criticized for letting this information be known, for the subject was not yet decided and should have remained a government secret.

At the same time, Livingston had been sending Madison an exhausting number of proofs about his great many talks with the highest French authorities as well as near breakthroughs on Louisiana. As before, the secretary of state seemed to take little notice. For weeks, Madison had busied himself with updates on Monroe's preparations for the trip to Paris. He had blandly written that he was expediting Monroe's departure, as if Livingston was supposed to be pleased about that. It was good that Madison had spared him the full details of his friendship with the Monroes. He and Mrs. Madison were buying for cash some of Monroe's solid silver tableware and Sevres porcelain plates, knowing that he could replace these splendid items for a much lower price in Paris, as one of several ways of augmenting the skimpy Monroe finances. Madison was also trying to raise Monroe's spirits by writing to him of his confidence that war between England and France was now nearly certain, making him sure that Monroe would soon be able to "turn their fol-lies…to our just interests."

⌒

It is not certain whether Talleyrand had already learned from Marbois that Napoleon's decision had been made or whether he had only sensed from his presence of the day before that Napoleon was about ready to authorize an outright sale of Louisiana. He had been in the room the night before and heard Napoleon talking about a pos-sible sale. Napoleon had seemed less decisive than usual, but that may have been a ruse to prevent Talleyrand from injecting himself into the deal. Talleyrand's rush to be ahead of Marbois in mentioning it to Liv-ingston could have been a last-minute effort to make the Americans feel indebted to him or, more likely, an attempt to muddy the waters in hopes that confusion might ruin the deal and therefore keep alive his hopes of enrichment from the British bribe he had been offered. That would have been a typical Talleyrand coup, a moneymaker for him and also a great benefit to France, for he always believed Napoleon should have been making peace, not war, with England.

Whatever the foreign minister's motivation, Monroe reached Paris to learn from Livingston that a whole new situation—on which he had no instructions—would be the true nature of his mis-sion. Fate had at least seen to it that Monroe—after all the briefings from Jefferson and Madison—would be forced to stand on the same numbing ground as his less-favored colleague. How differently two persons can react to a similar challenge was soon made clear. As they sat in the small study of their Paris legation, Livingston—feeling somehow relieved now that the responsibility could be shared—said he was "in favor of making a push to buy the whole territory." He repeated this idea more than once to Monroe, stressing that any part the Congress did not wish to keep could be sold for a profit to some other power that would pose no threat to the United States.

Monroe did not even dignify that comment with a response. Nothing could have been less acceptable to the man whose Monroe Doctrine twenty years hence would forbid other powers from intruding on any part of "our" hemisphere. Monroe had decided almost at once that a purchase would be far preferable to any makeshift plan for the protection of New Orleans, and he thought they should all have realized that Napoleon was in a situation that made an outright sale his best way out.

Livingston even wrote in an uncharacteristically breezy way to Madison now, "It is so very important that you should be apprized that a negotiation is actually opened, even before Mr. Monroe has been presented....The field opened to us is infinitely larger than our instructions contemplated....We shall do all we can to cheapen the purchase; but my present sentiment is that we shall buy." As for the price, he repeated grandly what he had told Monroe: if the Congress didn't want to keep the investment, "I persuade myself that the whole sum might be raised by the sale of the territory west of the Mississippi to some Power in Europe."

From his talks with Madison, Monroe had become convinced that Napoleon's thought of a new empire in America was a mere dream—the First Consul should have realized that British naval superiority would always block his distant adventures. It was those same British, who might break him in Europe, that he must deal with. To do that, the First Consul needed cash and he needed to distract the English with other worries of their own.

The two Americans sat and talked for an hour about what price they might offer for the great prize. Livingston continued to be very expansive, while Monroe was noncommittal. He had an offering price in mind, but he wasn't yet ready to reveal it out loud.

Having had Napoleon's order to rush the negotiation even in advance of Monroe's arrival, it is not clear why Marbois took two days to reach Livingston. But there had apparently been no such approach until late on the night of April 13. Perhaps he had made efforts to contact Livingston and found that he was engaged in other activities. That could account for Marbois's apparently odd behavior on the 13th, creating a moment reminiscent of a Feydeau farce and one of the more humorous scenarios in diplomatic history.

The two American envoys, joined by two other Americans, Fulwar Skipwith, the U.S. consul general in Paris, and a Colonel James Mercer, who was going to serve as Monroe's secretary without pay, were having their first dinner together. They were just enjoying a final course when it was noticed that someone in the garden was peering in through one of the dining-room windows.

One of the guests said, "Doesn't that look like Barbé-Marbois out there?"

Livingston, incredulous, turned to see, then said excitedly, "It is. It is!" He seemed to hesitate between calling a servant or going to the window himself. At last, he rose. The Frenchman must have had to call on all his years of diplomatic experience to maintain his self-possession on having been spotted, but he came inside, made a brief excuse of having found himself in the area and deciding to look in, without even trying to explain why he had not gone to the door instead of a garden window. He was asked to join the party, and had a bit of cognac with the group, most of whom he already knew. But before leaving, he managed to get his real business accomplished: he quietly asked Livingston to come to his office after the dinner party ended to continue their talk about Louisiana.

It was a delicate touch on Marbois's part to ask Livingston without involving Monroe. There was a formal correctness to it, since Monroe had not yet been received, but it was also a great personal courtesy to Livingston. In this situation, a French official might have been expected to make the newly arrived Monroe, the person of the moment, his first concern. Instead, he showed more regard for his longer-standing relationship with Livingston. Clearly, the empathy between these two flowed in both directions.

When Marbois had heard that Monroe was on his way to France, he obviously must have imagined the hard sentiments that Livingston felt at seeing what might be taken as a no-confidence vote on the part of his superiors. What's more, Marbois felt that the First Consul was approaching a decision to sell Louisiana, and he hoped this would not be delayed until the new envoy came and robbed Livingston of the credit. Now, with Monroe on hand, the personal visit was as if Marbois were saying to Livingston, *You and I know each other, and I'm not dropping you in favor of this new arrival. After I give you the facts, you can decide how to handle it.*

Livingston, pleased, told Monroe of Marbois's request, and said that he was going to make the visit. But he was surprised when Monroe questioned the propriety of doing so, pointing out that the instructions from Washington had stipulated that they would do everything together as partners. Livingston firmly insisted that such a thing would apply only after Monroe had been received by the government.

As Monroe told Madison months later, "I hesitated on the idea of Livingston's going to see Marbois alone. I intimated delicately that this might be showing too much zeal—that a little reserve might have a better effect. He only talked of the government's rigorous etiquette, the impropriety of my going with him. I stopped trying to change his plan, but I reminded him that he had not even read the instructions I had brought for him. In short, I said, if you must go, go to hear and not to speak."

Livingston went alone to the treasury minister's office and stayed until about midnight—to be told that "the whole country of Louisiana" was offered to the United States for one hundred million francs (slightly less than twenty million dollars). Livingston correctly took that to be a bargaining offer, and he frankly called it exorbitant. Marbois delicately said that he would not deny the truth of this observation, but he urged Livingston to think hard and make the very best possible counteroffer as quickly as he could, because the First Consul might not leave this opportunity on the table for long.

Livingston is usually accused of behaving in a devious way with Monroe on this occasion because he stayed up until three o'clock in the morning writing a dispatch to Secretary Madison with the latest news of the offer. It has often been made to appear that he went to see Marbois without telling Monroe and that he wrote to Madison as if this were none of Monroe's business. This was not at all the case. He had not hidden from Monroe the fact that he was going to see Marbois, and he did not hide from Madison that he was writing him before telling all these facts to Monroe.

Perhaps a little untruthfully, he told Madison, "I think it necessary to write this while the impressions are strong upon my mind, and also as I fear I shall not have time to copy and send this letter if I defer it until morning." His actions were largely in the open, although it might be said that he could have waited until morning and discussed Marbois's offer with Monroe before writing to Madison. But the accusations of pettiness usually lodged against Livingston are themselves rather petty. Yes, he was trying to make the point now that this was his deal. He had first heard of it from the French foreign minister, then received the price information from the treasury minister, and now he was relaying the idea and asking for instructions from home—but none of it was written as if Monroe did not exist. He made it plain that the very next step would be to take the subject up with Monroe. And he included his comment that he thought the deal was wise, repeating his infelicitous suggestion that the cost could be recovered by selling part of the property to some other European power.

Livingston did, however, compound all the stylistic mistakes he habitually made in writing to Madison in this letter, dated "April 13, 1803 midnight": there were five very long pages, filled with paragraphs of dialogue on what Marbois had said to him about their friendship, what he himself had said about America's hopes for peace with France, and how cleverly he was reminding the French that by pushing for a price that America could not pay, they might "strengthen the hands of America's war party, which was restrained only by the prudence of President Jefferson." As latter-day readers, we might find it delightful of Livingston to have added that Marbois, in return, explained his own problems in dealing with Napoleon, "trying to promote a better price while dealing with…the temper of a young conqueror; everything is rapid as lightning; we have only to speak to him in a crowd. When I am alone with him, I can speak more freely, and he attends, but this…is always accidental." Interesting for the historian, but these were just irritating comments to Madison.

Unfortunately for Livingston's place in history, events moved too swiftly to favor his apparent hope of seeing himself acknowledged as the principal deal maker. He may have thought the final negotiations would continue until he had a reply from Washington that would strengthen his position. But such a reply would have taken a minimum of seven or eight weeks. And why should Livingston have expected a personal reply at all? Based on past performance, Madison would have addressed any reply to the pair of them, at best.

Chapter Twelve

THE TREMULOUS PAUSE

We were all resting on our oars" was Robert Livingston's description of the floating state in which all the participants found themselves in mid April 1803, as the moment of possible decision seemed in sight. But it was an uneasy rest, for success was by no means a sure thing. Not only was the question of price still a major obstacle, there was even said to be a basic uncertainty as to whether France had the right to sell the property that was under discussion. But calling it an uncertainty was a euphemism to mask a truth that all the parties wanted to ignore. There was, without any doubt, a major impediment that stood in the way of France's right to sell the Territory.

Spain, in the Treaty of San Ildefonso, had given Louisiana back to France with the firm proviso that the French were not to dispose of it except by returning it to Spain. So in the technical sense, there was not really anything for the French and American negotiators to discuss. The only reason to continue the negotiation was that an eager seller and buyer do sometimes agree to trade a piece of property even if the title is encumbered. France needed the money; the Americans suddenly longed for the land. Both were willing to dispute or ignore the protests that Spain might mount. And the impropriety was just one more worrisome technicality they hoped the Congress would overlook if and when the time came for it to ratify a treaty.

Equally astonishing was the fact that America was considering the purchase of a property that had no precisely defined extent or boundaries. The two Floridas may or may not have been included. The western part of the Territory was simply *terra incognita*. Marbois is said to have once told Napoleon that those boundaries were rather obscure, causing the First Consul to smile mischievously and say, "If an obscurity did not already exist, it would perhaps be a good policy to put one there." In other words, the less definite the description, the more liberties one can take in claiming a very expansive area.

When Livingston asked Talleyrand, who was far more nuanced than Marbois, what the eastern boundary was, he settled it easily by saying, "You must take it as we received it."

Livingston pressed on. "But what did you mean to take from Spain?"

Talleyrand shrugged, "I do not know."

Livingston saw from Talleyrand's arch look that he was trying to convey something with that unbelievable statement. "You mean," he asked, "that we should construe it in our own way?"

"I can give you no direction," Talleyrand replied. "You have made a noble bargain for yourselves, and I suppose you will make the most of it."

With all the uncertainties, then, why were the principal players not actually negotiating? Why were they not holding active discussions from morning until night? Partly there was the usual necessity for each side in a bargaining contest to hide its keen anxiety for a decision. To seem anxious might give the other side the advantage. Partly, too, there was the very deliberate pace at which most things were done because even the simplest message required a handwritten letter, and no letter from a diplomatic person could go out without a handwritten copy for the embassy's file and another copy to be sent to the mother country—to the State Department in the case of American letters. The original could not go out until at least one extra copy had been made, for there was no other way to ensure that each subsequent copy would be identical. So the principal players were forced to sit and wait for this to be done—or often to do the writing themselves.

But the days were not as empty or wasted as they seemed. It is known that Monroe and Livingston—in their different ways—were pondering the choices before them with growing intensity. A decision that had suddenly been expanded to involve the size, shape, productive power, and trading strength of a country—its whole future course as a nation—called for more thought than two men alone felt able to give it. Each time they came to what seemed a stopping point, where every detail appeared to have been covered, one or the other of them gave a start and brought a fresh question. A lesser version of this must have been going on among the French, and Marbois' *Histoire* gives some idea of it; but in their case, the tendency to think on their own was limited by the knowledge that the First Consul, wherever he might be, was considering the same ideas, making their thoughts of little account, for, at any moment, he might come forth with an overriding announcement.

Meanwhile, a litany of points being considered in Washington was dramatized in the form of a letter from the secretary of state to Messrs. Livingston and Monroe—one written without any certainty that Monroe had even arrived safely in Paris and certainly not knowing in what state their negotiation stood. Conducting international affairs was an onerous process. It might take two to three months to reach another interested party and receive a response, which meant that many hours of thought and writing had to be expended on subjects that may have long since been settled or that might well be settled before this day's letter would reach its intended reader.

An outstanding example of this problem can be seen in correspondence written by Madison on April 18, 1803, showing how something like a modern computer programmer's successive possible choices had to be devised to guide the recipient when alternate instructions were given. This moment deserves attention because few official letters have ever given such an insight into the management of foreign policy two hundred years ago, and also because the need to be critical of this great man in some earlier pages makes it important to recognize what Madison at his best was capable of.

The scenario is this: a month had gone by since Monroe's departure. To Madison in Washington, Paris might have been as remote as a star whose light takes months to reach Earth. He could only work on an assumption—that Monroe and his family had arrived in Paris and that the two ministers had had talks with the French, clarifying that country's position.

Madison, therefore, began by telling Monroe and Livingston that in case they had made a deal with France, or if they had at least a clear picture that the French government meant to respect American rights, then they must tell the British promptly that they have done nothing that jeopardizes the good understanding between Britain and the United States.

If, on the other hand, the French seem to be thinking about hostilities, or to have formed projects that will force the U.S. to resort to hostilities, said Madison, Livingston and Madison must naturally be careful to word their communications in such a way that they

THOMAS JEFFERSON. The president-elect, shown here as he was a few days before his inauguration, in 1801.

NAPOLEON BONAPARTE. A particularly striking picture of Napoleon Bonaparte, showing how youthful he was when he became First Consul and virtual dictator of France.

JAMES MADISON. As he was while serving as secretary of state and also playing an actor's part in President Jefferson's strategy for dramatizing America's readiness to fight for New Orleans.

CHARLES-MAURICE DE TALLEYRAND-PÉRIGORD. This rare portrait of Talleyrand several years before the Louisiana negotiations seems designed to show his interest in the worlds of learning, the arts, and the salon.

ROBERT LIVINGSTON. The look captured here shows the bright and creative side of the envoy who was so much mistrusted by his superiors in Washington.

FRANÇOIS DE BARBÉ-MARBOIS. The finance minister whom Bonaparte trusted implicitly, who loved America and wanted to see it win Louisiana—but at a price that benefited France.

JAMES MONROE. One of the best portraits of James Monroe, for it reveals the firm determination that enabled him to agree to the Louisiana Purchase without specific instruction.

PIERRE SAMUEL DU PONT. This brilliant thinker's practical words in both Washington and Paris turned the subject of Louisiana from troops to money and earned Jefferson's high tribute.

MONTPELIER. "Montpelier," the gracious but simple home of James and Dolly Madison, where the secretary of state worked while he was ill during the early months of the Jefferson administration.

LOUISIANA BECOMES AMERICAN. As a formality, France took over Louisiana from Spain for twenty days. Then, complying with the Louisiana Purchase, French troops saluted as their flag came down and the American flag was raised.

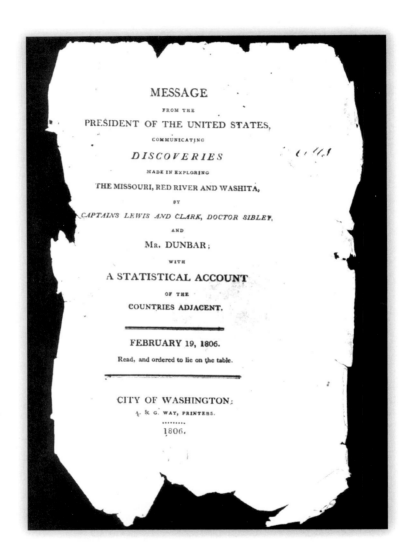

MESSAGE

FROM THE

PRESIDENT OF THE UNITED STATES,

COMMUNICATING

DISCOVERIES

MADE IN EXPLORING

THE MISSOURI, RED RIVER AND WASHITA,

BY

CAPTAINS LEWIS AND CLARK, DOCTOR SIBLEY,

AND

MR. DUNBAR;

WITH

A STATISTICAL ACCOUNT

OF THE

COUNTRIES ADJACENT.

FEBRUARY 19, 1806.

Read, and ordered to lie on the table.

CITY OF WASHINGTON:

A. & G. WAY, PRINTERS.

1806.

LEWIS AND CLARK. President Jefferson saw to it that the exploits of Lewis and Clark, which he had inspired, were made known to the members of Congress, and through them to the voting public that had long appreciated Jefferson's efforts to expand the nation westward.

LIFE ON THE RIVER. An itinerant artist depicts the primitive loneliness of a point along the Mississippi at the time of the Louisiana Purchase.

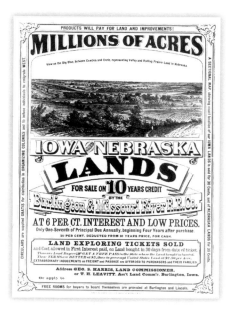

HOW THE WEST WAS SOLD!
The astonishingly modern sales strategy gives an example of how thousands of Americans were attracted by the promise of more and richer lands in the Louisiana Territory.

NAPOLEON AT AUSTERLITZ. Here Napoleon is shown surrounded by his marshals among the enemy dead after his greatest victory at Austerlitz. This triumphant campaign was aided by the money Napoleon received from the Louisiana Purchase.

THE BATTLE OF NEW ORLEANS. General Andrew Jackson held off a British armada that aimed to take Louisiana, and lost only 14 men compared to 2,700 British casualties. The Louisiana Purchase was final at last.

would not be precipitating France into hostile operations; on the other hand, to keep Britain thinking that the U.S. would be the one to decide on war or peace, and that America's choice of war would depend on Britain's participation in it.

He went on to say that if war were to be the result, it would be best to delay the start of it until this result was known for sure, so that the legislative and other provisions could be made. He also reminded them that Britain should not learn of the certainty of war, for it might take advantage of America's exposed position to make her accept disagreeable terms before Britain would agree to enter the war.

In exchanging ideas with the British, Monroe and Livingston were told to do it through the British minister in Paris, rather than either one of them going to London, for that might rouse the French to act and also make the British more smug in their attitude towards the United States.

Madison confessed his inability to give precise instructions, since he could not foresee what price the British might exact for their cooperation. If they insisted on a stipulation that neither party would make peace or truce without the consent of the other, he would consider it a reasonable condition. But he asked the two envoys to try to learn what Britain's objectives were, so that when the war had achieved American objectives, the United States would know what its British partner would require before agreeing that it was time to stop fighting. "It is only fair to ask this of them," he said, "since the U.S. objectives are so fair and so well known."

Madison foresaw, however, that the British would also require a stipulation of commercial advantages along the Mississippi— beyond those in the existing treaties. He authorized Monroe and Livingston to answer at once that Britain would enjoy free trade with all the ports to be acquired by the U.S., on the terms allowed to the most favored nations in U.S. ports. If pressed, they could even agree that in the ports to be acquired within the Mississippi, British subjects would be on the same footing as American citizens for about ten years. But the U.S. was not to be required to exclude the trade of any particular nation.

In case Britain asked for a mutual guarantee of existing possessions or of conquests to be made, the answer was to be no, for the United States did not want to be entangled in that other nation's wars with other powers.

Madison looked next at Britain's obvious anxiety to extend her domain to the Mississippi, beyond the western limits of the U.S., and to the northwest coast of America. He feared the likelihood that England would see a war as an opportunity to acquire the country west of the Mississippi, which was understood to have been ceded by Spain to France. He referred to these as evils that would be extremely displeasing to America's western citizens, and warned that their bearing on South America would arouse the jealousies of France and Spain and prolong the very war that was under discussion. So he instructed the two men to resist this demand "as altogether repugnant to the sentiments and policy of the United States." But he thought it might ease Britain's disappointment to agree that France would not be allowed to keep any part of the territory either.

Madison reminded the envoys that the minute war might arise, they must not fail to give confidential notice to U.S. ministers and consuls and to its naval commanders in the Mediterranean, and perhaps also to the collectors in the principal ports of the U.S.

The secretary of state enclosed a separate letter, authorizing the two to enter into such communications and meetings with the British minister as France's conduct might require. While hoping that France would not make this necessary, he said the president relied on their on-the-spot information and their best discretion to open communications with the British government and to shape the degree of understanding to the likelihood that war with France was indeed approaching. "But note this," he said. "If France should seem about to deny to the U.S. the free navigation of the Mississippi, you can consult with Great Britain as if war is inevitable."

If the navigation were not disputed, and only the right of deposit were denied, Madison deemed it wise to limit these consultations, having in mind the possibility that Congress would not consider this grounds for an instant resort to arms.

Here follows a whole new scenario: up to this point, Madison's instructions were based on the assumption that Britain and France were at peace. If war between them should have commenced, however, or if its approach seemed certain, he foresaw that France would be more apt to concur in friendly negotiations with the U.S. and Britain more desirous of engaging the U.S. on her side. So he reminded the envoys to profit from this by not having to consult with the British, or if it would be necessary to do so in order to make arrangements connected with the war, let the arrangements not be entangling.

Thus Madison's letter concluded. Although the length of the letter makes it seem so unlike most of Madison's communications, this four-page correspondence is actually as crisp as the rest, for in the fewest possible words, it gives firm instructions on how to handle at least twenty-two separate occurrences or nonoccurrences. Whatever may be thought of a secretary of state who unaccountably left unanswered so many inquiries from his diplomat in a critical foreign post, it has to be said that when he wrote on a subject of the highest importance, he produced a masterpiece of order and logic.

Meanwhile, the two ministers in Paris were sending the secretary of state much less edifying letters, although the disputes about their Louisiana agreement would make their words echo into the future.

On April 15, 1803, Monroe wrote in confidence to Madison, offering critical comments about Livingston that he did not wish to put into an official letter, but his words are nonetheless known. Monroe told how an American embassy employee, Consul General Fulwar Skipwith, had revealed to him how mortified Livingston had been when Monroe was assigned to Paris. Livingston said that having a new man come had jeopardized a good result that might have been easily obtained. In other words, that the coming of Monroe had disturbed a transaction that he was about to conclude. Monroe also told about the dinner party, at which Marbois had been seen in the garden and then come in to quietly arrange for Livingston to "come to his house" later that night. (This is incorrect, implying a more personal involvement. Marbois asked Livingston to come to his office.) "All this attention to my colleague, etc., may be an intrigue on the part of Marbois," wrote Monroe. But this point about Livingston's closeness to Marbois had never been hidden. Livingston had boasted of it.

Historians have almost unanimously tended to be pro-Monroe and anti-Livingston in this dispute, due to the latter's behavior after negotiations were concluded. However, it should be noted that Livingston had endured considerable ill treatment from the administration. And in this letter, we see that despite his sterling character, even Monroe is capable of grumbling and carrying tales to his patron. In fact, his complaining tone is not so different from Livingston's.

More important, Livingston's claim to have had a deal almost in hand is very close to the truth (although it was based more on Napoleon's growing desire to sell, rather than Livingston's persuasiveness). Those who deny that there had been anything close to a deal point out that there had not been a final, firm agreement on a price. But it should be acknowledged that the French and Livingston had moved a very long way toward a likely arrangement, despite

Livingston's great disadvantage in having been denied the directions for which he had pleaded. And although there is a real question of whether Livingston's tentative personality would have enabled him to make a deal on his own, no one would deny that his hard work over the two previous years had a great deal to do with making Monroe's task easier.

On April 17, another very personal letter was on its way to Madison. This letter was a rather free-swinging complaint of Livingston's, clearly written in an angry state since the language is less diplomatic than his normal style, in which he says bluntly:

> There are two circumstances with which I am not quite satisfied; one, indeed, of very little moment because it only respects me personally; and the other very important as it may defeat all that we may do, even at the moment of signing. The first is that I have not the same rank in the commission with Mr. Monroe. It is important that I should be thought to stand as well with our Government as any other person....The second thing is that the commission has power only to treat for lands on the east side of the Mississippi. [At this point in the letter, he actually lectures Madison on what should be proper behavior for a secretary of state.] It is absolutely necessary, my dear Sir, to repose confidence in ministers who are placed so far from the seat of government. You will recollect that I have been absolutely without powers to the present moment; and though I have hazarded many things upon a presumption that I should have them, none have been received till now, and they are unfortunately too limited.

A few paragraphs later, Livingston was in an even more aggressive mode:

> I am sorry you have not thought it proper to attend to my
> request as to the Italian Republic. It has, I believe, been
> acknowledged by all the Powers of Europe except Great
> Britain. [Apparently, Livingston had asked for permission
> to recognize or congratulate the newly inaugurated Italian
> Republic, and no answer had been given.] Compliments
> that cost nothing should, I think, always be paid, where
> you have points to carry. Be so obliging, in answering my
> letters, as to notice any project I throw out; because it is not
> enough to have them passed over in silence, as that leaves
> me in doubt; whereas the approbation or rejection of them
> would inform me of your sentiments, and enable me to act
> accordingly.

The touchy matter of "not having the same rank as Monroe" to which Livingston refers was an overblown issue then, and has been in subsequent accounts. They were both known as "envoy plenipotentiary," meaning that they had full power to sign for their chief of state, and that was obviously a major distinction. But Livingston seemed to feel that the additional word "extraordinary" in Monroe's title elevated him higher. Some of the French officials seem to have thought so, too, and a few dictionaries have defined "extraordinary and plenipotentiary" as the highest designation given to an ambassador. But many at that time took the extra word to mean only that Monroe had come for a special mission and purpose, as compared with the envoy who had all the ordinary duties. In any case, it will be noted that both men would become signers of the treaty, both taking an equal part in setting up promises and obligations on the part of their president. In this, as in other cases, Livingston raised unnecessary questions about his own status.

There is nothing to show whether Madison responded to this letter. It must have made him angry, but since his usual treatment of Livingston was to ignore his communications, there is no reason to think this brought the minister any better result.

ॐ

One undocumented but believable event that is said to have occurred during this time was a mysterious morning visit paid to Monroe. A gentleman who said he had been sent by "a confidential friend" represented two separate British banking firms, Hope and Baring. He made it clear that London banks knew a great deal about Monroe's mission, expected to see a positive result, and knew that he would have to borrow a large sum. The British knew, of course, that Napoleon would then use these proceeds to make war on them. But they preferred, at least, to benefit from the interest earnings, since they knew that otherwise, the Americans would get what they needed from Dutch bankers—which they eventually did. The confidential friend would seem very likely to have been Pierre Samuel du Pont, for he knew a great deal about the state of the negotiation and Monroe's mission, and it will be recalled that he had once told Jefferson that he could advise him how to borrow the necessary funds if the United States was not in a position to pay cash.

Listless as these weeks appeared, they brought a significant movement in the relationships. The decision was settling more and more firmly into Monroe's hands—not because the French had chosen to wait for the "extraordinary mission" that Washington was sending, nor for any other reason of rank or designation. It was because he was by nature a decision maker, with the special form of intelligence that is not brilliant, but balanced. He was being deliberate, using these days to consider and reconsider all the pros and cons. He was evaluating the allowable price on his own, considering the fact that America would be paying for something France had no right to sell, and trying to assess how many senators back home were going to denounce the acquisition of empty territory that would need to be populated and governed at a huge cost. It was a stressful time, but it was not—as with Livingston—a search for a way to avoid making a mistake. Ego never seems to have been a problem with Monroe; finding the way to a decision did not involve a detour to search for self-esteem. With him, it was a search for the right choice, regardless of its effect on his own position or reputation, and that was trouble enough in this case.

Chapter Thirteen

MONROE'S HISTORIC DECISION

Just before Monroe left Washington, Jefferson had told him in confidence that he could offer France a maximum of more than nine million dollars (fifty million francs) if it gave the United States possession of a substantial part of the Floridas in addition to Mississippi River navigation rights. This was more than four times as much as the two million that Congress had mentioned. But the disparity is not as great as it has been made to seem if note is taken of the way the Congress had worded its message.

The president's instruction to Monroe began with a reminder that the only figure that was remotely like a commitment from Congress was, indeed, a ludicrously small one, but it was cleverly stated in a way that hinted at possible enlargement. It came from the report of a congressional committee which, on January 12, 1803, had authorized the executive branch "to commence with more effect a negotiation with the French and Spanish governments relative to the purchase from them of the island of New Orleans and the provinces of East and West Florida." It pointed out that the Mississippi and its branches, with other rivers referred to, "drain an extent of country not less, perhaps, than one-half of our whole territory, containing at this time one-eighth of our population and progressing with a rapidity beyond the experience of any former time or any other nation. The Floridas and New Orleans command our only outlets to the sea, and our best interests require that we should get possession of them." Then, said the legislators cannily, "The Committee have no information before them to ascertain the amount for which the purchase can be made, but it is hoped that, with the assistance of two million dollars in hand, this will not be unreasonable."

That last phrase could have meant a number of things—from a bribe to induce some foreign minister to arrange a cheap purchase to a down payment on a very large purchase of the kind that eventually occurred, although no such thought had ever been discussed. Jefferson had spoken rather dismissively of the two-million-dollar amount, however, telling Monroe in confidence that he could go to a maximum figure of fifty million francs. Monroe knew that this represented a gamble for the president, because it so far exceeded the only figure that Congress had specified. He didn't know how Jefferson's greater number had been arrived at, but he assumed that the president had gone through some mental process of imagining the arguments of each leading legislator and finally assessing a level of political pain that they would all consider bearable.

But while the amount that Monroe now thought of offering seemed to him easily in line with Jefferson's criteria, considering the much greater purchase, he was really on his own in trying to determine whether Congress or even the president wanted to take on such a large transaction—not only as to its price, but even as to what many in the United States would consider the burden of dealing with so much land.

Jefferson, after all, had talked only of adding Florida territory to the equation. But the congressional pros and cons that Florida alone would have raised were limited. The political forces that would be set in motion by taking on the entire Louisiana Territory were incalculable. One by one, Monroe mentally reviewed the power centers that would bless or damn this treaty. The Republican-oriented westerners could boast that this virtual seacoast of their own would enrich the nation, could even show their own flair for industrialization with the rise of a boomtown called Pittsburgh at a well-located spot that had once been known as Fort Pitt, and now had taken to calling itself "The Gateway to the West." The northeast's business interests might lobby the Congress with strong facts and figures that pretended to show the westward tilt as a destabilizing force. Then there were the southerners, trying to ignore their fear of a possible slave rebellion while rejoicing at how the great rise in the value of a healthy slave made each slaveowner's net worth great enough to silence most of their doubts. These people might see the new land as more potential slave states—but in doing so create a major new split in the fabric of America.

A logical price evaluation, therefore, was far from being the sole issue. This decision involved the whole philosophy of what kind of nation Americans wanted. If he made it virtually alone, Monroe had no way to know what he might be condemning his great friend in the president's house to—impeachment, perhaps? Would Jefferson want him to use the extraordinary power he had been granted for such a different purpose as doubling the size of the country?

He must have tried to imagine Thomas Jefferson's own impression of the benefits versus the terrible risk to him and to the presidency itself. He knew that the president had no explicit right to buy foreign property. He was comforted, on the other hand, by knowing that nothing in the Constitution explicitly forbade it, and that some thought a part of the great document's genius was that it allowed wide latitude for action that was not strictly forbidden. This liberty inherent in the Constitution was what they saw as permitting ingenious and constructive activities that were already, in less than two decades, propelling the nation forward at a rate that intrigued and frightened the rest of the world. But these unimpeded federal activities were not the policy of Jefferson's party, which believed in limiting the power of a central government.

Another negative thought was that Monroe knew that financial subjects were primarily matters for the House of Representatives to deal with. What right did he have to pay cash for territory? It was consoling to keep in mind that the president would not be ordering the treasury secretary to disburse any funds. He would be asking Congress to appropriate what was needed, and, in this case, to authorize the borrowing from foreign bankers. It would be a request, not an order.

One thing that lessened the sense of impending doom was that the Senate could refuse to ratify any treaty Monroe might make, ending the subject of any kind of payment. But what a disgrace that would be—for a young country to have sent an envoy who exceeded his authority, bungled his mission, and came home with none of the vital assurances he was sent to get. Again, being Monroe, he worried less about personal disgrace than about harming the standing of the United States.

Jefferson, he imagined, would be as stupefied by the newness of this French offer as he himself had been on first hearing about it. Monroe was slightly off on that point, for he apparently didn't know about Jonathan Carver's book and the impression its estimate of the continent's expanse had made on Jefferson years earlier. If he had, Monroe might have imagined, at least, that Jefferson was going to be exhilarated by the idea of acquiring title to such a huge property. He did know that Jefferson wanted to see westward development. But he was even more aware of the president's caution as a politician. Favoring development didn't mean risking impeachment for totally ignoring the size of transaction that Congress had apparently intended to see on this subject. Monroe couldn't even recall hearing others in their party voice any idea that would be a guide. The very notion of such a purchase had not once come up during a conversation to help him assess whether other men he respected might deplore or cheer having that much wilderness heaped onto the country's responsibilities.

Monroe personally had no doubt that the huge acquisition was right, but he was shackled by thinking that the "supreme right thing" was to do what Jefferson would want, for his only power, he thought, was the mantle of authority Jefferson had placed on his shoulders.

Monroe and Livingston were together during part of this critical process, and the latter offered frequent words in favor of accepting the Marbois figures and making the purchase. "All France's lands west of the Mississippi!" he would say unbelievingly. "My, my. Why, no one even knows how much land that is. How many square miles, have we any idea?" And Monroe would shake his head silently. He later recalled that he also "was constantly having to overrule Livingston, who kept returning to 'the claims, the claims.'" Conversation with Livingston was not helpful, for Monroe was much closer to having a feel for the subject. While still in his twenties, he had helped Jefferson consider ceding Virginia's claims in the Northwest Territory to the federal government. He recalled the time in his youth when he had set off on a tour of observation, writing to Jefferson that he would "commence for the westward upon the North River by Albany. I shall pass through the lakes, visit the posts, and come down to the Ohio and thence home…hoping to acquire a better knowledge of the cause of the delay of the evacuation by British troops, the temper of the Indians toward us, as well as the soil, waters, and in general the natural view of the country."

He had even written Jefferson a confidential letter about the relationship between Canada and the United States. Without having gone west of the Mississippi, he could picture what the land would be like. But although Monroe knew that Jefferson had recently ordered two men named Lewis and Clark to explore the upper Mississippi, and perhaps beyond, it would be years before the extent of these French holdings he was contending for now could be even estimated. Livingston's random thoughts were not helpful for the present purpose of deciding what must be done. There were times when Monroe, with no sign of irritation, simply left the room for quiet moments of thinking alone in the orderly way that his mind liked to work.

Monroe knew that the land he thought of buying did not even exist in the minds of most Americans. The fact that the land west of the great river was much more extensive than the better-known eastern part was not only unknown, but quite unthinkable. Most of his countrymen, if they thought about it at all, would be chiefly concerned with the great river—so the value of the mysterious Louisiana Territory lay mainly in barring any other country from controlling the southern end of the Mississippi. It would either prevent any traffic from moving in and out of the Gulf of Mexico or keep ratcheting up the fees for such commerce—both being opposite to the free-trade principles that George Washington and other Virginians had enunciated for the Potomac River over twenty years earlier and that many other businessmen were declaring to be the right path to prosperity and population growth. So, more than the threat to land, it was the whole idea of a freer life that could be threatened—an existence in which the ability to grow and develop economically was as uninhibited as the new attitude toward personal fulfillment. Quite a new idea called "the pursuit of happiness" was at stake.

Despite all the westward migration that had occurred, the essential United States was still only a little more than a strip of land close to the Atlantic coast at the time. At most points, it extended inland no more than about fifty miles from the ocean. Even the largest states reached only about halfway to the Mississippi, and it is seldom realized that the other half of that distance belonged to the U.S., too. The nation had it because of a rare piece of generosity in the peace treaty it had won from the British in 1783. Many Americans had been quite prepared to accept the Allegheny Mountains as the western boundary line, but this very substantial strip of prime territory had also been ceded to the new nation by England as part of the Revolutionary War settlement—one of the providential pieces of good fortune that kept coming America's way. Some maps called this land on the right-hand side of the great river "Eastside Louisiana," and some states behaved as if their property extended westward right into that additional land. They were allowing settlers to claim acreage there, building population rapidly. But such purely eastern states as Delaware and Maryland protested this use of the land vigorously, and they eventually forced the federal government to treat the massive extra acreage as the whole nation's property, divisible into new states later on.

Everyone agreed that the Mississippi was the legitimate western boundary of the United States. (Spain had insisted that the midline of the river was the true boundary, giving American settlers no rights to the western bank, but there had been little enforcement of this rule.) Between that dividing line and California was largely a mystery land, and nobody knew how much of it there was or how many inhabitants it had. The number of Native Americans appeared to be sparse. There was some fretting about a few old British outposts that the British had agreed to dismantle, but were delaying in doing so. The surges of excitement that would be aroused by the successes of Lewis and Clark and the two journeys of Zebulon Pike were only a few years away, but until then, the impression of an uninteresting wilderness prevailed.

A huge part of that emptiness was often called "Spanish Louisiana," even though the key city of New Orleans in the south was occupied mostly by the French-oriented Cajuns, who had not been changed much by the last twenty years of Spanish rule. From there, the land extended north and west for great distances that had never been surveyed or even seriously estimated; it was only known that it held vast expanses of wilderness, some of it reputed to be quite beautiful and rich with promise. Up to the mid-eighteenth century, that unknown area to the west had still been thought of mainly as a route to China. Many were intrigued with the conviction of early French explorers that there must be a Northwest Passage somewhere above the North American continent. The notion of a passageway far outstripped any interest in the place itself. The fabled wealth of Cathay had seemed infinitely more attractive than mere empty land, so the few who meditated on what the rest of the continent might hold thought of it mostly as a pathway to a richer place.

ᓚᓂ

It is almost impossible to imagine what it was like, faced with a decision surrounded by such mystery, to have no way to consult with a superior. At one point, Monroe thought he would tell Marbois that they would have to wait until he could send a message to Washington, since he had never been authorized to commit his country to such an acquisition. Why should the French even have imagined that two men so far from their own capital might, without notice, negotiate for half a continent? It would have been a perfectly normal request to ask for more time, not in the least small-minded or embarrassing. But the risk of losing the opportunity would be very great. Napoleon was in a constricted situation. Money was very tight, the Saint Domingue uprising had forced him to divert troops intended for New Orleans, and the British were being especially threatening. That picture could change within days or less. Word might come that the violence in Saint Domingue was over, some new loan might ease his cash problems, or Talleyrand might give the restless ruler a brilliant idea that took his plans in a new direction. Then today's eagerness to deal would be replaced by shrugs and cold looks.

This new appraisal finally made Monroe turn away from the idea that his job was to discover what Jefferson wanted him to do. Not so! he decided. There was no earthly way he could accomplish that. His mission was to do what was right for the United States. That, after all, was what the term "plenipotentiary power" meant, not the right to act as someone else might act. Because that king or president could not be on the scene, he had invested you with the obligation to use your own best judgment. If you did that to the very best of your ability, neither man nor God could ask anything more.

It became easier for him after that. Instead of recoiling from the fact that he would be obligating the United States to borrow from foreigners, he reviewed more clearly the probable amount of the loan that would have to be sought from the Dutch, and thought of the interest and the terms. Others would step into the picture by that time, but it was right for him to be aware of all the costs that the United States would be incurring. Mostly he thought of the gap that existed between what Congress had quite eagerly agreed to and the entirely different transaction he would be handing back to those legislators. And—he had to face this squarely—his country's politicians might very well respond by strapping both him and his president with total, career-ending disgrace for having misused their authority. No American from that day to this has ever had to make so great a decision alone, with no way to contact his government. But the risk would be purely personal; the opportunity was national.

How high a price they should consider might change as the bargaining went on, but Monroe knew that an offer, to be significant, would have to be far beyond any sum that the Congress or even the president had ever hinted at. Livingston was not really an equal partner in the price decision, for Monroe had clearly been sent as the special emissary to deal with this issue. On this one subject, the power and the risk of being president were his alone. The negotiation was now between the French government and one man, James Monroe, in full charge of America's destiny.

Chapter Fourteen

THE MOMENT
IN HISTORY

Knowing that it had no chance of acceptance, the Americans first proposed a token figure to Marbois on April 15. It was the same amount that Livingston had previously mentioned offhandedly to Talleyrand: twenty million francs plus twenty more for the claims (or less than eight million dollars total). Marbois made it plain that he could not even take the First Consul's time with such a proposal. By the following day, they agreed to raise the amount to a total of fifty million francs—including the claims—which was the amount Monroe had first thought of as the maximum, and also happened to resemble Jefferson's limit of between nine and ten million dollars. Marbois showed great reluctance about taking this sum to the First Consul, saying that he felt sure a price at least thirty million francs higher would be his minimum, but he did agree to present it to Napoleon the next day. He soon reported to the Americans that he had gone to Saint Cloud to do so and had received such a cold response from Napoleon that he thought the whole plan was dead. (This may well have been untrue. More likely, Marbois never risked going back to

Napoleon with an offer he knew to be the barest minimum.) Whichever the case may have been, Marbois urged the two Americans to press forward with a better offer.

In the very personal way that he often talked to Livingston, the finance minister now took him aside and reminded him that it was not only "the extent of the country and the exclusive navigation of the river" that should be computed, but also the incalculable importance "of having no neighbors to dispute you, no war to dread." It was a telling point, indeed.

A delay of nearly two weeks followed. Napoleon had become distracted by other matters that were not explained to the Americans. Talleyrand also kept putting off the formality of presenting Monroe to Napoleon, probably still in the hope that some political event would kill the sale. And a back injury that confined him to bed prevented Monroe from taking part in talks for several days more.

The two Americans acted like comrades during this hiatus, going over boundary issues that they thought might have to be specified in a treaty, such as the Floridas, the northern boundary with Canada, which was constantly in dispute with Britain, and the uncertain border between Louisiana and Spanish Texas. In the end, they agreed that these would have to be left for later discussions with each of the other countries involved, and that a treaty with France would have to accept Louisiana just as France took it from Spain, which is to say undefined.

By Saturday, April 27, 1803, the endgame had begun. Monroe was able to sit on a sofa in his lodgings while meeting with Livingston and Marbois. The latter had brought a draft of a projected treaty that he felt the First Consul would sign. It called for the total of eighty million francs that he had been advocating all along. They talked pleasantly for a time without studying the treaty, and the Americans promised to see Marbois on the following day.

As Monroe wrote in his diary, he and Livingston went to Marbois's office in the Treasury the next day and began by restating their offer for a total of seventy million francs:

> Barbé-Marbois declared that he would not proceed in the negotiation on a sum less than 80 Millions, since it would be useless....Indeed he assured us that his government had never positively instructed him to take that sum, but that as he had told the Consul it was enough, that he would ask no more, and to which he understood the Consul as giving his assent, he Mr. Marbois had thought himself authorized to accept and propose it to us, but that he could not proceed unless we agreed to give it. On this frank and explicit declaration on his part and after explaining to him the motive which led us to offer the sum we agreed to accede to his idea and give 80 Millions.

The sudden release of tensions can be sensed from Monroe's typically simple language. It is believed that toasts were drunk, and that, according to Marbois, Livingston said, "We have lived long, but this has been the noblest work of our whole lives." But Monroe's plain statement of eighty million francs (fifteen million dollars) paid with no reference to the enormous property that had been gained shows the almost unimaginable disproportion that he saw between the cost and the substantial section of the continent that had been acquired.

There has been speculation about whether Monroe should have trusted Marbois when he said so firmly that a deal would require eighty million francs, nothing less. Marbois was not really being "frank and explicit." He could have taken less and still been within

Napoleon's limit. But he was working for France, trying earnestly to gain a significant amount of money in return for giving up a huge colony. At the same time, Marbois genuinely wanted to see America make the purchase, knowing that the rising American economy would easily be able to borrow and repay that sum. And it should be borne in mind that Marbois had been instrumental in cutting Napoleon's price from a hundred million francs. The amount he then persisted in demanding was his own reduced figure. So he out-bargained the buyers, but did them a great favor while winning an acceptable price for his government.

At this figure, France would get only sixty million francs net ($11,250,000), because the other twenty million ($3,750,000) would be used to pay off France's obligations to Americans who had valid claims for the seizure of American ships, crews, and cargoes. This meant that the U.S. government would be relieving France of a debt—paying its own citizens the compensation that the French owed them.

Monroe was aware that the overall figure of eighty million was the number that Congress would have to consider and that would be excoriated by Jefferson's enemies. Around fifteen million dollars, more than seven times the amount that Congress had ever thought of dealing with, was what he had to risk signing. But he genuinely believed that it would seem a very small sum in a few years.

Later that day, when Marbois told Napoleon of the eighty-million-franc deal, the First Consul turned sharply and said, "But I told you I wanted one hundred million."

"No, Citizen Consul. Your last words were that you would take fifty million and nothing less." Napoleon gave him a long look and said nothing.

John Quincy Adams, whose judgement was of the highest order, called the Louisiana Purchase "next in historical importance to the Declaration of Independence and the adoption of the Constitution. It was unparalleled in diplomacy because it cost almost nothing."

There are many ways of calculating the cost for the 875,000 square miles that the U.S. acquired. All of them yield a ridiculously small price per mile or per acre; four cents per acre is one of the figures. But since the deal had to be financed over a twenty-year period, a more accurate assessment would include the cost of the claims and then compute interest on the entire amount to the time in 1823 when the final payments were made. As with home buying, the cost of financing rivaled the price of the property. By that method, the total outlay has been set at a little more than twenty-seven million dollars.

Several different days are given as the date of the Louisiana Purchase. Full verbal agreement on all points, without signatures, was reached on April 29. The three negotiators met again on the following day, Tuesday the 30th, and made things a little firmer by having all three initial the agreement. That was also when wine was poured for another toast. An official reception at the Louvre was held on May 1, after Monroe and Livingston dined with Napoleon. The formal Louisiana Purchase treaty was dated and signed on May 2, 1803.

Chapter Fifteen

THE SENATE'S PRETENDED RELUCTANCE

Getting the new Louisiana Purchase treaty to Washington and into Secretary of State Madison's hands was naturally an urgent concern for Monroe and Livingston, but their first move was directed just across the Channel. Bizarre as it may seem, it was Britain, the country Jefferson had successfully pretended to be courting as a potential ally, that was feared as a last-minute troublemaker. Knowing that Britain coveted New Orleans, the danger that it might make a move to grasp it during a moment of uncertain ownership had been a worry for months. Now the two envoys in Paris moved instantly to advise Rufus King, the American ambassador in London, that the purchase of Louisiana was an accomplished fact, adding the assurance that due care had been taken to safeguard British interests in navigation of the Mississippi. They rushed this message out so hastily that it appears to have been undated; and in any case, it certainly went several days before their letter to Madison. So King George knew of the treaty long before President Jefferson did. Lord Hawkesbury, the British foreign minister, was quick to respond that his sovereign had received this intelligence with pleasure and with great appreciation for the protection of British interests.

On May 13, Livingston and Monroe sent a joint letter of many pages to Madison, transmitting the treaty and covering numerous details of the reasoning behind the decisions they had made. It began by recalling the earliest intimations that a purchase might be possible, touched on their attempts to estimate the true extent of the territory, the dubious status of West Florida and East Florida, their consideration of various factors affecting the price they might offer, and the estimate of what the cost of financing a purchase might be. It took them so long to prepare this letter that a French courier named M. Dirieux, who was named as the bearer on the first page, had left for Bordeaux before it was done; so at the end, they had to explain that they were entrusting it instead to an embassy employee named Mr. Hughes, who was to embark at Le Havre.

The vital documents are believed to have reached the White House on July 3, and to have sparked a burst of rare happiness. A month earlier, Jefferson had seen Livingston's letter to Madison reporting on Talleyrand's talk of selling the entire Louisiana Territory, and it had set up a feeling of excitement, although coupled with a nagging doubt about anything that came from Livingston. But the long messages and the treaty that finally were placed before him made the following day, Independence Day, 1803, a time of real joy for the president.

Curiously, the usually dependable *New York Morning Chronicle* did not refer to this important happening until July 21, and then it said—perhaps self-exculpatorily—that Mr. Hughes had delivered these documents on the previous Thursday evening, which would have meant that the delivery took a little more than two months. The July 3 date seems the likelier one, and it also would have allowed time for the involved thought process that President Jefferson went through.

After the initial delight of studying the letter of transmittal and the treaty itself, Jefferson began an agonizing period of doubt about the propriety of what he had done. Secretary Madison and the inner circle of cabinet members and executive-branch employees who heard the news were unreservedly happy. Some were ecstatic about the staggering amount of new territory that the United States had acquired. They fully expected to see lavish public joy, but they had to wait a bit before it manifested.

The news spread unevenly. Americans did not all awake on a single morning and find that their young nation was more than twice as large as they had thought the night before. Even the leading big-city newspapers were somewhat haphazard in reporting the Louisiana Purchase, and some merely referred to the news belatedly in the form of letters from thoughtful readers, giving the impression that the editors hardly dared to take responsibility for printing such news as a story of their own. This may explain the curious treatment by the important *New York Morning Chronicle*. In the previous month, on June 30, it had confidently run an unusual "extra" edition and banner headline reading WAR IS DECLARED—referring to England's new war with France, based on a reliable major statement from the British prime minister. But it waited until July 21, when it had a Proclamation by the President of the United States to add its own report on the Louisiana Purchase treaty and its terms.

As the people of this suddenly aggrandized country absorbed the news, it was no surprise that the westerners reacted like lottery winners who find their good fortune unbelievable. In Kentucky, Tennessee, and Ohio, the wild, tub-thumping, roaring joy exceeded anything seen before. Not even the end of the Revolutionary War had brought such a flag-waving delirium. But, most significantly noted by the members of Congress who were home on recess, this enthusiasm swept along even many of those who had been opponents of expansion.

The old Federalist opposition was still heard, but it was balanced by a new sound of lively approbation, of easterners actually thinking that not only was the Mississippi River safe for navigation, it was their own river now, even if they had never seen it; they owned it and great stretches of territory far beyond it. And this approval by easterners had to be reflected in the stand taken by many legislators. No one had seriously imagined such growth before the summer of 1803. After that, it struck many as being America's obvious destiny. Even many citizens who had no intention of going west wrote to their newspaper editors to say, in effect, that there would be no stopping the United States now. Especially reflective citizens pointed out that having the run of the continent would give the country unlimited capacity for good or for error.

The Federalists—the opposition party in Congress—thought up snide, half-humorous ways to attack the bargain purchase of nearly half a continent, calling it an extravagance. "When you consider that Manhattan was bought for twenty-four dollars, doesn't fifteen million dollars seem excessive for a wilderness?" they asked. But the senators who would shortly be faced with having to ratify or reject this treaty had to note that the nation's emotional response was somewhere between those who were filled with sheer patriotic joy at seeing their country's land area doubled, exceeding the size of all of Europe, and those who still feared the cost and inconvenience of enormous dimensions.

At just such a moment, Thomas Jefferson, who so often had to be different from the throng that adored him, became the Hamlet president. He was unquestionably the chief architect of this superb new vision, but he was not so sure about what he had done. Jubilant as he saw many of his fellow citizens to be over the grand enlargement of the nation, he was gripped by the suspicion that "he had gone beyond the Constitution" and against one of his firmest principles in purchasing a huge new territory. And—as is usually true of a Hamlet—there was a point in his brooding.

Jefferson had always stood for broad states' rights and very narrowly drawn federal powers. His political enemies, the Federalists, believed in the implied right of a federal government to assume any powers that were not specifically banned by the Constitution. The president abhorred that idea, believing it to be the passkey to a massive central power that would strangle the rights of the states, which he considered the only protection of the people's liberty. Now, he feared that he had traded liberty for territory—that his huge acquisition might be cited in the future as evidence that great decisions could be made without any consent from the states. Jefferson made his way exhaustively through many convoluted arguments, even debating whether the constitutional right to make war might be used as an argument; making war envisioned the right to acquire foreign property, did it not? His counselors all agreed that was so. Then, if the founders envisioned acquisitions by force, they certainly could not have been opposed to peaceful ones. He was heartened by this view, but not yet convinced.

This crisis of conscience went on for ten days, and it genuinely frightened James Madison to realize that the president was, indeed, leaning toward the idea of asking for an amendment to the Constitution. If such an amendment were passed to give the federal government a specific right to acquire territory, Jefferson felt that would be only a limited new power—the right to add new territory, but not necessarily any sweeping federal power in a variety of other fields. This would be far less fearsome than the open-ended force that said, by implication, "anything that is not specifically prohibited by the Constitution is permissible."

Madison had first believed that Jefferson was merely proposing this amendment idea as a bit of symbolism—a sign of how strongly he believed in the need for consulting the states. When he saw that Jefferson was seriously considering such a proposal, Madison stiffened his opposition to the notion. It was one of the few times that he displayed the steely backbone that was seldom needed to enforce his winning voice. "Any mention of a constitutional amendment could destroy this whole result," he warned, quoting from a June 7 letter he had from Monroe and Livingston. The two men in Paris reported that, "The First Consul, in a moment of chagrin at what he may have considered to be a bad bargain," had insisted that he still had the power to kill the treaty. "They beg you, Sir, to convene Congress promptly, get an early approval of the Treaty, and get funds provided for immediate compliance with the arrangement," Madison told the president. Much more forcefully than he usually talked to Jefferson, Madison now argued that any hint of a long constitutional impasse could cause the impatient French ruler to renounce the treaty and revive the whole specter of a French move to retake New Orleans, perhaps blocking U.S. navigation of the Mississippi.

Jefferson was quickly persuaded, for although his constitutional concern was genuine, it could not compete with his ardent wish to conclude the purchase that promised to lead to a continental United States of America. Anxious as he was to show that the treaty's adoption should be seen as a genuinely popular wish, and not a lone initiative of the executive branch, he had to act promptly. On July 21, major newspapers carried a Proclamation by the President of the United States appointing Monday, October 17 for the Senate and Congress to meet and consider the treaty. Some of the main provisions of the agreement were given, and as a loyally pro-Livingston New York paper added, "that without derogation to the talents of Mr. Monroe, previous to his arrival the negotiations had already been effected by Mr. Livingston in all material points." Despite the early sounds of approval, some of the thoughts expressed by members of Congress from their home areas during this recess period began to make it appear that the vote was going to be very close. As August and September passed, opinions apparently were evenly divided between proponents and opponents of the treaty.

And that was the apparent status of the affair when the senators reconvened on October 17 in response to a presidential call for haste in hearing and considering his special message, since the 30th was the stated deadline for ratification.

The Senate, even when it was less than a third of its present size, moved at its own pace. It voted twenty-eight dollars weekly for "such services as are usually provided by the Doorkeeper," solemnly resolved that each senator be supplied during the present session with three newspapers printed in any of the states, and, after a chaplain had been chosen, named the Hon. Nathaniel Macon as its Speaker. The ballots having been collected and counted, the whole number was declared to be twenty-eight, of which fifteen made a majority.

With all such business out of the way, a message that President Jefferson had directed to the Senate and House of Representatives was read and five hundred copies thereof were ordered to be printed. Jefferson began by apologizing for the need to call the members back into session earlier than the expected date, but there was a new forcefulness in his words as he explained that the "extraordinary public agitation over the status of the port of New Orleans" made it clear how great a danger to the nation's peace existed as long as "so important a key to the commerce of the western country remained under a foreign Power."

Jefferson's words touched on major issues and on minor details, chiefly intended to warn that the European powers were again at or very close to war (strange wording, since Britain had declared war on France in May), and to show the many dangers that the United

States would be evading if the recent Louisiana Purchase treaty were approved and implemented. In the last paragraph, he openly referred to the decision that would now be in the hands of the Senate, urging the members to consider the state of Europe and to be:

> sensible how much it is our duty to look on the bloody arena spread before us with commiseration, indeed, but with no other wish than to see it closed, I am persuaded you will cordially cherish these dispositions in all discussions among yourselves, and in all communications with your constituents; and I anticipate with satisfaction the measures of wisdom which the great interests now committed to you will give you an opportunity of providing, and myself that of approving and of carrying into execution with the fidelity I owe to my country.

The early rash of objections proved to have been so flimsy and had given way so promptly to the generalized desire for the exciting new land that the Senate voted in favor of the treaty three times by more than a three-to-one margin. This has been misstated in a variety of ways in the past, because the so-called "History of Congress" in that era was not an official organ, but a commercial product with frequent errors. The official *Congressional Record* that is known today did not appear until two decades later. However, there had always been an official and reliable *Executive Journal of the Senate*, and it shows that the treaty was read three times—on October 17, 18, and 20, with votes being taken on each occasion, the result being a thumping twenty-four to seven in favor each time. The 20th was the official date of ratification. (It will be noted that the higher vote total than the number cited earlier in the week occurred because three new members had presented their credentials, including the young

John Quincy Adams of Massachusetts, who crossed party lines to vote for the treaty.) On Saturday, the 22nd, the resurgent president was hailing the ratification and asking to be granted the power to employ any part of the army and navy of the United States for the purpose of taking possession of the territories ceded by France. This, too, was quickly granted. And the House of Representatives, which had to consider the financial arrangements called for by the treaty, approved it by the even greater margin of eighty-nine to twenty-three.

Twelve days later, however, on Wednesday, November 3, there was ample evidence that the American politician's penchant for talking merely to be seen and heard goes back a very long way. A financial subject required Senate approval (although with a looser deadline) because it consisted of a separate "Convention" appended to the treaty. It called for the creation of a special stock in the amount of $11,250,000 for the purpose of giving France an interest-bearing asset that could be used to turn the deferred payments into spendable cash. For little reason beyond mere posturing, some of the strongest objections now erupted.

As if the positive spirit of the recent ratification had never existed, Delaware's Senator Samuel White was back to ask:

> What is the hurry about passing this? We have already passed a bill that authorizes the President to take possession of the Louisiana Territory. The French officer who is authorized to make the cession is already at New Orleans. But we have authorized the President to take possession without knowing whether the First Consul can or will carry this treaty faithfully into operation. But, Mr. President, it is now a well-known fact that Spain considers herself injured by the Treaty. [Just before the

ratification, Spain had registered a complaint, stating that it should have been consulted by both parties to the Treaty before they reached this agreement, and especially raising the Florida issue, but not threatening any specific action.] And why should we make the President the sole and absolute judge of what shall be a faithful delivery and possession? While he may think a delivery sufficient to justify the payment of the money we may not. What would the payment be for? It would be buying France's authority to make war on Spain. What reason would we have to think the French prefect in New Orleans can give us peaceable possession of the country?

He went on at length to warn that the Creeks and other Native American nations "from the howling wilderness never to be trodden by the foot of civilized man" might find it impracticable to relinquish these territories so lightly traded by persons who have never seen them.

On the next day, the second Delaware senator, William H. Wells, tore into the treaty with multiple objections, starting with the fact that it failed to make specific mention of payment, pretending instead that the First Consul was doing the transfer "to give the U.S.A. a strong proof of his friendship." He called the language of the treaty "dark, obscene, and unintelligible." He pointed out that perhaps the Spanish would refuse to obey the French prefect in New Orleans, and instead attack and slay half the men sent to take possession. "In that case," he asked, "would we be satisfied to have paid the sum of fifteen million dollars for this privilege?"

Almost talking over each other in their haste to be heard, some expostulated about whether or not Louisiana should be taken into the Union at once, and, in case not, surmised that the treaty itself might be rendered null and void, because France could claim that its chief reason for entering into the arrangement had been to secure American citizenship for the people of Louisiana.

The very basic question of whether the United States had the power to add new states to the Union was explored at great length, especially focusing on whether this was implied by anything in the Constitution or only by common sense. Clearly, it had already admitted new states that had taken the initiative of applying for entry, but could the federal government become the instigator, the creating agent?

Mr. Uriah Tracy of Connecticut embellished on that question by asking whether an assumption that the U.S. could admit new states to the Union would not also give the federal government the power to cede states. This challenging query caused John Breckenridge of Kentucky to taunt him by pondering whether it might, for example, cede Mr. Tracy's Connecticut to France? But mercifully he said, "I think not. The U.S. could not cede Connecticut because in doing so, it would be giving up part of the sovereignty of the nation, which is whole and entire."

Perhaps the most pointless comment was by New Jersey's Senator Jonathan Dayton, who insisted that he was not present as a champion of small states, but did want to protest that although he represented a relatively large one, he objected to being bound hand and foot to the interests of five large states. Having said that, he gave no clue as to which way he planned to vote or was urging other members to vote.

These generalities gradually gave way to lesser, but quite practical, details. Should persons born in Louisiana, for example, be considered the equals of native-born Americans for the purpose of eligibility to become president or vice president? Would French and Spanish ships, being given free access to Mississippi River ports, be considered to have locked in a commercial parity with Britain, one that the latter, as our greatest trading partner, would come to resent? All such issues were soberly declared to be worthy of further study, but in no way serious enough to imperil the outcome of any pending decision.

As the week wore on, it became clear that the handful of hold-outs who continued their opposition would not disturb the *fait accompli* that had prevailed from the beginning. Oddly, however, Jefferson's glorious victory meant the defeat of his most cherished political belief, and the crushed opposition Federalists saw their philosophy become the law that the U.S. was destined to live by. Just as Jefferson had feared, the Louisiana Purchase made the use of implied rights the all-purpose tool with which the federal government would grow great and the power of the states would appear to recede for a time. Many, however, consider this to have been a force that propelled the United States toward today's historic stature. The marked narrowing of the gap between states' rights and federal power appeared to put the nation on a path that some would call a self-correcting balance.

Chapter Sixteen

THE ANTAGONISTS MOVE ON

The four Americans who had brought about the brilliant result could have been optimistic for their own futures, for they all shared in the success that lay ahead for the expanded nation.

Of the four French participants, two, Napoleon and Talleyrand—whose mental agility dealt with ups and downs like mountain goats—still had their greatest days ahead, in spite of France's turmoil. But Marbois and Pichon were buffeted by the wild politics of the coming years in ways they could not have imagined when the Louisiana Purchase treaty was concluded.

Looking back on their work in the spring of 1803, the great individual responsibility that had been thrust on the American subordinates, Monroe and Livingston, was clear. The time required to communicate between Washington and Paris would have forced even the most demanding superior to delegate many of his key prerogatives to others. Yet a curious and counterintuitive fact emerges: despite his distance from the center of action, despite the decision making he had to entrust to others, President Jefferson had unquestionably been the indispensable player. He had been forced to rely on a set of unruly aides who repeatedly veered from his wishes, and still it was his program and his strategy that carried the day. No heavy-handed dictator could have seen his commands more thoroughly enforced in the end.

Thus, Jefferson was the one person without whom the Louisiana Purchase treaty would have been inconceivable. For one thing, Monroe could never have made the buying decision without having had Jefferson's clear instruction that the figure named by Congress could be substantially exceeded. Monroe went far beyond anything the Congress had imagined, but he would never have considered doing so if the president had not told him that some elasticity was envisioned. Just as important was Jefferson's dogged opposition to any incursion into America's neighborhood by French troops. It was like a preview of the Monroe Doctrine, and it succeeded brilliantly, even though the United States was totally unprepared to mount the brand of opposition the president threatened.

Jefferson could have looked back with satisfaction at having won the day by making Napoleon believe that America was ready to fight for New Orleans, and to join with Britain if necessary, so that accepting cash for it instead seemed like victory to the First Consul. As Napoleon said, "I count Louisiana as already lost." But once his first joy at seeing the treaty had passed, Jefferson was less ebullient than most others because he had the dual problem of making the Congress come aboard, while also questioning whether the Constitution gave him the power to purchase foreign territory. He admitted that he "had stretched the Constitution until it cracked," and wondered if he would be impeached because his treaty-making powers did not specify the acquisition of territory. He need not have worried.

Jefferson's opponents had often grumbled wonderingly at the man's way of gaining political support without seeming to go after it.

Now that was happening again. A country alive with the exuberance of youth told Jefferson that his afterthoughts were groundless. The idea of an "America—from sea to shining sea," seemed to be taking shape. Many were laughing at the Federalists' attempts to deride the Louisiana Purchase as a terrible mistake; "spending a great fortune for a desert" they had cried, moaning that some of the nation's best young blood would be dissipated in trying to protect a far greater area than the United States was ready to swallow. But in the early months, at least, few were lining up with the naysayers. Jefferson had gambled shamelessly and come out of it with more than popularity—he came out with glory. The entire Congress fêted him at a gala dinner.

He went on to complete two very productive terms, and he has been called our first successful president, because Washington and Adams, despite their personal prestige, had rough sailing in the uncharted waters of the presidency. Jefferson proved to be a surprisingly good administrator of the nation's business, considering how unsuccessfully he managed his personal life. In his own affairs, he was a profligate spender, ready to buy anything that took his fancy, to enlarge or embellish dwellings beyond his means, even homes that he knew to be temporary, and to entertain an incredible mass of house guests at great expense. Consequently, he approached the end of his life with the certainty that his estate would be in the hands of creditors and his heirs would have little or nothing.

James Madison's steadiness in channeling and containing the Jeffersonian fury about protecting New Orleans was what had made it into a workable strategy. Regardless of his curious treatment of Livingston, nothing can take this achievement away from the secretary of state.

Only in hindsight does it become clear how thoroughly Jefferson and Madison had operated almost as a single person with the benefit of two viewpoints during these months. The nature of their teamwork had been unique. For example, Jefferson projected determination to fight the first French footfall in Louisiana. Madison's pretense of indifference, based on confidence that the American people would snuff it out, prevented the agitated Congress from moving prematurely toward war. Historian George Dangerfield called the president and secretary of state "one of the subtlest intellectual combinations in American history." Perhaps their greatest asset was frequent disagreement, so that they were not limited to a single mind-set. They often set out with opposite views of a question, but usually came to a conclusion that accommodated both their approaches. Any tendency to think of Jefferson as the great man and Madison as the supplier of ideas and balancing opinions—a pairing that is often seen among partners—would be very misleading. James Madison was very much his own man, even though in his years as secretary of state he insisted on starting nearly all pronouncements with "The President wishes…" or "The President has decided…" This apparent reticence to put himself forward was actually a method that he believed would clarify and strengthen anything that he set down as policy. It did not illustrate how the two men behaved when they worked together. Then, it would very often be Madison who was correcting Jefferson's suggestion or countering his errant idea. If he was the one who said less, it was because each of his words counted for more. Another person's long and seemingly balanced thought was very often reduced to a single sentence by the Madison brain— a sentence that separated the balanced words like a cleaver and simply said, "This is what needs to be done."

The president may have seen to it that even Madison was taken in by his saber-rattling threats to keep France from moving into New

Orleans, for they had to be totally convincing. What appear to have been misgivings on Madison's part had shown through at times, as his letters and remarks to Pichon tended to soften the president's approach, though never enough to damage its effect. Almost invariably, the Madison version showed a controlling mind and hand, and sometimes a fallback position to be sure that any disappointing turn of events would not be fatal to the final objective.

However cool he may have seemed during the negotiations, Madison's all-consuming interest was shown when he reacted to the treaty with an ejaculation that was so unlike his normal speech: "A truly noble acquisition" were his exact words. This revealed what a masterpiece of fakery he had pulled off when he had once told Pichon, "How sad it would be if French intransigence forced us to conquer the country west of the Mississippi," and listed the several unfortunate consequences he pretended it would bring.

Looking back, Madison knew perfectly well that his own words had been absorbed and copied by Napoleon when the First Consul gloated about how this deal would not only make trouble for the English, but would also confront the Americans with all those misfortunes that he absorbed from Madison's sly falsehoods to Pichon. The exact Madisonian reasoning that Pichon had passed on to Paris was now the dictator's explanation of why he had chosen to sell: "We must expect rivalries in the bosom of the Union. Confederations which are called perpetual last only until one of the contracting parties finds it to its interest to break them."

But the secretary of state never once drew attention to how many of the words used by others were lifted from him. As one of Madison's biographers pointed out, "Like nearly everything else relating to Madison that leads in the direction of pre-eminence, this has to be dug out of the records." While others were competing for glory in Paris, this rare man never tried to get his brilliant contributions noticed, which helps to explain why he loathed such boasts from others.

In only five years, James Madison would be elected as America's fourth president, and by 1809 he would move into the White House, facing a simmering quasi-war with Great Britain. The underlying factors are discussed in the final chapter, leading to the moment when Madison, having survived the highly debatable War of 1812, had to wait in suspense to know whether the Louisiana Purchase that he had helped to bring about would be confirmed and validated by General Andrew Jackson or tragically negated by the giant British armada that attacked the New Orleans area in 1814.

ᥟ

The troubled future of French *chargé d'affaires* Louis-André Pichon can appropriately be seen at this point because he and Madison were virtually each other's counterparts during the negotiations. It is not rare for a secretary of state and a key foreign ambassador to maintain an active relationship, but never had one been so decisive as theirs. The intimacy and the result should have been a triumph for Pichon. It was, instead, a professional shipwreck.

Professor Albert H. Bowman, writing in the *Journal of the Society for Historians of American Foreign Relations*, has credited Pichon, who was only twenty-nine years old when he became France's envoy and consul general in Washington, with being the principal influence on the First Consul's decision to abandon his dream of an American empire. While we have seen how Madison's long and frequent sessions with Pichon had transmitted disinformation to Napoleon, Bowman insists that Pichon was not at all taken in; almost from the start, he had concluded on his own that New Orleans could be a disaster for France, and he made that clear to his superior, Foreign Minister Talleyrand. This contribution would devastate his own career.

Less than two months after taking office in Washington, late in 1801, Pichon (who had been told by Talleyrand to avoid discussing French colonization with the Americans), wrote to report that American newspapers were announcing that the Spanish had ceded Louisiana back to France. And in his forthright way, he told his foreign minister—who was a strong advocate of creating a French empire in America—"If this event has taken place, you can be assured that it is one of the most delicate operations we could undertake, and there is no safety or advantage at all to us in this acquisition without two things: First, the complete freedom of the port of New Orleans, and second the cession of the Floridas, or at least one of them, to the United States."

Month after month, Pichon's reports had been accurate, effective in making Napoleon realize how little chance he had to succeed in the New World, and inflammatory to the colony-minded fraternity in the Ministry of Marine and Colonies. As soon as the treaty was concluded and Pichon rotated back to Paris, he was highly praised for his work by Talleyrand, who also nominated him for the Legion of Honor; but he was almost instantly attacked by Admiral Dénis Décrès and falsely charged with irregularities in his financial accounts. He was tried before a special council and, although a majority is said to have favored his acquittal, a decree was handed down that dismissed him from the foreign service in disgrace. He would never return to the diplomatic service or to any very significant public office.

Only in 1809 did Pichon reappear in public service as a royal councillor of state and intendant-general of finances for Napoleon's brother Jerome, who had become king of Westphalia. He resigned from this presumably boring work in 1812 and returned to Paris to write a book on France under Napoleon, which was published in 1814. He had never approved of Bonapartism, but he had served the emperor's government loyally, so he wrote of the period with measured disapproval. He received a minor royal appointment under King Louis XVIII, then, in 1820, became councillor of state and secretary general in the Ministry of Justice. Between that time and 1830, he also had frequent—and unenviable—missions to inspect French West Indian colonies. After the French conquest of Algeria in 1830, he became the first civil administrator of that country. Pichon retired from public service in 1832, and he was treated courteously under the Restoration, being made a baron and an elected officer of the Legion of Honor. He died in Paris in 1850.

James Monroe must have looked back happily at the fact that he had doubled the size of his country. What is known for sure is that he wrote Jefferson, saying that having used his plenipotentiary powers and signed the agreement, "I can only hope for mercy!"

It was fortunate for him that his bargaining with Marbois had not been carefully analyzed. Monroe had simply been himself—with no guile of his own, he had trusted the Frenchman's words; shrewd bargaining had no place in his makeup. By resisting, he could certainly have made Marbois accept ten million dollars less, for that would have been well within Napoleon's figure. But the traits he showed here were the same ones that later made him one of the most successful and widely respected of all America's presidents. A cleverer person might have struck a sharper bargain, but his trusting manner ultimately won nearly unanimous support.

For a time after the Louisiana Purchase, Monroe reverted to the perverse luck that had usually dogged his political life. Even after the triumph of the Louisiana Purchase treaty, he suffered another mortification that plunged him again to the lower rungs of the political ladder. Monroe had not been called home to receive the acclamation for Louisiana in person; instead, he was quickly shifted to a mission to England that ended too poorly to add any luster to his image. He struggled for two difficult years in London, failing to make progress against the disagreements that later led to the War of 1812.

By the time he returned home in 1805, the fact that James Monroe had doubled the size of the United States had been taken for granted too long to afford him much acclaim. The Louisiana Territory, in fact, had come to seem more troublesome than glorious because it was exacerbating slavery and Native American problems. When Monroe came back to center stage, he was noticed mainly because of disappointment over his British treaty. Its terms were so poor that Jefferson did not even send it to the Senate. (Other American attempts to set new treaties with European powers had met similar fates—not due to inept diplomacy, but to arrogant older powers believing they were entitled to dictate terms to a young nation.)

Monroe went back to his old starting point for a third time, served again in the Virginia General Assembly, was elected governor again, and finally reemerged into national high office in the cabinet of James Madison. Stepping into a crisis during the botched War of 1812, he served doubly as secretary of state and of war. It began to be recognized that he was—as Jefferson had once said with perfect simplicity—"honest and brave."

One of the few who troubled to write a biography, Daniel C. Gilman, then president of Johns Hopkins University in Baltimore, wrote in 1898, "The conclusion has been forced on me that Monroe is not adequately appreciated by his countrymen....He has suffered by comparison with four or five illustrious men—Washington, Marshall, Hamilton, Jefferson, Madison—his seniors in years and his superiors in genius....He was in early life enthusiastic to rashness; but as he grew older his judgment was disciplined, his self control became secure, his patriotism overbalanced the considerations of party. Political opponents rarely assailed the purity of his motives or the honesty of his conduct."

The phrase, "his patriotism overbalanced the considerations of party" is especially noteworthy, for the lack of this trait—the increasing tendency of most leaders to let political opportunism outweigh other considerations—was becoming almost toxic. George Washington, in particular, found it hard to understand how men he relied on, such as Jefferson and Hamilton, could allow political enmity to outweigh the need for national unity.

As Monroe's higher principles became clearer to his fellow citizens, he was elected to two full terms as president from 1817 to 1825. His reelection was memorable because he was nearly chosen unanimously. One elector voted for John Quincy Adams only because he did not want anyone other than George Washington ever to be a unanimous choice. Monroe must be judged a very successful president, even though he did not preside over wars or other catastrophic events that usually make for memorable presidencies.

The enduring policy that bears his name, the Monroe Doctrine, has to be called a truly historic initiative because it was, right from the moment of being enunciated, "an exact expression of the general opinion of his countrymen," in his biographer's words. This doctrine, like all major international policies, had been taking shape somewhat earlier. There are at least ten instances, dating back to 1780, of American statesmen, including Washington, Jefferson, Adams, and Monroe himself, warning another nation or group of nations to "stay away from our hemisphere." And just five months before Monroe wrote the doctrine in full, John Quincy Adams, then secretary of state, told a Russian minister on a question dealing with the northwest coast, "we should contest the right of Russia to any territorial establishment on this continent, and we should assume distinctly the principle that the American continents are no longer subjects for any new European colonial establishments."

President Monroe's doctrine, expressed in his annual message on December 2, 1823, is a little less than nine hundred words in length. It is curious that Monroe is best known for a piece of writing, because he was not an especially fluent or elegant writer. But it is altogether appropriate that this man who was so closely associated with the Louisiana Purchase should also have been the one to set forth the natural sequel to that great event. The Louisiana Purchase had signaled that the United States was probably destined to cover most of an entire continent. In the Doctrine, Monroe broadened this claim to go far beyond the continent and to insist that the entire hemisphere was to be free from foreign interference.

Robert Livingston quite astonishingly survived a post-treaty period of anguish, stupid behavior, and even contempt to move on to another decade of life that was happy and prosperous. It is almost novelistic, but a part of his success during this time was directly linked to New Orleans, Louisiana, and the Mississippi.

If the Louisiana negotiations had taken the very small turn needed to make them into a tragedy, the tragi-comic Livingston would have been its central figure. Coming so close to a lifelong wish for greatness, he earned only sympathy, at best, and appeared to be the ill-favored of the gods. In fact, he was extremely fortunate to have avoided censure and dismissal for his misdemeanors as an envoy who tried to act as a policymaker. It was probably only Madison's wish to avoid a breach with New York political leaders that saved Livingston from this.

If Livingston's backward look included any self-examination, which is not evident from his writings, he would have seen that his natural cleverness was overcome by a massive failure in dealing with any superior. The relationship apparently robbed him of confidence, which he demonstrated in two ways: by trying too hard to show how much he was doing, and by avoiding any situation that called on him to make a final decision.

Livingston would have been astonished to hear himself described as lacking self-confidence. There was no timidity about his approach to the great, so he did not stand in awe of a fabled individual like Talleyrand, and certainly not of the young Napoleon. He could match wits with them, and could propose intriguing new ways of looking at a subject. But his failing was most like that of the athlete who avoids taking the crucial last shot in a close game.

Thinking back to his work in Paris, Livingston knew he had sparked ideas that may have been central to the final settlement, but he may never have realized that every time affairs approached the possibility of an offer that could be decisive, his mind had turned to ways of skirting or diminishing the deal.

The players had never been so separated, so different in their ideas, as they were after the treaty was concluded. Livingston was trying to forget, deny, and readjust the fact that as recently as three days previously, he had written a note to Madison, saying indelibly, "I would rather have confined our views to smaller objects; and I think that if we succeed, it would be good policy to exchange the west bank of the Mississippi with Spain for the Floridas, reserving New Orleans." Up to the very end, Livingston was suggesting to Monroe and Madison that something smaller than the entire Louisiana Territory would be best. To him, the goal tended to shift as the end neared: it was no longer to gain a victory, but simply to avoid a mistake.

The fair-minded Monroe stretched a point to say that Livingston, "has manifested an invariable zeal to promote the object of the cession and to extend our rights on the Mississippi." Still, there was a hassle over Livingston's demands to have the payment for claims kept separate from the treaty of cession, so that if the latter were not ratified, the claims could still be collected. Livingston said that was important, because failure to collect claims might lead to Republican defeat in the coming election. Ridiculous, thought Monroe, forgetting that he had used a similar argument in Paris years earlier.

In the aftermath, Livingston could not have handled the matter worse. He wrote numerous accounts to friends, all telling how close he had been to the deal, and how wrong and unnecessary it was for Monroe to have been sent, arriving just in time to take all the credit. In fact, Monroe did no such thing. He had tried to include Livingston as an equal colleague in victory. But it was hard to send any compliments in Livingston's direction when the latter was making himself so shrill and petty. Monroe ended by saying of Livingston, "The most difficult, vexatious, and embarrassing part of my labor has been with my associate."

Since Monroe's behavior was so far above reproach, Livingston took to saying that "friends of Monroe" were trying to give him all the credit, as in this fatally lengthy letter of November 15, 1803, to Secretary Madison, who was bound to deplore the effort. It included this passage:

> This letter [one in which Livingston had warned that no course but war could possibly save New Orleans] is very imprudently shown and spoken of by Mr. Monroe's particular friends as a proof that he had been a principal agent in the negotiation. So far, indeed, as it may tend to this object, it is of little moment, because facts and dates are too well known to be contradicted. For instance, it is known to everyone here that the Consul had taken his resolution to sell previous to Mr. Monroe's arrival....

Even this short excerpt contains a stark untruth. When he says that "facts and dates are too well known," Livingston is referring to his own version of facts and dates, which are fictitious. Napoleon had authorized Marbois to sell Louisiana, but at the price of one hundred million francs, which Livingston had called exorbitant (and Marbois agreed). There had been no counteroffer by Livingston, and there was simply no agreement. The approach to a negotiation and a potential agreement was obvious, but its effect is sullied by being wrapped up with a lie.

Perversely, Livingston persisted in showing his disappointment rather than accepting the equal credit that Monroe was quite willing to give him. Under pressure from his party and his state to clarify how the Louisiana Purchase was achieved, Monroe finally sent a written statement to Virginia legislators, making it clear that Napoleon had not finally made up his mind until he had learned via the semaphore that Monroe was arriving. He did not, however, claim that any merit of his had brought about the conclusion. In the main, he correctly attributed success to the firmness of the administration's policy, which caused Napoleon to see that the arrival of the special envoy was a time for decision.

Monroe tried hard to avoid a challenge that would have hopelessly exposed Livingston. And even when the latter went on with behavior that led to the greater disgust of Madison and Jefferson, Monroe asked that there be no public exposure "with respect to this old friend...who should be treated with the utmost kindness possible."

But not even Monroe's astonishingly forgiving nature made him want to see anyone with such a flawed character as Livingston brought close to the presidency of the nation. To be on the safe side, Monroe suggested that his colleague be kept on in Paris long enough to ensure that he could not get back home in time to seek the vice-presidential nomination. Because it was Monroe's idea, it can be accepted as a high-minded one; but it also happened to contain a political component that made Madison accept it at once, adding a typically demeaning thought that Livingston "would probably be flattered at being asked to stay." Political developments had already put the vice presidency out of Livingston's reach, as George Clinton had clinched the nomination in February 1804 before Madison's suggestion reached Madison. Livingston was nonetheless happy to stay in Paris for two more years.

That Livingston was trying to take credit for the Louisiana Purchase became well known after the treaty was concluded. And while some, especially in New York, agreed, Livingston's aggressiveness diminished the number of well-wishers. Worse yet, any sympathy he might have enjoyed was damaged when insiders whispered suggestions about his outright wrongdoings. For one thing, he had widely broadcast the fact that Americans with claims against France were going to be paid—in order to boost his vice-presidential chances—when that information was still a state secret. (Livingston later finessed this rather well in a letter to Jefferson, writing flatly that he had made sure the claimants were informed, lest they abandon their claims to speculators for trifling sums when their success was almost assured.)

He further infuriated Madison by publishing in the gazettes a letter from his supporter James Swan that credited Livingston's long memorandum proposing a new trade policy for France with having brought about the Louisiana Purchase and was written in a way that, in Madison's words, "makes him Magnus Apollo." Madison "found it hard to believe" that Livingston had publicized his suggestion of a Franco-American alliance, for that amounted to a confession of guilt. In effect, it proposed a new foreign policy for the United States, despite the fact that no qualified American authority had approved any such notion. As Madison saw it by that time,

Livingston had been guilty of serious misconduct in his job—and then took pains to unwittingly spread the word of what he had done.

Livingston went farther and actually falsified documents, attempting to prove a point by altering dates—and in one case, on a letter of which the original, bearing the right date, was in the State Department files! He wrote Madison that his hasty note to Monroe, with the unfortunate remark that nothing but war would accomplish any purpose, was written "under the influence of...ideas excited by these prevarications of the minister." Blaming Talleyrand for his own skewed remarks would have been simply silly, even if the dates had supported his argument. But his note to Monroe had been written on April 10, whereas Minister Talleyrand's "exciting" suggestion was not made until the following day—and copies of both documents were in the State Department's files. Livingston's note begging Talleyrand for a statement is in the French Archives, clearly showing April 12 as the date. But he actually altered this date in his own letter book, scratching a 0 over the 2 to make it appear that it had been done on Easter Sunday, the 10th. The altered figure is not craftily inserted, and the 2 is visible under the 0.

Despite this period of dangerous imbalance, Livingston regained his equilibrium, thoroughly enjoyed the farewell dinner that Marbois gave when he left his Paris post in 1805, and lived on for a happy decade as lord of the manor in Clermont, New York. Livingston resumed being a distinguished agricultural pioneer, and his handbook *Essay on Sheep* became well known in its field, although it is safe to say that James Madison never bought a copy.

Livingston would have been greatly distressed had he lived to see the whole of the devastating turn that was to come in the life of Marbois, for whom he felt real affection. Marbois, in turn, had been so loyal to the New Yorker that he risked embarrassment and possible censure from the First Consul in his repeated attempts to steer any new proposals toward Livingston, rather than Monroe. But astonishingly, the normally dismissive Napoleon, who had been a little more respectful to Livingston than to most foreigners, seemed to join in this Marbois-Livingston chemistry. In the late stages of negotiation, one of Napoleon's firmest remarks was "Don't wait for Monroe." And to Marbois, he said, "Well, you're the Finance Minister. You tell him the price." That meant, *You, as opposed to Talleyrand*, and it has often been taken to include the thought, *I know you won't take a big slice for yourself,* as Talleyrand would.

Marbois was given a very handsome bonus by Napoleon, who belatedly remembered that the price his treasury minister won for him was many millions more than the minimum he had set. He gave Marbois 192,000 francs (nearly $40,000) with these words: "To give evidence of my satisfaction with your important work. You have won for the Republic ten millions [two million dollars] more than the amount called for by your instructions." And there were more sentences of praise for his achievements in general.

But after further honors had been bestowed on him in 1805, rumors of a financial scandal in the Imperial Army caused a loss of confidence in France's money and sent the value of banknotes down by 15 percent. The people were infuriated, and public disorders erupted. The minister of finance was the natural one to blame, although his only fault was in having looked rather helpless during the affair. Napoleon, returning home from his brilliant victory at Austerlitz, called Marbois on the carpet, talked to him scathingly, and dismissed him on the spot. With tears in his eyes, Marbois said only, "I dare to hope that Your Majesty does not accuse me of being a thief."

"I'd prefer that a hundred times over," was Napoleon's retort. "Misbehavior at least has its limits. Stupidity has none."

But Napoleon remembered Marbois's honesty and accuracy, so in 1808 he named him first president of the Court des Comtes (Court of Accounts), which was a perfect assignment for the numbers-oriented public servant. He plunged into this new work joyfully. But in a sense, it dealt Marbois a deadly blow. The man who had once been hardy enough to survive a tropical island that killed most others and who had come back to Paris full of energy was now so overwhelmed to be recalled from his disgrace that he became the worst flatterer in France. His love for Napoleon was boundless, and he stood to shout it in public. In 1809, when the emperor returned from a trip to Spain, Marbois greeted him with, "When you are away, there is no basis for happiness. Your presence fulfills all our hopes, all our affections." The flowery talk grew even worse and continued almost until Napoleon fell for the first time. But then, in April 1814, it was Marbois, as head of the Court des Comtes, who had to process and sign some of the separation papers that sent the emperor on his way and other documents that welcomed the returning Bourbon royals.

At that point, it was noticed that Marbois's flattery was not reserved for Napoleon alone, but for anyone who had power over him. He was soon heard to lavish on the Comte d'Artois, lieutenant general of the new regime, some of the very same phrases that he had slathered on Napoleon. His obsequious praise became well known, and when Napoleon escaped from Elba and returned for the "Hundred Days," Marbois had to go into hiding. After the emperor was sent to his last exile, Marbois came back yet again with the honeyed phrases that he did not deliver especially well, and it is suspected that one of the Bourbons told him of his disgust and ordered him to leave Paris permanently. His life ended in disgrace three years later, in 1834, at age ninety-two.

There are French persons who recall this historical figure as one who had long fooled the whole world about his true nature, then was exposed as the characterless buffoon that he had always been. Considering the fact that nothing of this kind had even been suspected through sixty years of a very active political life, it seems likelier that the early Marbois was a decent public figure, while the later performances were tragic evidence of how a ruler's hunger for praise can destroy his own judgment and that of the people around him.

Napoleon Bonaparte was justified in seeing himself as a winner for having sold Louisiana. Letting go of the Territory had not been a sentimental wrench, even though some imagined that it was. The First Consul found it easy to sell land he had never seen and that would be valueless to France if Saint Domingue were not available as a base and source of supply.

After Britain's 1803 declaration of war on France, the British were soon blockading Saint Domingue and bombarding its coast. The mere fact that the island was totally lost by the end of 1803—with all the remaining French soldiers and eighteen thousand civilian refugees departing in November—shows how little value nearby Louisiana would have had for Napoleon if he had retained it.

On January 1, 1804, the island that had been the heart of France's interests in the Americas would become an independent black nation under Dessalines, who later imitated Napoleon by having himself crowned emperor. But the once-beautiful land had suffered so much destruction that it had only the bleakest legacy to pass on to the republic that took the old Arawak name of Haiti. Dessalines wrote a proclamation, saying, "Accursed be the French name! We declare eternal hatred for France!" But he was assassinated within three years, and as a small new Haitian elite formed, it turned out to be completely French, in language, law, and letters.

The deal that Napoleon won was also remarkably good in view of the fact that some of the land he sold had never actually belonged to France at all. When Spain gave Louisiana to France, it apparently did not intend to cede either of the Floridas. But Napoleon slyly pretended to believe—and encouraged the U.S. to believe—that the Louisiana Purchase included the Floridas. Marbois, writing years later about the negotiations, said the Americans insisted on a definition of this "Louisiana" that their country was buying, and he told them that Florida could not be mentioned, for it would cause problems with Spain. They were to accept the idea that they were buying exactly what France had received from Spain—whatever that was. On this flimsy basis, the United States quietly considered that it had a claim to Florida, and then was able to confirm it by waging a minor military action and making a small cash payment years later. But Spain never did agree that it had let Florida go before that. So Napoleon's sale of such questionable holdings for any kind of spendable cash appears to be—to put a polite word on it—rather astute.

A critic of Napoleon could find reason to say that after having cleverly taken Louisiana from Spain, he had conducted this whole matter in as haphazard a way as anyone could imagine, setting two ministers on the same task, tossing out random numbers as the sale price he would accept, and then appearing to have forgotten what he had said. But it is more instructive to focus on the astonishing fact that Napoleon calmly digested the words of both Madison and Livingston—actually using some of their very phrases that had been reported to him—as reasons for favoring the sale over the retention of the Louisiana colony. Then, far from "squandering the money on war," as some might see it, he used it in setting up a rise to new heights.

The war that came almost immediately was a very successful one, bringing him his greatest victory, and should not be confused with the eventual disasters that led to Elba and St. Helena. In March 1803, Napoleon had staged a violent tirade against the British ambassador,

Lord Whitworth, over the English insistence on occupying Malta. This caused the envoy to leave France, and led George III to declare war against France on May 18, two weeks after the Louisiana sale had been made. In the three turbulent years that followed, Napoleon contrived to be crowned emperor and mounted a project to invade England, but swerved away from it at the last moment and marched his Grand Army into Germany instead. This surprise set the stage for his most brilliant victory at Austerlitz, crushing the armies of Austria and Prussia and setting the Russians to flight, making him the master of the entire continent. It would be wrong to pretend that the American money had made this possible. More accurately, the money helped, and the freedom Napoleon gained from being diverted by any Louisiana adventure helped far more.

The First Consul seemed to feel the need of defending his decision to sell by dramatizing his cleverness in giving up the Territory. This has led to colorful quotations, some of which appear to be credible. It is said that he cited the problems he was creating for Britain by making their former colonies into a growing giant that would be hard to deal with. According to Marbois's *Histoire de la Louisiane,* it was more simply stated, "I regard the colony as already lost, and it seems to me that in the hands of this newborn power, it will be more useful to the policy and even to the commerce of France, than if I should try to retain it." He probably offered various versions of this theme at different times. Because Marbois was so conscientious about protecting the man he served, it is likely that he selected this statesmanlike remark in preference to the one quoted by another serious biographer: "I have given to England a maritime rival which will sooner or later humble her pride." But since few Europeans in that day felt much confidence that the young United States would survive as a nation, Napoleon may not have been all that certain of what the sale would mean in terms of American greatness and British discomfiture. He was much more convinced that the cash benefit would be important to him in the new war he was facing.

But the prescient wisdom of one thing the First Consul definitely said overrides all the others. Although the robustness of today's United States is no guarantee of its duration, this rather wistful remark of Napoleon's appears likely to remain valid for many more years: "Perhaps it will be objected that the Americans may be found too powerful for Europe in two or three centuries. But my foresight does not embrace such remote fears."

Of the French players, only Talleyrand might be said to have had a more successful post-treaty life than the emperor. His honors kept multiplying to the end. Talleyrand's recollection that he had been the least influential of the French negotiators in the Paris talks distressed him very little, for his long-term thinking and constant search for new openings made any failure merely a prelude to the next opportunity. And, in fact, some of the brightest moments in his half-century diplomatic career were still ahead of him.

The secret cornerstone of that career was, quite unbelievably, to work toward "lasting brotherhood between France and England," as he had said frankly to the French Assembly in 1791. This remained a fixed idea, even when he was to be a leading counselor of men who steadily planned war with England, and especially of Napoleon, who lived for such a war.

While Napoleon seemed out of sorts with his foreign minister during the Louisiana talks, he never let many weeks go by without soliciting new ideas from him and taking soundings of how Talleyrand was assessing the ongoing situation. Their close association continued until 1807, when Talleyrand resigned as foreign minister because Napoleon was determined to destroy the Spanish Bourbons.

Only then did Napoleon realize how strongly his foreign minister opposed his policies, putting the welfare of France ahead of the emperor's glory.

Nevertheless, as a going-away gift, the emperor did name him His Most Serene Highness, the Prince of Benevento (a small enclave in the kingdom of Naples), and he was called Prince Talleyrand from then on. The emperor also named him Vice-Grand Elector of the Empire (which a wag said was, "The only Vice he lacked.") Both titles carried substantial annual revenues. And up to the time of his death, Napoleon frequently moaned, "Why on earth did Talleyrand give up the Foreign Ministry? My affairs always prospered when he was handling them."

However, after Napoleon's fall, Talleyrand supported a return of the Bourbons to the throne. He had the personal triumph of seeming so much the true soul of France that the Czar Alexander and the Triple Alliance that stormed into Paris would not hear of any new government that was not headed by Prince Talleyrand.

The prince arranged this elevation by declaring himself president of the Assembly in a totally illegal fashion. He had 64 Senate votes out of 140 members, announced that he had won, and closed the meeting, instantly becoming the most powerful man in France. The Allies found it useful to accept him as being the voice of the nation, and the victorious Czar Alexander again declared himself impressed. At Talleyrand's behest and without hesitation, the Senate then confirmed Louis XVIII as king. So he had put the Bourbons back on the throne, but Napoleon's prediction, "They will kick Talleyrand out," proved exactly right. The Bourbons had never forgiven him for having helped Napoleon to set up his own throne. The prince was not distressed by this decision, for his old physical laziness still made him prefer to avoid administrative duties that went with forming and running a government.

Talleyrand, however, was not through. After almost fifteen years of comfortable retirement, he came back to help Louis-Philippe become king in 1830. He was not anxious to be given other responsibilities, but this king was, at last, one who wanted the close relationship with Britain that Talleyrand had always sought. So when he implored the prince to become his envoy, Talleyrand accepted. This time around, as ambassador to London, he was treated as an almost mythical figure, and his brief stay was a thoroughly happy one.

His personal life was as scandalous as ever. There was an unusual bond between him and a niece, Dorothea, that made the young lady leave her husband in order to be with her uncle. The relationship made other women of the court tend to snub Dorothea, but Talleyrand paid as little attention as ever to the opinions of others.

He was eighty when he retired from the London post. He went back to beautiful Valençay, in the Loire Valley, and lived sumptuously to age eighty-three. His last three and a half years there were tranquil and happy. He knew himself to be the most honored elder statesman of France and of Europe. He was enormously rich. His house was almost always full of guests, who never seemed to be put off by his caustic wit, and no visitor left without a supply of sharp remarks to spread throughout Paris. Typically, one of the last of these *bon mots* concerned an especially flat-chested lady who insisted on wearing outrageous decolletage: "It would be impossible for her to uncover more or to reveal less." And Parisians, hearing this witticism, rejoiced that the sly old prince was still himself.

But he also wrote numerous notes and documents of a very serious nature toward the end of his life. One strange paper set forth assertions about what he claimed was his lifelong adherence to certain guiding principles. Some historians believe he wrote out these views in order to contradict anything against him that might be found in Napoleon's memoirs. But Talleyrand, at the end of his self-

The Jim Click Automotive Team

FORD - LINCOLN

CHRIS SCHRELL
Service Advisor

6244 E. 22ND STREET
TUCSON, AZ 85711
cschrell@jimclick.com

BUSINESS (520) 519-7226
FAX (520) 570-7302

justifying paper, appended these further lines that are less easily explained:

> Placed by Bonaparte himself in the position of having to choose between France and him, I could only make the choice dictated by my primary duty....Nonetheless, I shall remember even in my last hour, that he was my benefactor, for the fortune that I leave to my nephews comes to me, in large part, from him. My nephews should not only never forget this, but they should teach it to their children, and their children to their own children, so that the remembrance of it shall become perpetual in my family, from generation to generation. If ever a man bearing the name of Bonaparte shall be in a financial position where he has need of aid or assistance, he shall obtain from my immediate heirs, or from their descendants, whatever assistance that it may be in their power to render him.

One of the happier reflections on the Louisiana Purchase came from a man who might well be considered a member of the U.S. team, even if his status was unofficial. When the treaty was concluded on April 30, 1803, Pierre Samuel du Pont wrote to Jefferson, "Let me congratulate the United States and yourself on the wisdom through which, avoiding a war that would have thrown you into the arms of a redoubtable ally, you have acquired without shedding blood a territory ten times in extent and in fertility as the one you desired."

Jefferson replied, "For myself and for my country, I thank you for the aids you have given...and I congratulate you on having lived to give those aids in a transaction replete with blessings to unborn millions of men, and which will mark the face of a portion of the globe so extensive as that which now composes the United States of America."

More tangibly, Jefferson also wrote to Henry Dearborn, the secretary of war, urging him to consider placing some of his orders for gunpowder with the E.I. du Pont Company, explaining, "I should be the more grateful as it would gratify his father, who has been a faithful and useful friend to this country." After explaining some of Pierre Samuel's specific aid to Jefferson when he was serving in France, he added words that embody a volume of meaning, considering how rarely presidents can be expected to share credit for their accomplishments: "On the late occasion too of Louisiana, though he does not bring himself into view, I am satisfied that his just views of the subject have enabled him to make those energetic representations to Talleyrand, Marbois, and others about the Consul, which his intimacy with them favored, and must have sensibly favored the result obtained."

Secretary Dearborn was very anti-French, and he was much annoyed at being told to order the "foreign" gunpowder. But as the shipments came in and the material was tested, Dearborn relented and agreed that it was not only a fine product, but the finest in the world, even superior to the British.

✑

Like a symphony that seems to have had a triumphant ending but then goes on, the loudest sounds were yet to come. As subsequent conflicts have demonstrated, wars are seldom won until troops move in on foot. The United States owned Louisiana, but another power, Great Britain, had not stopped resenting the magnificent purchase, and was planning to take it by force.

Chapter Seventeen

A TERRITORY ON THE MOVE

On November 30, 1803, Pierre Clément de Laussat, a representative of France, was part of a ceremony in which France finally took formal possession of Louisiana. After the keys to the city and the forts were handed to him on a silver platter, he went out to the balcony with the Spanish officials, and saw the Spanish flag taken down and the French flag raised. He declared that the Spanish government of the territory no longer existed, and he appointed French Creoles to all the offices that had been vacated. France then began its twenty-day rule over Louisiana.

On the next day, December 1, Laussat gave a huge fête to honor the French flag. The seventy-five guests were French, Spanish, and American. Toasts were drunk to all three nations in their three languages. The remaining nineteen days followed a similar pattern, with banquets where twenty kinds of gumbo were served, and balls that went on for six or eight hours. Laussat, who wrote repeatedly about the great beauties who had been assembled "to adorn all the balconies in the square and to fill the eleven galleries of the city hall," also noted that these lands were some of the richest areas in the entire world and that "the Americans would have given $50,000,000 rather than not have possessed it."

According to the new American governor, William C.C. Claiborne, who took over on December 20, "the Government of the United States was received with joy and gratitude by the people." Others said that the French Creoles, in particular, were less than enthusiastic when they found France forcing them into the arms of American strangers, although Delaware's Senator Wells must have been relieved to learn that there was no move to "attack and slay" the small force of American troops that had been assembled at Fort Adams in Mississippi and brought in under the command of General James Wilkinson.

The first time France had given away Louisiana, to Spain in 1762, the French residents had been utterly dismayed. It is said that some wrote back to France declaring that because theirs had been a French colony for more than sixty years, they considered themselves just as much Frenchmen as if they had lived in Paris. When the next change of title occurred, however, there was no such definite sense of loss. Although Spain had owned the area since 1762, French had continued to be the predominant language. The officials had been Spanish for nearly forty years, but the people had become so mingled and diversified that mixed race and mixed ethnicity was the order of the day. Moreover, being such a near neighbor of the United States had been more meaningful than the matter of ownership. It is astonishing to realize how early in its life the United States became a super-nation, in the sense that it had an above-normal effect on other countries. Part of this was from the appeal of its Constitution, its democracy, and its emphasis on freedoms. But a substantial part was due to the speed of growth that was enriching so many persons and the promise that this held for many more.

There were people in New Orleans who feared the loss of their old ways and resented the new power. There were probably more who felt stimulated by the thought that these Americans were going to bring new ways that might spell better living. And there was presumably a majority who felt a nonchalant willingness to see what the new era would bring.

ℭ৹

The total area that was to become the state of Louisiana had no more than fifty thousand people, only ten thousand of whom lived in and around New Orleans. The city was described as having unpaved streets littered with trash and garbage. The wooden buildings were unpainted. Yet an observer who was more forthright than diplomatic said, "It compared favorably with most Latin American, French, or Spanish towns of its size."

A few hundred American businesspeople lived there, mostly working for commission houses that had been opened by companies based in New York, Philadelphia, and Baltimore. These enterprises began to expand and to be joined by other American firms soon after 1803. To the people living there at the time, progress in modernizing and improving the city and state seemed very slow. But in fact, an astonishing amount of progress occurred in the nine years until Congress approved a constitution and accepted Louisiana as a new state. Governor Claiborne, who had been only twenty-eight years old when he became the territorial governor, continued in the office until an election could be held, and he showed sound judgment, both in normal administration and in dealing with the unusual threat that the Spanish still presented.

It was worrisome that some of the Spanish officials who had governed Louisiana remained in New Orleans long after the American takeover. Claiborne thought they might be stirring up trouble in the area where Spain's Texas holdings bordered western Louisiana.

Early in 1806, he sent Casa Calvo, the former governor, a passport with a note that said, "Best wishes for the health and happiness of the nobleman whose presence has become so unacceptable." The furious Casa Calvo and other former officials left, but there was still a Spanish army operating in east Texas and making an issue of where Louisiana's western border should be. The Louisiana Purchase treaty had not fixed the definite line, and the Americans claimed it to be the Sabine River. The Spanish said it should be east of the Calcasieu River, making the land between the two into the infamous "Sabine Strip"—land that many lawless people fled to, where robberies and murders of traveling traders were all too frequent. An American military post had to be established at a border town called Natchitoches to patrol the area.

A more normal administrative problem was dealing with crime in New Orleans itself, and Claiborne had to create a police force from scratch. This consisted of men armed with spears and heavy swords, and it was called the *garde de ville* because Claiborne tried to cater to the feelings of the French population whenever possible. For the same reason, all laws were written in both French and English, and all juries were made up of both French- and English-speaking persons. In short, this neighboring area that some Americans had long thought of as virtually a part of the United States now had to be treated as newly acquired foreign territory, yet Americanized as rapidly and thoughtfully as possible.

Building new roads, establishing a mail service carried by men on horseback, and, most of all, education were key issues to be addressed. This last was the knottiest of problems, because the Creoles were nearly all Catholics and wanted only church-run schools for their children. Governor Claiborne was a firm believer in public education, demanding "a school in every neighborhood." But although he got an act passed in 1805, there were only three public schools in existence when statehood came to Louisiana seven years later.

⌒

One of Claiborne's closest advisers, and a leading lawyer in the community, was Edward Livingston of New York, the brother of Chancellor Robert Livingston, who had played such a large role in the purchase of Louisiana. Although Robert was seventeen years older than Edward and had overseen his education because of their father's death, Edward was even more brilliant and had a much steadier character. He had been admitted to the bar at age nineteen, and as years went on, it became clear that under his agreeable manner lay one of the finest legal minds of his day. His presence in New Orleans helped to make the years after the Louisiana Purchase exciting ones for his older brother.

Robert Livingston, while staying on for a time as American envoy to Paris, had come to know Robert Fulton and even put his own creative mind into proposing certain engineering changes for Fulton's newly invented steamboat. Fulton had given a number of demonstrations of his invention in Brest, one ending badly, followed by several more that were triumphs.

Napoleon Bonaparte, who was just then considering a variety of bizarre methods for somehow floating an army across the Channel on a foggy day to invade Britain, had refused even to look at Fulton's steamboat. The First Consul said, "In all capital cities there are hordes of adventurers and schemers offering to all sovereigns various alleged miracles which exist only in their imaginations. They are nothing but charlatans and impostors, and this American is one of them. Don't tell me any more about him."

No one will ever know whether that snap judgment may have been Napoleon's greatest mistake, but it is a curious fact that his old negotiating adversary, Robert Livingston, turned this invention into an enormous personal success. In addition to his technical suggestions, he invested cash in Fulton's venture, and the partners had a peerless New Orleans lawyer, Edward Livingston, of course, to process their request for monopoly rights to operate steamships—not simply in the immediate area of New Orleans, but for the entire length of the Mississippi River. This extraordinary privilege was ultimately reversed by the United States Supreme Court some years later, but by then, Fulton and Livingston had prospered far beyond their original hopes.

☘

When Louisiana formally became a state on April 30, 1812, exactly nine years after the Louisiana Purchase treaty had made it American property, its state-wide population had already risen from fifty thousand at the time of the Purchase to more than seventy-seven thousand. It was expected that the free citizens who could now vote for their own government would topple Claiborne, whose service up to that time had continued to be as an appointed governor. The Creoles had a favorite of their own, Jacques Villeré, who was considered a sure winner.

The result was a surprise, showing that Claiborne's earnest efforts to teach responsible self-government had taken hold with unusual speed. Enough Creoles understood the merit of Claiborne's efforts, and crossed ethnic lines to vote for him. He won and served four more years as governor before being elected a United States senator in 1816.

Populating the huge territory north of the state was not a uniformly swift process. Most of the nearly nine hundred thousand square miles was remarkably empty at the time of the Purchase. The best estimate for total population of the entire area purchased in 1803—excluding Florida, which was not confirmed as belonging to the United States until 1819—is approximately one hundred forty-six thousand persons, of whom about half were in the part that was to become the state of Louisiana. (For perspective, the entire nation's population was about five and one half million in 1803, with less than four hundred thousand classified as "urban dwellers" and the rest as "rural." So while the Louisiana Purchase added 100 percent to the nation's land area, it increased population by only about 3 percent.) Beyond that, only Missouri, Mississippi, Iowa, and Oklahoma barely touched double digits in population count. Some other areas that would be reaching for statehood within decades were virtually empty, with only one or two persons per square mile. Of the few white inhabitants, a considerable percentage were fur trappers, some of whom had very profitable businesses; but they were active competitors and had no reason to form communities. Similarly, breeding horses for sale to the Native Americans had become a bustling business without creating cities or villages. The relatively few settlers who had managed to build homes and to coexist with the Native Americans were clustered along the banks of rivers, such as the Arkansas River and the Red River. A number of years passed before settled farmers or merchants began to appear well north of Louisiana.

Thomas Jefferson, who had underplayed the need for expansion in his first inaugural address by calling America, "a chosen country, with room enough for our descendants to the thousandth and thousandth generation," had already been active much earlier in encouraging and helping to fund expeditions into the west that would invade the territories of European powers. Just a month before that inaugural occasion, he had asked young Meriwether Lewis to be making plans for a major western exploration, relying partly on the usual excuse that botanical and other scientific research was the principal object. But with the conclusion of the Louisiana Purchase, subterfuges were no longer needed. Lewis and his partner, William

Clark, set out with a forty-man party early in 1804, leaving Illinois and moving up the Missouri River as far as the region that was to become North Dakota.

As authors Robert V. Hine and John Mack Faragher have shown in a recent interpretive history of *The American West,* there had been truth in the French claim that they became closer to the Native American tribes than the British or Americans ever had. Lewis and Clark found French traders with Native American wives living comfortably among Native Americans who were settled farming people. And these same authors have pointed out that the surge in use of horses by Native Americans had enabled them—rather than Europeans—to reclaim the North American heartland and exploit the huge buffalo herds after a long drought had depopulated the plains.

The Native Americans themselves had already dropped to an astonishingly small number. Some believe there were no more than one hundred thousand alive in North America in 1803, a great many having perished in wars between tribes, and even more having been killed by the long drought, by disease, and by the privations forced on them by white expansionism.

This makes it all the more tragic to find that Professor Anthony F.C. Wallace, University of Pennsylvania anthropologist, has pointed to Thomas Jefferson as "the planner of cultural genocide," one that further decimated the native Americans. He believes Jefferson's deeply controlling temperament, his conviction that he knew what was best for everybody, was the reason he could have presided over policies such as he advocated in this letter to a friend, which was able to make a harsh program of extinction sound like beneficence:

> I believe the business of hunting is insufficient to furnish clothing and subsistence to the Indians. The promotion of

Agriculture, therefore, and household manufacture are essential in their preservation, and I am disposed to aid and encourage it liberally. This will enable them to live on much smaller portions of land....While they are learning to do better on less land, our increasing numbers will call for more land, and thus a coincidence of interests will be produced....It is probable that this idea may be so novel as that it might shock the Indians, were it even hinted to them....Of course you will keep it for your own reflection.

President Jefferson put these thoughts into action. In 1803, at the very time of his exceptional achievement in expanding the nation, he made a plan that resulted in a dramatic shrinkage of the land area held by the large Kaskaskias tribe that lived in a village along the Mississippi about sixty miles south of St. Louis. The tribal chief, Jean-Baptiste du Coigne, had met Jefferson twenty years earlier and named his infant son after Governor Jefferson, as he was at the time. Now Jefferson suggested to one of his operatives that a spy be sent into du Coigne's village to learn facts that would help them arrange a deal whereby they would take all the tribe's lands and give them a reservation of just 350 acres. In return, the United States promised to protect the Kaskaskias from other tribes, grant them a $1,000 annuity, and pay the expenses of a priest who would give them seven years of basic schooling. For du Coigne himself, a special house and the use of one hundred acres was given as reward for approving this larcenous exchange.

To Jefferson and to many other Americans of the time, this treatment of the Native Americans was a necessary and sensible part of the ongoing growth of the white population. Although statistics are not reliable, it is estimated that the country's urban population grew eightfold in the fifty years between 1790 and 1840, so it may have increased as much as 50 percent in the first decade after the Louisiana Purchase. Just as important as numbers was the great surge in quality of life. The demand for food products and for bread-stuffs drove farms to produce more meat, milk, vegetables, and the grains that would make cheaper and better-packaged flour a new staple of American life. The interchange between city dwellers and their nearby suppliers began to make transportation a much livelier subject. The improved roads and canals gave a great impetus to the American desire to travel just for travel's sake, which was noted by every observant foreign visitor.

The *Universal Traveller* said soon after this, "The great thorough-fares heading west are thronged with a singular assemblage of travelers, a great wave of motion." A Louisville, Kentucky, newspaper noted that, "Several times during the last week the road was literally filled with movers," although there were complaints that they were often traveling on inferior roads because America's road-building methods lagged behind those of Europe. Kentuckians and Ohioans who could pole their flatboats down the Mississippi to market at New Orleans were far better off than the teamsters who tried to drive huge wagons along rutted roads. Still, with a six-horse team pulling a four-ton load, good teamsters could do twenty-five to thirty miles per day. The most important thing was how much business there was to be done—how much new demand for services resulted from production and the turnover of goods and money. Very soon after the Louisiana Purchase, planners were talking about starting stagecoach connections from Boston through to New Orleans and from New York City as far west as St. Louis. It took another dozen years to accomplish this feat, but by then Boston travelers could choose from more than sixty different stage routes, linking New England with many parts of the Louisiana Territory.

Like so many things American, the filling and enriching of the whole Louisiana Territory proceeded swiftly by European standards, even if it seemed ponderous to Americans during the first decade. This impression of disappointing expansion had briefly revived the old thought that the country may have taken on a burdensome amount of space. The excitement over the doubling of America had cooled. In the usual way that joy becomes jaded and victory begins to age, the problems of bigness had begun to seem weightier than its glories for a time.

A Connecticut congressman, Roger Griswold, sounded a theme that many Americans started to feel within months of the great acquisition: "It is not consistent with the spirit of a republican government that its territory should be exceedingly large, for as you extend your limits you increase the difficulties arising from a want of that similarity of customs, habits, and manners so essential for its support....Our views were confined to New Orleans and the Floridas....[But now] the vast and unmanageable extent which the accession of Louisiana will give the United States...threatens at no very distant day, the subversion of our Union." It was more than just talk. Griswold and numerous other New England politicians were seriously discussing secession—forming a Northern Confederacy under the leadership of Vice President Aaron Burr, as part of a new nation divided into three republics: northern, southern, and western.

Most people had a mental picture of what a normal country size should be. They were accustomed to smaller ones, as in Europe. The United States suddenly seemed in danger of becoming clumsily huge, as a giant would appear among men. Nearly nine hundred thousand square miles of almost virgin territory was emptiness indeed, and at first, it had seemed to fill hardly at all. Most of it was still a wilderness, largely uninhabited and not yet demanding much governance; this was not an immediate concern, only a fear for the future. But for a time, the fear was shared by many Americans. The very thing that Madison had once told Pichon—falsely, attempting to send a message to Paris—seemed capable of coming to pass: the acquisition of the Louisiana Territory might break the country into parts.

Jefferson, determined to maintain his deep belief in states' rights, at least pretended that he could live with this division if it made the population of each portion happy. He talked, however, of two sections, not three—and called them the Atlantic and Mississippi Confederacies. "Those of the Western confederacy will be as much our children as those of the Eastern," he said, "and I feel myself as much identified with that country in future as with this."

An even more serious problem that would not be settled for more than half a century was whether the blight of slavery would be allowed into the new territories. Although statistics were questionable, there were thought to be about one million slaves in the Union, if men, women, and children were all included. Some 70 percent of the slaves were clustered in a few southern states. But states that were in the process of formation tended to ask for the right to have slavery, which distressed a great many Americans who did not want to see the balance between slave states and free states worsen. The expansion of slavery eventually became a major issue, referred to as the Missouri Question, which was considered a wedge that might separate the Union. In this case, a compromise was arranged whereby Missouri entered the Union as a slave state while Maine, which separated from Massachusetts, became a free state. This division preserved the balance between slave and free states. Also, while there were to be no restrictions on slavery in Missouri, slavery in the rest of the territory acquired in the Louisiana Purchase was banned north of the parallel 36°30′ (north of Missouri's southern border).

The disagreements over great size faded soon after the 1821 Missouri Compromise, as it became evident that much of the newly acquired area showed signs of quickly forming into more states that wanted to be part of the original United States. As if blown away by a fresh wind, the distaste for bigness soon gave way to complacency about the nation's new shape and even a happy premonition that one day a single flag would fly over the whole continent.

Everything seemed to come together in ways that encouraged more and more growth and feeling of community among people whose roots were so different and separate. Even a total eclipse of the sun on June 16, 1806, had been greeted with amazement as people in Massachusetts were told that the same strip of darkness was shadowing fellow Americans near the Canadian border who were barely starting to dream of the statehood that might take them decades to win.

While some parts of the Louisiana Territory would remain underpopulated (such as North Dakota, which took eighty-six years to become a state with six hundred thousand people in 1889), others showed notably rapid growth: Louisiana, Mississippi, and Missouri led the way. Each of them could have been compared in area with some of the leading European nations. And they entered the Union as quite populous states, Louisiana with seventy-seven thousand people in 1812, Mississippi with more than twenty thousand in 1817, and Missouri with over forty thousand in 1821. Iowa, bristling with pride in its "Grade A Premium" land and boiling with scrappy politics, kept resisting statehood because of border disagreements and also because it liked having the federal government paying many of its general expenses. It finally, almost reluctantly, agreed to become a state in 1846, when its population exceeded forty-five thousand. Many of the territories around it joined in the boast that they were "in the middle of the middle west," and the nation had

firmly accepted them as fellow Americans even before formal statehood was declared.

A considerable rise in material standards was under way, too.
Western houses up to that time had had primitive heating arrangements, very little furniture, and often a deep earthen hole in front of
the fire where cooking was done. But by the early 1800s, goods that
had been the trappings of luxury in colonial days were expected in
most eastern white households. Soon, the homes that began to be
built in the new states, while they seldom compared with homes in
long-established cities of the northeast, were very close to the standards of villagers in those older states. And whereas less than four hundred thousand Americans were classed as "urban dwellers" in the early
1800s, that figure would climb even more steeply than the overall
population with each decade, reaching two million by mid-century.

The enormous expanse to the north and west of New Orleans,
the key city that had been the primary object of the Louisiana Purchase, meant that thirteen new states would eventually be created, in
whole or in substantial part, from the eight hundred seventy-five
thousand square miles that had been bought. These, ascending from
the Gulf of Mexico to the Canadian border, are Louisiana, Arkansas,
Oklahoma, Missouri, Kansas, Iowa, Nebraska, Minnesota, South
Dakota, North Dakota, Colorado, Wyoming, and Montana. Their
movement into statehood would take most of the nineteenth century, but during that period, there was little question that the people of the east were part of the process. Even those who never
planned a trip to the west coast thought of it as part of their country, and most would have fought to defend it.

The importance of expansion for America was no longer an
issue. James Madison had won another major point, for he had long
insisted that expansion was at the heart of the American political

system, saying, "Extend the sphere, and you make it less probable that a majority of the whole will have a common motive to invade the rights of other citizens." He foresaw, "One great, respectable, and flourishing empire." As was so often the case, Madison's words came to be heard from others. Several of the founding fathers, including George Washington, used the word "empire," not in the sense of dominion over other nations, but of sheer national expanse, and it was taken for granted that movement from east to west would be the means of achieving this grandeur.

Chapter Eighteen

THE
LONG SEQUEL

For all Jefferson's talk of war, the excitement of the Louisiana Purchase had been entirely cerebral. But its true end came only with war—and a battle that was to go down as a memorable event in military history. Before this, however, there were nine intervening years on the edge of conflict with England.

The problems between America and Britain that had churned on throughout the negotiations for Louisiana continued unabated. The British attitude toward the United States was uglier than modern Americans imagine, for bad memories were later dimmed by the twentieth century's years of intensifying alliance. But in the early 1800s, the English were still thinking of Americans as renegades who deserved no respect and who would probably be brought back into line before very long. The blockading of U.S. maritime trade, the impressment of its seamen, and the ongoing fight over the boundaries between the U.S. and Canada were negotiated year after year by James Monroe and others, without success because there was a shortage of goodwill on the British side, and America, perhaps with some cause, was seen by the British as a smug and arrogant upstart.

Most Americans felt thoroughly righteous about their troubles with England, considering the British to have no sense of fairness and, in fact, to be trying with great cruelty to force them back into a colonial status. The specific reasons given by those who advocated going to war against Britain were these:

—They violated U.S. rights of commerce on the high seas.

—They cruelly snatched U.S. seamen, often torturing them as "traitors" who should be British subjects. They sometimes impressed them into the British service, where they were subject to bad treatment and great danger.

—They armed Native Americans along America's frontier and incited them to murder its people.

—They hurt the South economically by depressing the prices of its products.

—They insulted the young country's national honor and self-respect.

In addition, there was one American ambition that inclined many to war: once the fear of a large size subsided, the wish to annex Canada and Florida proved strong. This last point made opponents of war say that some Americans simply wanted to incite a war of conquest. But it was not so much a greed for land as a wish to be free of unpredictable neighbors. Those who felt this way pointed out, for example, that Britain was backing Native American Chief

Tecumseh in his many raids against white people, so they considered their desire for more annexations as being a matter of self-defense.

The rhetoric on both sides was elevated and powerful. An 1811 report of the House Committee on Foreign Relations said, "To wrongs so daring in character, and so disgraceful in their execution, it is impossible that the people of the United States should remain indifferent. We must now tamely and quietly submit, or we must resist by those means which God has placed within our reach."

The British had a few bitter thoughts of their own, to be sure. They felt that the new nation was unbearably opinionated and self-righteous, expecting to trade very profitably with both sides in a serious conflict and to be allowed a freedom that no other nation was granted in a time of war. Americans gave the impression of feeling so superior that no constraints whatever should apply to them. They alone, of all the world's countries, had a divine right to national solitude. It was an early version of the incredible glory that the U.S. assumed in later taking over most of the entire continent and, just a bit further along, warning the world that the whole Western Hemisphere was off limits to any other power.

One particularly vicious British tactic that was deeply resented by Americans was the practice of arming of Native American warriors and inciting them to attack anyone they found vulnerable—almost always helpless civilians, and often women and children. This was done repeatedly in Florida, where the Spanish also joined in any stratagem that offered a chance of holding off the spread of American influence. The practice played a great part in bringing General Andrew Jackson to public attention, for his gritty personality gave him a unique ability to act as if the Americans' right to Florida was God-given and not to be infringed upon by Englishmen, Spaniards, or Native Americans, regardless of what prior claims these others might plead. He also was free of doubts about what game the British were up to, saying, "Britain is in conjunction with Spain arming the hostile Indians to butcher our women and children."

There were anti-war people in Congress who made each of the points cited by their opponents seem false. John Randolph, a brilliant states' rights Republican, ridiculed the notion that Native American massacres were organized by the British. On one occasion, he said:

> An insinuation had fallen from the gentleman from Tennessee that the late massacre of our brethren on the Wabash had been instigated by the British government. Has the President given any such information? Has the gentleman received any such, even informally, from any officer of the Government?...It was indeed well calculated to excite the feelings of the Western people particularly, who were not quite so tenderly attached to our red brethren as some modern philosophers; but it was destitute of any foundation....

It was much more likely, he pointed out, that the House of Representatives itself was responsible, the Native Americans having acted out of fury that treaty after treaty had been concluded, but none had given the Native Americans real help in coping with their new conditions. They had been given only bits of money while "extinguishing their title to immense wilderness...It was our own thirst for territory that had driven these sons of nature to desperation...."

None of these reasons adequately explained why America went to war against England in 1812, however. The economic explanations, the theories about the undue influence of westerners, the desire to expand into Florida or Canada, even the standard explanation that the election of 1810 had overturned nearly half the seats in Congress, showing a disillusion with the Jeffersonian approach—all these dwindle on close examination of the political forces and the voting in Congress. The overwhelming reason—more than in any other war the U.S. ever fought—was the honor and integrity of the nation. The West had only ten votes in the Lower House, against thirty-nine for the South Atlantic states, and most of the southern congressmen were veterans of years in the legislature. Their seats were safe, and there was no popular pressure on them to vote for war. Where young men had taken over seats, they did not stand for very specific attitudes on the issue, but they were "war hawks" with great ability as speakers. Especially in the Select Committee on Foreign Relations, this talent was channeled toward exhortations to fight—for honor—and they convinced the others that war was "the only alternative to national humiliation and disgrace." Regrettably, this determination was not matched by any reasonable effort to achieve readiness for combat.

There is still a lively dispute among historians on how a strong executive branch could have allowed its country to slip into war under such conditions, but it is difficult to escape the administration's responsibility for the unreadiness and the botched beginning. In any event, President James Madison did finally declare war in 1812, heard it generally referred to as "Madison's War," and saw one disgraceful defeat after another. Jefferson and Madison had had such total faith in commercial restrictions as a weapon that they had left the country virtually without an army. The declaration of war had come when the nation was dismally unprepared. It became a source of humor that the United States didn't seem to have a general who was capable of winning a single engagement. This made General Andrew Jackson stand out, even though he was mostly defeating Native Americans, while lacking a conventional military background.

And it was this unique man—almost more spirit than substance—who was destined to defend and ultimately to rescue the great Louisiana Purchase from near disaster.

When Jackson was fixed on a central goal, he appeared to ignore all obstacles—physical, political, even legal—so blindly that he caused them to vanish. He was not bothered by the technicality that the U.S. was not at war with Spain, as it was with Britain. Jackson wrote the Spanish governor of Florida a letter charging that "Refugee banditti from the Creek nation are crowding into Florida, drawing rations from your government and under the drill of a British officer." The United States would retaliate if further provoked, he warned, citing his creed, "An Eye for an Eye, Toothe for Toothe, and Scalp for Scalp."

The conduct of the whole 1812 war had been abominable up to that point, leading Madison to appoint James Monroe secretary of war as well as secretary of state. Monroe applied his methodical mind to the confused situation. He knew that Jackson was anxious to invade Florida, in order to put a real end to the threat of Native American cooperation with the British, and he sent Jackson a letter ordering him not to attack Florida because it was territory that the Spanish still claimed, and the U.S. did not want to arouse Spanish hostility. But Jackson pretended not to have received the letter until he had made the move "for the security of the country, even if it cost him his commission." It was a sound move, sealing off avenues of possible invasion, and it helped to secure his position in the East.

But even though "Old Hickory" had a special role in totally crushing the Creek Native Americans, pushing their remnants back to lands far from the coast and out of contact with the Europeans, he had no real training in the science of war and had never commanded troops in normal combat. His firmness in negotiating with enemy leaders secured many of his advantages more than actual combat did. But along with the remarkable things that his personality could do to enemies and to his own men, Jackson had one other great quality that a general needs: he was extremely lucky. His finest biographer, Robert V. Remini, has said: "A remarkable string of good fortune trailed Jackson throughout the War of 1812, some of it earned, most of it entirely accidental." This man and this long run of pure luck are the only reason that the great Louisiana Purchase was not largely obliterated in 1814 by the loss of New Orleans, which was, after all, the crown jewel and focal point of the entire territory. It was a state, fully a part of the United States of America, and no part of the Union has ever again come so close to being captured by a foreign power.

Time and again, toward the end of that year, bizarre incidents and simple careless mistakes came within a whisker of wrecking the great accomplishment of the Louisiana Purchase. It has often been said in later days that either new technology or a single oversight had an effect supposedly never seen before in world history, enabling "a few men to accomplish what used to require an army." But this principle has never been new. Even more than new weaponry, war situations have always involved the chance that one person's failure could open the way for massive loss. But probably there has never been a case in which the fate of a nation as large as the United States in 1814 was nearly shattered by an unknown person's careless error.

Jackson, having subdued the Native American "menace" and firmed the American claim to Florida, was a very sick man looking forward to retirement, even though he was just forty-seven years old when he received word that his country would need him to defend Louisiana. It became known that the culminating battle of this bizarre war would apparently take place on short notice because the

British had assembled an armada of sixty ships, loaded with crack troops, to conquer and take over New Orleans. "I owe Britain a debt of retaliatory vengeance," he told his wife, recalling the horrors he had suffered during the Revolutionary War, when, at age fifteen, he nearly died of starvation and disease as a British prisoner. "Should our forces meet, I trust I shall repay the debt."

While British troops under Sir George Cockburn had invaded the Chesapeake area and another army had come down from Quebec into New York, hoping to secure Lake Champlain, Vice Admiral Sir Alexander Cochrane mounted an expedition to invade from the Gulf of Mexico. He expected that Native American troops would join with his men to drive the Americans back from the coast and bottle them up in the Mississippi Valley. He spoke openly of making the Americans prisoners in their own country, living on an island surrounded by Great Britain in the north, west, and south. He had asked for and received the Admiralty's permission for a plan that seemed foolproof, and it was indeed a very serious threat: not only to take New Orleans, but to cripple and encircle the United States.

The British moves and Jackson's countermoves began in August 1814. Because Jackson had correctly guessed that Cochrane would go through Mobile to reach the Mississippi Valley, he moved his army with amazing speed from Fort Jackson down the Coosa and Alabama Rivers to reach Mobile first. Cochrane, learning of this tactic and also being told by his intelligence that New Orleans was totally unprotected, decided to strike New Orleans directly, which strategists now consider a major mistake, for a full frontal assault would carry huge risk. The move that experts consider the obvious wise one would have been to move overland north of New Orleans, cutting off the city before attempting to capture it. But for several months, Jackson can also be said to have repaid the favor with his own sins of omission. This exchange of errors, and the fact that the administration in Washington did not seem clear on what it really wanted done, was keeping the situation fluid.

By mid-November of 1814, Jackson received intelligence reports that the British were about to make a full-scale assault on New Orleans. He still feared that they were actually planning to start by striking through Mobile, so he left some troops there, but he did begin sending troops in groups of two thousand men at a time to New Orleans. And despite being very ill and going eight days without food, he managed to get onto his horse and move with two thousand more men on an eleven-day march to New Orleans.

The city of destiny was virtually impossible to attack from the west, because the river is broad on that side and the current is swift. It was difficult to attack from the south, because a post called Fort St. Philip stood downstream, well-manned and ready to fire a great battery of twenty-four-pounders, and another fort offered further protection just twenty-five miles south of the city. So the two possible eastern approaches were by far the likeliest to be chosen by the British attackers—a water route from the Gulf and the land route from Mobile that still worried Jackson the most.

But a frantic letter from Secretary Monroe reached him, saying, in effect, forget Mobile—the massive sixty-ship British invasion armada had already left for New Orleans. It had been a full year in preparation, with veteran troops that had been specially held aside in earlier phases of the war against America to make this one massive blow against that "one spot on the globe" that had been prized and threatened for decades. It was one of the most elaborately equipped fleets ever assembled, with even many of the officers' wives on board, facilities for music and dancing, and printing presses to publish a regular newspaper.

The great armada had left England on November 27, so it was still far away at sea when General Jackson, gaunt and pallid, but with his usual military bearing, entered New Orleans on December 1. But this was quite a late arrival considering how much there was to be done in preparing a defense—closing water routes into the city, blocking bayous that connected the city to the outskirts, inspecting every fortified site and ordering repairs on many of them, and studying each important street to determine the route likeliest to be taken by the invaders. Among the many political and military figures there to meet Jackson was Edward Livingston, younger brother of Robert. He and Jackson had known each other before, and Livingston quickly became a great favorite of the general's, who is said to have admired his intelligence and judgment.

One of the trickiest problems was deciding what to do with the pirate Jean Lafitte and his brothers, whose great band of freebooters did so much of the city's business and were aided by some of the town's most prominent citizens. Even the highly respected Edward Livingston served as their lawyer. The British had offered Lafitte complete respectability and great rewards if his forces would help them in the fight. The pirate shrewdly asked for two weeks to consider the proposal, then sent the British letter to the governor of Louisiana, offering his services to the defense of the city in return for an amnesty for all his band. The governor was disinclined, and, in fact, had already taken strong action against the Lafitte brothers before Jackson arrived. But when Jackson saw Lafitte's letter, offering the services of a thousand men who were said to be incomparable marksmen, his penchant for acting on instinct asserted itself. The tone of the letter reminded him of a courageous Native American chieftain he had once admired, and he accepted the offer.

Jackson also accepted the aid of free blacks, despite the distrust and opposition of many citizens who feared that a fully armed black battalion might turn its guns on the whites. The men were to be commanded by white officers, but treated exactly like other volunteers and paid the same bounty of 160 acres of land and $124 in cash. When two full battalions of black soldiers had been formed, Jackson showed the citizens how highly he regarded these units by making them some of the first troops that he reviewed, along with one from leading New Orleans families. This last was commanded by a person who had become a favorite and personal friend, Major Jean-Baptiste Plauché, the Creole whose rise in fortune and friendship with General Jackson was described in a previous chapter. The talent for personal emotion and interaction was an intangible skill that gave Jackson a mysterious edge in encounters with ordinary commanders. Knowing how badly outnumbered his forces would be and perhaps even outclassed by the highly experienced and professional British troops, he used every imaginable device to create a passion for the coming fight.

In addition to taking control of the city by declaring martial law, Jackson issued declarations that he liked to model on the orations that were addressed to Greek soldiers before battle. He had Edward Livingston, who had been appointed a volunteer aide-de-camp, read pronouncements like the following:

> Fellow-Citizens and Soldiers: the general, commanding in chief, would not do justice to the noble ardour that has animated you in the hour of danger if he suffered the example you have shewn to pass without notice.
>
> Natives of the United States! They, the British, are the oppressors of your infant political existence with whom you are to contend—they are the men your fathers conquered whom you are to oppose. Descendants of Frenchmen! natives of France! they are the English, the hereditary, the eternal enemies of your ancient country....Spaniards,

remember the conduct of your allies at St. Sebastien, and recently at Pensacola, and rejoice that you have an opportunity of avenging the brutal injuries inflicted by men who dishonor the human race....

He had special words for each battalion, adapted to their history and main interests, as well as words that specifically mentioned "men of colour," stressing how he wanted them not only to share in the perils, but also to divide the glory of the coming action with their white countrymen, and telling them of the great qualities and noble enthusiasm he had found in them. It seems likely that no one had ever before sung such praises to a group of blacks in America. The spirits of the Orleanians seemed to glow under this treatment, observed Edward Livingston, who would become President Andrew Jackson's secretary of state two decades later.

However, the city was almost lost on December 22, when an advance army of British soldiers discovered that one bayou, ominously called Bayou Bienvenu (Welcome Bayou), was not only big and deep enough to be navigable for large barges, but that it was unprotected. Someone, and the guilty party has never been identified, had failed to obey Jackson's command to seal off every bayou. And it must be noted that Jackson had failed to double-check each such danger point. The British got all the way through underbrush and came out into an opening of a home owned by a general of the militia. They captured the general's son, Major Gabriel Villeré, whom some believe to have been the careless culprit. In any case, Villeré was now the hero. He escaped in a hail of gunfire and ran several miles into the city to sound the alarm.

Even so, the city was only saved because the first of a series of exceptionally timid decisions by British officers gave the lucky General Jackson time to recover. If the British column had moved swiftly toward the city, it might have captured the city almost without a struggle. But the officer who had found the great opening decided that it was too dangerous to pursue until reinforcements were brought up. Before that could be done, however, Jackson, whose famous "luck" consisted largely of an instant energetic response to each crisis, had rushed to the scene and forced a night battle that was inconclusive, but at least halted any further advance. This was only one of several incidents during these fateful days when the main point of the Louisiana Purchase hung tremulously in the balance.

Soon afterwards, the officer who would command the British army troops arrived on the scene. Lieutenant General Sir Edward Michael Pakenham, the Duke of Wellington's brother-in-law, was one of Britain's most respected military men, who had survived repeated wounds and performed gallantly. But here, taking command of troops that were squeezed between a swamp and a river, facing Americans in a position that General Jackson had fortified well, his decisions were less than perfect. Once again, what had been a British opportunity to break through Jackson's line was lost by hesitation.

Days followed during which Pakenham moved heavy naval cannons to a position where he could pound and perhaps destroy the American guns. Jackson used that same period to reinforce his own rampart, digging a deeper ditch and building a mud bank higher and higher. By the evening of December 31, Pakenham's preparations for a massive shower of lead were complete; a tremendous threat, even without knowing that Jackson planned a foolish event for the following morning—a military review to bolster the morale of his troops. Jackson's morale-building efforts had paid off, sending his forces' spirits ever higher while the British morale sank from inattention. But on New Year's morning, 1815, the flashy American parade that began as the fog lifted could have been a suicidal move. The British battery exploded, sending Americans running in all directions.

The British had a chance to breach the American line, but again lost the opportunity. A long exchange of heavy cannon fire followed, with the American accuracy creating heavy casualties among the British gunners. But then it was Jackson's turn to err on the side of caution, a rarity for him. He might have sent troops to capture some of those guns with very little risk, but he made no such attempt.

Pakenham decided that his best chance of victory was to punch straight ahead through Jackson's position, which would require more men. So he waited for some reinforcements that were on their way, and this gave Jackson precious time to thicken his rampart. The American general also welcomed the arrival of two thousand Kentucky militiamen whom he knew to be crack shots, although a shortage of weapons—about which he wrote a furious letter to Monroe in Washington—was a drawback.

At four o'clock in the morning of January 8, a column of redcoats stole closer to the mud rampart under an incompetent officer who forgot to bring sixteen ladders that were needed to scale the rampart. By the time some of the men turned back to fetch the forgotten ladders, the attack had begun and the timing was thrown off. Still, with great discipline, British soldiers moved forward all across the field. The American lines cheered, as if asking the foe to step right up, for everyone knew this was the critical moment. Then, as the American band struck up "Yankee Doodle," artillery and rifles erupted, blasting the oncoming Englishmen. Line after line of Americans stepped forward, fired, then stepped back to reload while an alternate line moved up.

The American fire was deliberate and deadly. British men crumpled and fell, many on top of one another. Kentuckians, who had looked scruffy and inept to the people of New Orleans, turned out to be sharpshooters who seemed never to miss. British officers later said they had never seen such destructive fire. Gallant efforts to get more of the attackers moving were made, but the troops had lost their nerve. General Pakenham, already wounded, came riding up, shouting to the soldiers to remember their duty, but he was still calling out in vain to bring up the reserve when he was hit by two more salvos and died within minutes. Several other generals perished in the devastation.

Creole Jean-Baptiste Plauché had become a major by then, commanding an all-volunteer group that took part in a show of force to give the citizens confidence. It was Plauché who brought his contingent up just in time to save General Jackson's line from being turned by a sudden British advance. And it was Plauché who nearly captured an entire regiment of the British army, but was prevented because another officer from the general's staff mistakenly stopped him from giving the order for a bayonet attack.

Although the undermanned American defenders on the west bank of the river were being overrun by the British at that same time, not much came of this threat, because the English general who was left in command ordered a general pullback, and Jackson did not risk pursuing them. In the end, a massive British force that should have won easily was destroyed with enormous losses, while the Americans had only minimal losses. The country had very nearly given up hope as days passed with no word about the outcome of the battle. Then the cry of a great victory was greeted as the Second Independence from Britain, for the new nation had truly been on the point of losing all.

Even his generally admiring biographer has scathing words for Andrew Jackson's miserable taste in blaming others for each of his own mistakes that detracted even minimally from his great victory. He refused to face up to the fact that others had warned him about the inadequacy of the west-bank defenses and that he had ignored them. But the British armada, after a few tentative attempts to renew an attack, finally withdrew for good. Jackson's luck held fast. He was adored and cheered at a series of open-air meetings and heard the Almighty praised for having had the wisdom to send New Orleans such a great savior.

The Battle of New Orleans went down in military lore as one of history's memorable battles, not because of great strategies, but because of the unbelievable casualty ratio of well over twenty to one. This encounter is considered a special feature of world military history for the massive disparity in the losses of the two sides. The British later admitted to casualties of 2,037 against 71 American casualties, of which only 13 were killed. Like the Louisiana Purchase itself, which was now confirmed and secure, the price paid was incredibly low.

It would be a dangerous precedent to read too much into the fact that both the acquisition and then the retention of Louisiana were powered primarily by impulsive actions. Robert Livingston's quixotic insubordination, Pierre Samuel du Pont's insistence on cash bargaining, Louis Pichon's warnings against seizing New Orleans, James Monroe's decision to trust his own opinion of Louisiana's worth—these succeeded not because they were impulsive, but because bright individuals reached the right conclusions. It was the caliber of these men on both sides that shaped the deal. And if the final rescue of New Orleans was facilitated because Andrew Jackson ignored instructions given by the same James Monroe whose confidence had purchased the land, again, it was not impulsiveness, but good judgement that prevailed. The person on the spot knew more than a distant superior. If any single principle that was at work here has to be credited most, it is that intelligent persons who understood the big picture were able to make wise decisions beyond their normal level in the hierarchy. In the controversy between the narrow "need to know" mentality that often prevails in military and law-enforcement organizations and the opposite rule of letting people think "above their pay grade," the latter approach would seem to have been a clear winner in the negotiations and battle for Louisiana.

The whole subsequent history of the nation flowed from these achievements: the treaty with Spain that confirmed American ownership of Florida and the Oregon Country, the annexation of Texas, the establishment of the northwestern boundaries, the acquisition of California, the question of an isthmus canal, and the overriding belief in America's manifest destiny. None of these could have been contemplated if Spain, France, or Great Britain had controlled the heart of the continent. But once the Louisiana Territory was so dramatically added and the new states started to form, the rest began to seem natural and preordained.

The Louisiana Purchase must be counted as a principal reason that many admiring or envious non-Americans have quipped, "God protects fools, drunks, and the United States of America." But for a country that, in 1803, had already made a noble start toward good government and blazing growth to have been given such an imperial gift as the Louisiana Territory must have convinced many of the seriously faithful that nature's design for the planet included a special role for America.

Short of that, one must credit the success of the negotiation to a long list of events that somehow all fell into place as if by design: Napoleon's growing need for money, the mosquitoes that brought death to Saint Domingue at a critical moment, Spain's baffling closure of Mississippi shipping, the perfect way that Congress unwittingly played its part, and the interaction among nine remarkable men who did indeed do "the noblest work" of their lives.

NOTES

ABBREVIATION

1903 St. P. "1903 State Papers and Correspondence Bearing Upon the Purchase of the Territory of Louisiana," Library of Congress, House of Representatives Serial Set no. 4531, 57th Congress, 2nd Session, doc 431.

CHAPTER 1: TOWARD THE GREAT RIVER

1   *"Where are your landmarks"*: Patrick Henry speech to the Continental Congress, Philadelphia, October 14, 1774, Senate Library.

1   *more Americans than anyone imagined*: Jack Larkin, *The Reshaping of Everyday Life* (New York: Harper & Row, 1988), xvi, 6, 204–7.

3   *"America has always had"*: "Week in Review," *New York Times*, February 18, 2001.

3   *years of drudge work*: Larkin, 149–53.

4   *By the early 1790s*: Larkin, 37.

5   *Great Britain still provided*: Irving Brant, *James Madison: 1800-1809* (Indianapolis: Bobbs-Merrill Co, 1953), 87–88.

5   *A sharp portrait*: Henry Adams, *History of the United States of America*

during the Administrations of Thomas Jefferson, (New York: Literary Classic of the United States, 1986).

6   *Jefferson had been attracted:* Fawn Brodie, *Thomas Jefferson: An Intimate History* (New York: W.W.Norton, 1974), 340–41.

6   *Pierre Radisson:* Marshall Sprague, *So Vast, So Beautiful a Land* (Boston: Little, Brown & Co., 1974), 19.

6   *"so beautiful, so fertile":* Justin Winsor, *The Mississippi Basin* (Boston: Houghton Mifflin, 1895), 37-41. Also Sprague, 58.

6   *total drainage area:* Sprague, 57 and 352, note 3.

7   *Spain had succeeded:* Sprague, 57.

7   *Jonathan Carver:* Sprague, 220.

8   *corroborating facts:* Sprague, 223.

8   *It raises the question:* John Keats, *Eminent Domain* (New York: Charter-house, 1973), 171–88.

8   *Andre Michaux:* Sprague, 250–52.

9   *donation from George Washington:* Sprague, 250.

9   *Many a mug of ale:* Donald Barr Chidsey, *Louisiana Purchase* (New York: Crown Publishers, 1972), p86-87.

10   *350,000 square miles:* Sprague, 226.

10   *Northwest Ordnance of 1787:* Sprague, 226–27.

10   *at least five thousand population:* Sprague, 227.

10   *full-fledged statehood:* Sprague, 227.

11   *Spanish had only acquired:* Chidsey 130–32.

11   *Duc de Choiseul:* Sprague, 181.

12   *Count Floridablanca, announced:* Sprague, 219.

12   *Jay's proposed trade treaty:* Sprague, 231–32.

12   *letter to James Madison:* Sprague, 232.

13   *would simply arm:* Chidsey, 103.

14   *The western parts of many states:* Sprague, 232.

14   *Constitutional Convention:* Sprague, 237.

15   *talk of deserting:* Sprague, 237.

15   *less than a thousand men*: Sprague, 241.

16   *On 12 Fructidor*: Andre Castelot, *Napoleon* (New York: Harper & Row, 1971), page 49.

18   *"One would"... "for many years...doubtful"*: The quotations from the letters of Joshua Coit on pages 18 and 19 are from: Daniel C. Gilman, *James Monroe* (Boston: Houghton Mifflin Co., 1883), 42–47.

18   *The easterners, their industries*: Sprague, 247.

19   *American newspapers*: The noted newspapers were examined at the Library of Congress, Office of Publications.

CHAPTER 2: FRIENDLY FRANCE THREATENS AMERICA

23   *Even months before*: Irving Brant, *James Madison, 1800-1809* (Indianapolis, IN: Bobbs-Merrill, 1953), 65.

23   *Then, as now*: George S. Bryan, *The Spy in America*, (Philadelphia: J.B. Lipincott, 1943), page 13.

24   *On the brink*: Brant, 65–67.

24   *Spain had twice threatened*: Marshall Sprague, *So Vast, So Beautiful a Land* (Boston: Little, Brown & Co., 1974), 219

26   *France's impeccably honest* : François Marquis de Barbé-Marbois, *Our Revolutionary Forefathers: The Letters of François Marquis de Barbé-Marbois, during His Residence in the United States as Secretary of the French Legation, 1779–1785* (New York: Duffield & Co., 1929), 8.

27   *But to Jefferson*: Sprague, 292.

28   *Repeatedly, one finds*: Brant, 65.

28   *"If Madison be"*: Brant 35.

29   *"The Western people believe"*: Brant, 90.

29   *But the wisest*: Brant, 482.

29   *Madison's rocky start*: Brant, 37.

30   *Actually, he felt that*: Brant, 43.

30   *A Chief Clerk named Jacob Wagner*: Brant, 48.

30   *Daniel Brent*: Brant, 48.

31 *Rufus King, from Massachusetts*: Letter of March 29, 1801, *1903 St. P.*

31 *once beguiled Lord Hawkesbury*: Letter of June 1, 1801, *1903 St. P.*

33 *spent his first money*: Bryan, 51. Also Jock Haswell, *Spies and Spymasters* (London: Thames & Hudson, 1977), 59–64.

33 *Not long after*: Bryan, 71–73.

34 *"even deceived"*: Bryan, 81. Also, an accumulation of undocumented references to George Washington make it appear that his lessons in espionage came in successive steps. One of these dated back to the time of his arrival in Cambridge, in 1775, when he established a secret correspondence with someone whose name he cautiously avoided putting into written form. Arranging for spies to watch over the movements of British ships also came soon afterwards—again handled so secretively that there are no written details. But it was in the fall of 1777, when the Pennsylvania campaign was in progress and the enemy held Philadelphia, that Washington took a more formal approach to intelligence. Personal talks with individuals who have been involved with the history of cryptanalysis and other intelligence specialties have shown that General Washington felt a desperate need to know what was happening in New York, but had to fashion his own system for gathering such facts. So in an undated letter to Major Alexander Clough, of the 3rd Continental Dragoons, Washington suggested sending several men, who would be from different localities and unknown to each other, into New York, then comparing their accounts of the situation they found. He gave Clough these instructions: "Procure some intelligent person to go into the city, and as it will be unsafe to give him a written paper, I desire you to impress the enclosed upon his memory by repeating them to him. When he returns, let me know the answer to each head [subject]. If the person that goes in cannot make an excuse of business, he must be allowed to carry a small matter of provisions, and bring something out by way of pretext." The man, of course, would be a spy and subject to immediate execution, as Captain Nathan Hale had been a year earlier when he had exchanged his uniform for a brown suit and gone behind enemy lines.

Nothing came of this instruction to Clough, for the major was trapped in a surprise British attack about ten days later, bayonneted, and killed.

By then, however, Washington recognized how great his need for intelligence was, and he spotted certain exceptional qualities in Major Benjamin Tallmadge, in a regiment of Connecticut troops. Like Hale, he had been a schoolteacher before going to war, and he proved to have a good eye for sensing how everything he saw fitted into the general disposition of troops. On patrol he was particularly observant and effective. He took on the job of spymaster for Washington, and set about urgently collecting a small group of bright men with knowledge of the Long Island topography, giving them secret pseudonyms, and asking Washington for enough funds to supply these operatives for their "dangerous and expensive business, because I am obliged to give my assistants high wages, even while being as sparing as possible." Washington succeeded in actually coaxing the dead-broke Congress to give him a small secret-service fund. He asked for metal, preferably gold, saying, "Valuable purposes would result from it. I have always found a difficulty in procuring intelligence by means of paper money." Repeatedly throughout the war years, there are notes showing that much of Washington's correspondence on espionage matters concerns frugality in the handing out of gold guineas. When Washington drew up an account in his own handwriting on July 1, 1783, it showed that in eight years the total expenditure for "secret intelligence" had been £1,982 10s. (This would represent some $9,900 if paid in the gold that Washington preferred to use, but it could have taken up to nine times as many paper dollars to equal the same value in the unruly currency trading of that day.)

The gradually increasing complexity of Washington's espionage methods is noticeable. The nature of the information on enemy movements is more detailed, and special stress was laid on proposed movements by water. There is also much talk of a new "sympathetic ink," invented by Sir James Jay (elder brother of American diplomat John Jay), a physician living in England. This wonderful fluid permitted invisible writing, and the good doctor sent a quantity of it to his brother, which General Washington and his close associates put to great use.

There had been something of a farcical flavor to Washington's intelligence service. The invisible ink was so prized that when Tallmadge's No.2 man, Abraham Woodhull, dropped a vial of it in a close encounter with British officers, he was so distraught over the loss that he took to his bed and had to be coaxed at length before he would stir. There were also incidents where Woodhull had to watch with a spyglass from a great distance to see whether the wife of a certain patriotic judge had hung white handkerchiefs or a black petticoat on her clothesline to signal the landing place of another spy. And there were constant problems caused by the fact that the use of false names made it nearly impossible for messages sent by post to reach their destination.

Tallmadge was an amazingly calm, placid person, who delegated much of the effort while giving a real shape to the organization he was building. He had created a number of codes—one had been made up by listing the most common words and assigning an Arabic numeral to each one. Enemy was 178, camp 73, infantry 309, New York 727. Tallmadge called himself John Bolton, and his number code name was 721. He also made up a substitution alphabet, in which the relationship of letters is haphazard. For instance, *a* is represented by *e*, *e* is shown as *i*, and *o* is rendered as *q*. Since there is no regular pattern to these substitutions, anyone who figures out a few letters has no clue to what the other letters might be. So even though it is extremely simple, it makes the deciphering hard enough to delay a full translation.

Tallmadge and his men survived their dangerous wartime adventures and led prosperous lives. Tallmadge became a congressman, Woodhull a judge.

38   *Such was the awkward position*: Madison to R.R. Livingston, Sept. 28, 1801, *1903 St. P.*

40   *made the feared move*: Sprague, 277–79.

42   *"Since France"*: Hawkesbury to King, May 7, 1802, *1903 St. P.*

42   *done the reverse*: Sprague, 279.

43   *"I am afraid"*: Sprague, 292.

43   *needed the extra time*: Brant, 75.

CHAPTER 3: THE FATEFUL ISLAND

45 *a crown jewel*: Irving Brant, *James Madison, 1800-1809* (Indianapolis, IN: Bobbs-Merrill, 1953), 62.

46 *The island's revolutionary troubles*: W. Adolphe Roberts, *The French in the West Indies* (Indianapolis, IN: Bobbs Merrill Co., 1942), 30–33.

47 *A new turn*: Roberts, 38-41.

48 *"a master of constructive duplicity"*: Roberts, 42–45.

50 *"Then treat with Toussaint"*: Donald Barr Chidsey, *Louisiana Purchase* (New York: Crown Publishers, 1972), 133

51 *"From the General in Chief"*: *Moniteur de La Louisiane,* June 11, 1802.

52 *"The slaves are forced"*: Roberts, 151.

52 *"As we know"*: Roberts, 151. Also Jan Rogozinski, *A Brief History of the Caribbean* (New York: Facts On File, Inc., 1999), 68-71.

54 *"I begged you"*: Roberts, 220.

54 *The May rains*: Roberts, 218.

54 *Command of the French forces*: Brant, 177.

CHAPTER 4: ONE SPOT ON THE GLOBE

55 *the follow-up operation*: King to Madison, February 5, 1802, *1903 St. P.*

55 *In a back-up effort*: Livingston to Madison, February 26, 1802, *1903 St. P.*

56 *"the most fertile countries"*: Livingston to Madison, March 24, 1802, *1903 St. P.*

56 *a Frenchman named Tatergem*: Livingston to Madison, March 24, 1802, *1903 St. P.*

57 *Jefferson penned a letter*: Jefferson to Livingston, April 18, 1802, *1903 St. P.*

59 *New Orleans was…*: These impressions, partly from personal contacts and observations, also drew on Harry Hansen, *Louisiana: A Guide to the State* (New York: Hastings House, 1941); Edwin A. Davis, *Louisiana: The Pelican State* (Baton Rouge, LA, Louisiana State University Press, 1975); and Harold Sinclair, *The Port of New Orleans* (Garden City, NY: Doubleday Doran, 1942).

62 *A telling case history:* A descendant of Jean-Baptiste Plauché, Dr. Mark Plauche Ryan, D.D.S., assisted in gathering information from his family's history for the account that begins in this chapter and then is concluded in chapter 18. This is further confirmed in the two books by Robert V. Remini that are listed in the bibliography.

65 *The understatement received:* Donald Barr Chidsey, *Louisiana Purchase* (New York: Crown Publishers, 1972), 126

67 *Livingston's notion of propriety:* Livingston to Talleyrand, Feb.20, 1802, *1903 St. P.*

69 *Bernadotte fell behind:* A friend of Talleyrand's captivated Parisian gossipers by saying that "Bernadotte looks like an eagle, but is actually a goose." Whichever identity was involved, the handsome general later became King of Sweden. While leading troops in Scandinavia during the Napoleonic Wars, Jean-Baptiste Bernadotte became Regent of Sweden. In 1818, he was elected King Charles XIV, and the present Swedish royal family is descended from him.

69 *innumerable instances:* Irving Brant, *James Madison, 1800-1809* (Indianapolis, IN: Bobbs-Merrill, 1953), 90-91.

CHAPTER 5: THE MISTRUSTED ENVOY

73 *Livingston could detect:* Livingston to Madison, [mis-dated September 1, 1808, but surely was meant to be 1802], *1903 St. P.* The same conditions are indicated by another letter to Madison on January 24, 1803, *1903 St. P.*

74 *Livingston had been surrounded:* The discussion of Livingston on pages 74–76 are my own impressions largely based on this excellent biography: George Dangerfield, *Chancellor Robert Livingston* (New York: Harcourt, 1960).

78 *How much more confidence:* Madison to Pinckney, May 11, 1802, *1903 St. P.*

79 *One letter of King's:* King to Madison, March 29, 1801, *1903 St. P.*

83 *Yet it was clear:* This statement is based on the 1903 State Papers, including several letters from Livingston to Madison, such as July 30, 1802 ("I

am sorry that you have not communicated to me what are precisely the utmost limits of the sum I may venture to offer.") and Aug 10, 1802 ("I am very much at a loss as to what terms you would consider it allowable to offer.")

83 *Livingston clearly describes*: Livingston to Madison, July 30, 1802, *1903 St. P.*

85 *An example from his earlier career*: Dangerfield, 265

86 *He once wrote*: Talleyrand to Livingston, February 19, 1803, *1903 St. P.*

86 *Some accounts have reported*: Livingston to Madison, April 11, 1803, *1903 St. P.*

89 *At a later stage*: Livingston to Madison, March 24, 1803, *1903 St. P.*

CHAPTER 6: NAPOLEON'S ODD COUPLE

91 *Napoleon gave a firm order:* François Marquis de Barbé-Marbois, *L'Histoire de La Louisiane* (Paris: 1830), 30. Also in English from Carey & Lee, Philadelphia.

92 *had come to the United States*: François Marquis de Barbé-Marbois, *Our Revolutionary Forefathers: The Letters of François Marquis de Barbé-Marbois, during His Residence in the United States as Secretary of the French Legation, 1779–1785* (New York: Duffield & Co., 1929). His dates in the U.S. are included in the book.

92 *aboard ship with John Adams*: Barbé-Marbois, *Our Revolutionary*, 15.

93 *roller-coaster career*: Barbé-Marbois, *Our Revolutionary*. Taken from the book's introduction, written by Eugene Parker Chase, pages 6–14.

95 *Livingston had prepared*: Memorandums dated July 30, 1802 and August 10, 1802, *1903 St. P.*

97 *made himself famous*: J.F. Bernard, *Talleyrand* (New York: G.P. Putnam's Sons, 1973), 87-89.

97 *A few impressionistic recollections*: Bernard, 14, 19–22.

100 *He explained*: Bernard, 48.

101 *"If Talleyrand's conversation"*: Bernard, 104.

102 *But when he saw Hamilton*: Bernard, 160.

102 *(When he failed)*: Bernard, 208.

103 *Life as he viewed it*: Charles Maurice de Talleyrand-Périgord, *Talleyrand in America as a Financial Promoter*, trans. Huth and Pugh, (Washington, DC: 1942).

104 *But Talleyrand meant*: Bernard, 115.

104 *In the summer of 1797*: Bernard, 177, 183.

105 *the Directory was to be dissolved*: Bernard, 220.

106 *first official acts*: Bernard, 227.

106 *last official acts*: Bernard, 313.

CHAPTER 7: CONFUSING BONAPARTE

111 *Napoleon was given to wide mood swings*: Drawn from the 1903 State Papers from Livingston to Madison, especially the letter of April 13, 1803, quoting Marbois as often confiding how hard it was to deal with Napoleon's flighty ways.

112 *in personal and psychological terms*: François Marquis de Barbé-Marbois, *L'Histoire de La Louisiane* (Paris: 1830), 20–28

112 *"Almost all the institutions"*: Robert Asprey, *The Rise and Fall of Napoleon Bonaparte*, vol. 2 (London: Little, Brown & Co., 2001), 186.

114 *the lowest-ranked player*: Albert H. Bowman, article in *Diplomatic History, Journal of the Society for Historians of American Foreign Relations* 1, no.3: 257–70.

115 *"His name and reputation"*: Irving Brant, *James Madison, 1800-1809* (Indianapolis, IN: Bobbs-Merrill, 1953), 66–67.

117 *There was the time* Bowman, 260.

117 *Now the French* chargé: Bowman, 262.

118 *The sessions did not*: Bowman, 263.

118 *On one visit*: Bowman, 264.

119 *For example, Talleyrand passed*: Bowman, 268.

119 *The tumult on Saint Domingue*: Brant, 65, 78.

120 *Whenever the key subject*: Brant, 74, 140.

122 *"I give full weight"*: Brant, 52.

123 *Monroe's role*: *1903 St. P.*, 185.

125 *A Spanish official at New Orleans*: *1903 St. P.*, messages of Hulings and Morales, 54.

126 *By March 1803*: *New York Morning Chronicle,* November 7, 1802.

128 *As it happened*: *New York Morning Chronicle,* November 7, 1802.

129 *The noisy demands*: Congress Quarterly, *Guide to Congress, 4th edition* (Washington, DC: 1991)

130 *Four years later*: Congress Quarterly, *Guide to Congress, 4th edition* (Washington, DC: 1991)

CHAPTER 8: THE DU PONT WAY

133 *From the letters:* Various *1903 St. P.*

135 *To prove his point*: Joseph Frazier Wall, *Alfred I. du Pont* (New York: Oxford University Press, 1990), 10.

135 *he was barely twenty*: Wall, 13.

135 *Eleuthère Irénée*: Wall, 38.

136 *Jefferson knew*: Wall, 30.

136 *when he feared*: Wall, 31.

137 *The president was asking*: Wall, 46.

137 *In the spring of 1802*: Irving Brant, *James Madison, 1800-1809* (Indianapolis, IN: Bobbs-Merrill, 1953), 118. Also Wall, 32.

138 *Jefferson was determined*: Jefferson to du Pont, April 25, 1802, *1903 St. P.*

139 *he asked du Pont to*: Jefferson to Pierre du Pont, February 1, 1803, *1903 St. P.*

139 *At one point*: Du Pont to Le Brun, February 26, 1803, *1903 St. P.*

140 *On the Paris end*: Letter of Livingston to Madison, and letter of late February 1803 from Pierre du Pont to Le Brun, *1903 St. P.*

CHAPTER 9: AN EXTRAORDINARY MINISTER

145 *shortly to be joined*: Madison to Livingston, January 18, 1803, and Jefferson to Livingston, February 3, 1803, *1903 St. P.*

148 *a surprise choice:* L Gilman, 40. Also Sprague, 293.

148 *Harrowing it was:* Daniel C. Gilman, *James Monroe* (Boston: Houghton Mifflin, 1883), 55.

150 *Secretary of State Randolph had not:* Gilman, 57–58.

150 *He wrote his man in Paris:* Gilman, 58.

150 *Monroe, fuming:* John Keats, *Eminent Domain* (New York: Charterhouse, 1973), 243.

151 *he spoke excellent French:* Gilman, 60.

CHAPTER 10: WAITING FOR MONROE

154 *These men around Napoleon were divided:* Livingston to Madison, November 11, 1802, *1903 St. P.*

155 *In Washington, tension mounted:* Irving Brant, *James Madison, 1800-1809* (Indianapolis, IN: Bobbs-Merrill, 1953), 104.

155 *In January 1803:* Brant, 71.

155 *Also notable as a clue:* Brant, 77, 90.

156 *Livingston hammered at the question:* July 1802; December 20, 1802; and February 18, 1803, *1903 St. P.*

160 *"a confidential citizen":* Madison to Pinckney, November 27, 1802, *1903 St. P.*

160 *"Private accounts":* Madison to Livingston, December 23, 1802, *1903 St. P.*

160 *"I have obtained":* Livingston to Madison, November 14, 1802, *1903 St. P.*

161 *"It is well":* Jefferson to Livingston, November 27, 1802, *1903 St. P.*

162 *"I am not satisfied":* Livingston to Madison, March 11, 1803 and March 24, 1803, *1903 St. P.*

162 *"I see with pleasure":* Talleyrand to Livingston, March 21, 1803, *1903 St. P.*

163 *On April 10:* Marshall Sprague, *So Vast, So Beautiful a Land* (Boston: Little, Brown & Co., 1974), 300

164 *On Monday morning, April 11:* Sprague, 301, 302. Also Gilman, 82.

165 *word came on the very next day:* Sprague, 303, 304.

CHAPTER 11: AGONIZING MOMENTS

167 *He even told his sorrows*: Monroe to Madison, April 15, 1803, *1903 St. P.* Also Donald Barr Chidsey, *Louisiana Purchase* (New York: Crown Publishers, 1972), 134-137.

168 *"I congratulate you"*: Daniel C. Gilman, *James Monroe* (Boston: Houghton Mifflin, 1883), 81.

169 *"Would you Americans"*: Marshall Sprague, *So Vast, So Beautiful a Land* (Boston: Little, Brown & Co., 1974), 303.

172 *an exhausting number of proofs*: The "exhausting proofs" referred to here are shown in almost every one of his letters cited in the 1903 State Papers.

174 *"It is so very important"*: Livingston to Madison, April 13, 1803, *1903 St. P.* Also Sprague, 306.

175 *Having had Napoleon's order...irritating comments to Madison*: Incidents described in these pages are drawn from Livingston to Madison, April 13, 1803, *1903 St. P.*

176 *"I hesitated on the idea"*: George Morgan, *The Life of James Monroe* (New York: AMS Press, 1921), pg. 243.

CHAPTER 12: THE TREMULOUS PAUSE

179 *"resting on our oars"*: Livingston to Madison, April 17, 1803 (third page), *1903 St. P.*

179 *French were not to dispose*: Donald Barr Chidsey, *Louisiana Purchase* (New York: Crown Publishers, 1972), 146

180 *When Livingston asked Talleyrand*: Marshall Sprague, *So Vast, So Beautiful a Land* (Boston: Little, Brown & Co., 1974), 279.

182 *The scenario is this...not be entangling.*: Madison to Monroe and Livingston, April 18, 1803, *1903 St. P.*

185 *On April 15, 1803*: Monroe to Madison, April 15, 1803, *1903 St. P.*

187 *On April 17*: Livingston to Madison, April 17, 1803, *1903 St. P.*

NOTE: Another group of letters that have proved marginally useful are known as *American State Papers and Correspondence between Messrs. Smith, Pinckney,*

Marquis Wellesley, General Armstrong, M. Champaguy, M. Turreau, Messrs. Russell, Monroe, Foster, etc. vol. 8, London: 1812, 187.

CHAPTER 13: MONROE'S HISTORIC DECISION

NOTE: Broad generalities in this chapter have been drawn from 1903 State Papers cited above (pp.187–88), and from the previously mentioned American State Papers

191 *Just before Monroe left Washington*: Irving Brant, *James Madison, 1800-1809* (Indianapolis, IN: Bobbs-Merrill, 1953), 109.

191 *It came from the report*: Brant, 68–69.

195 *Monroe personally had no doubt*: Daniel C. Gilman, *James Monroe* (Boston: Houghton Mifflin, 1883), 84–85.

195 *"'the claims, the claims'"*: George Morgan, *The Life of James Monroe* (New York: AMS Press, 1921), 203.

199 *This new appraisal*: Brant, 71, 90.

CHAPTER 14: THE MOMENT IN HISTORY

NOTE: In addition to the subsequent citations, this chapter is based on analysis of "The Third Article of the Treaty of Cession of Louisiana," vol. 8, p. 8, *The Louisiana Purchase and Its Influence on the American System*, New York: 1885 (American Historical Associated Papers, vol. 1, no. IV).

201 *the Americans first proposed*: Marshall Sprague, *So Vast, So Beautiful a Land* (Boston: Little, Brown & Co., 1974), 306. Also Irving Brant, *James Madison, 1800-1809* (Indianapolis, IN: Bobbs-Merrill, 1953), 128

201 *By the following day*: Sprague, 306–7. Also Brant, 127.

202 *A delay*: Brant, 127. Also Robert Asprey, *The Rise and Fall of Napoleon Bonaparte*, vol. 2 (London: Little, Brown & Co., 2001), 244–48.

202 *By Saturday, April 27*: Daniel C. Gilman, *James Monroe* (Boston: Houghton Mifflin, 1883), 84. Also Sprague, 310–311.

203 *"Barbé-Marbois declared"*: Brant, 132.

CHAPTER 15: THE SENATE'S PRETENDED RELUCTANCE

207 *Now the two envoys*: Monroe and Livingston to Madison, May 13, 1803, *1903 St. P.*

208 *The vital documents are believed*: Donald Barr Chidsey, *Louisiana Purchase* (New York: Crown Publishers, 1972), 141and Irving Brant, *James Madison, 1800-1809* (Indianapolis, IN: Bobbs-Merrill, 1953), 133 both appear to have wrong dates for the document arrival. July 3 is the likeliest date, base on comments from the president's office.

209 *As the people*: Chidsey, 141.

210 *The Federalists*: Chidsey, 141–42.

210 *At just such a moment*: Chidsey, 145.

212 *When he saw that Jefferson*: Marshall Sprague, *So Vast, So Beautiful a Land* (Boston: Little, Brown & Co., 1974), 315.

212 *Jefferson was quickly persuaded*: Brant, 141.

212 *On July 21 major newspapers*: Newspapers examined at Library of Congress, Department of Publications.

214 *The early rash of objections*: Confirmed by the Senate Library, from a study of the *Executive Journal of the Senate* for the dates of the debate.

NOTE: Research also from *American State Papers and Correspondence between Messrs. Smith, Pinckney, Marquis Wellesley, General Armstrong, M. Champaguy, M. Turreau, Messrs. Russell, Monroe, Foster, etc.* vol. 8, London: 1812, 187.

CHAPTER 16: THE ANTAGONISTS MOVE ON

220 *"I count Louisiana"*: Irving Brant, *James Madison, 1800-1809* (Indianapolis, IN: Bobbs-Merrill, 1953), 143.

220 *"had stretched the Constitution"*: Brant, 141. Also Marshall Sprague, *So Vast, So Beautiful a Land* (Boston: Little, Brown & Co., 1974), 315–16.

221 *"spending a great fortune"*: Donald Barr Chidsey, *Louisiana Purchase* (New York: Crown Publishers, 1972), 144. Also Gary Rosen, *American Compact, James Madison and the Problem of Founding* (Lawrence, KS: University Press of Kansas, 1999), Introduction and 10–22.

222 *"One of the subtlest"*: George Dangerfield, *Chancellor Robert Livingston* (New York: Harcourt, 1960).

223 *"A truly noble acquisition."*: Brant, 133.

224 *The troubled future*: Albert H. Bowman, article in *Diplomatic History, Journal of the Society for Historians of American Foreign Relations* 1, no.3: 257–70.

225 *Less than two months*: Bowman, 259.

225 *Month after month*: Bowman, 265.

225 *Only in 1809*: Bowman, 267.

226 *"I can only hope for mercy."* Monroe to Jefferson, May 5, 1803, *The Letters of President Monroe.*

228 *The enduring policy*: Daniel C. Gilman, *James Monroe* (Boston: Houghton Mifflin Co., 1883), 164.

228 *Adams, then secretary of state*: Gilman, 160.

229 *Robert Livingston quite astonishingly*: Because George Dangerfield's *Chancellor Robert Livingston* stands alone as a superior biography of Robert Livingston, points in this section have been checked against it. However, they have been used merely as background for my own observations on his character and actions.

235 *Marbois was given*: Gilman, 87. (Letter from Bonaparte to Marbois saying that, "*192,000 francs seront a votre disposition*" and adding that, "*vous voyez dans cette disposition mon desir de vous temoigner ma satisfaction de vos travaux importants.*")

235 *But after further honors*: This information is based on a detailed account in *Dictionnaire de Biographie Francaise,* vol. 5, 246–54.

237 *On January 1, 1804*: W. Adolphe Roberts, *The French in the West Indies* (Indianapolis, IN: The Bobbs-Merrill Company, 1942), 210–21.

237 *The deal that Napoleon won*: Brant, 150.

239 *This surprise*: Brant, 151, 169. Also J.F. Bernard, *Talleyrand* (New York: G. P. Putnam's Sons, 1973), 262.

239 *"I regard the colony"*: Stuart Jerry Brown, *Thomas Jefferson* (New York: Washington Square Press, 1963). Also Brant, 143.

240 *But the prescient wisdom*: Marshall Sprague, *So Vast, So Beautiful a Land* (Boston: Little, Brown & Co., 1974), 302.

240 *The secret cornerstone*: Bernard, 79.

240 *Their close association*: Bernard, 265.

241 *"They will kick Talleyrand out."*: Bernard, 444.

242 *Talleyrand, however, was not through*: Bernard, 527.

242 *His personal life*: Bernard, 531.

243 *One of the happier reflections*: Joseph Frazier Wall, *Alfred I. du Pont* (New York: Oxford University Press, 1990), 48–49.

CHAPTER 17: A TERRITORY ON THE MOVE

245 *On November 30*: Harry Hansen, *Louisiana* (Hastings House, 1941), 44.

246 *the new American governor*: Hansen, 44.

246 *The first time France*: Hansen, 54.

247 *The total area*: Hansen, 43.

247 *"It compared favorably"*: Hansen, 308.

249 *Claiborne's closest advisers*: Robert Tallant, *New Orleans* (Boston: Houghton Mifflin Co., 1952). Also William B. Hatcher, *Edward Livingston* (Baton Rouge, LA: Louisiana State University Press,.1940).

249 *come to know Robert Fulton*: George Dangerfield, *Chancellor Robert Livingston* (New York: Harcourt, 1960), 403.

250 *When Louisiana formally*: Hansen, 45.

250 *The best estimate for total population*: These are my personal computations after consulting *Historical Statistics of the United States: Colonial Times to 1970, Part 1*, U.S. Department of Commerce, Bureau of the Census.

251 *"a chosen country"*: Robert V. Hine and John Mack Faragher, *The American West* (New Haven, CT: Yale University Press, 2000), 109. Also Jack Larkin, *The Reshaping of Everyday Life* (New York: Harper & Row, 1988), 17–18, 341–34, 78–82; and Joseph Frazier Wall, *Iowa, A History* (New York: W.W. Norton & Co, 1978), 34.

252 *Lewis and Clark found*: Hine & Faragher, 137.

252 *"I believe the business"*: Anthony P.C. Wallace, *Jefferson and the Indians* (Cambridge, MA: Belknap Press of Harvard University Press, 1999), 223.

253 *President Jefferson put these thoughts*: Wallace, 227.

254 *"The great thoroughfares"*: *The Universal Traveler* (a specialty travel publication), March 1811, 1.

255 *A Connecticut congressman*: Irving Brant, *James Madison, 1800-1809* (Indianapolis, IN: Bobbs-Merrill, 1953), 247.

256 *Jefferson, determined to maintain*: Brant, 171.

257 *Even a total eclipse*: Larkin, 62.

258 *less than 400,000 Americans*: *Historical Statistics of the United States,* as cited above.

CHAPTER 18: THE LONG SEQUEL

262 *Most Americans felt* George Rogers Taylor, *The War of 1812* (Boston: D.C. Heath & Co., 1963), 12.

263 *An 1811 report*: Taylor, 13.

264 *"An insinuation"*: Taylor, 14.

266 *Andrew Jackson stand out*: Robert V. Remini, *The Battle of New Orleans* (New York: Viking/Penguin, 1999,) 15.

266 *Jackson wrote the Spanish governor*: Robert V. Remini, *Andrew Jackson and the Course of Empire* (New York: Harper & Row, 1977), 29.

266 *The conduct of the whole*: Taylor, 29.

267 *"A remarkable string"*: Remini, *Andrew Jackson,* 42.

267 *It became known*: Remini, *Andrew Jackson,* 58.

270 *One of the trickiest problems*: Remini, *Battle of New Orleans,* 48.

270 *Jackson also accepted*: *The Letters of President Andrew Jackson,* vol.2, 76.

271 *a favorite and personal friend*: How smoothly New Orleanians made themselves a part of America's fabric is further demonstrated by an unusual personal favor that Jean-Baptiste Plauché was able to do for the proud and frugal General Jackson, who had never borrowed in his life. When Jackson's adopted son was deeply in debt some years after the Battle of New

Orleans, Plauche borrowed $6,000 and reloaned it to Jackson. Plauché refused to take any security or other assurances except a signed note. General Jackson went on to become president of the United States, but his cash position was still tight, and he fretted over the debt to Plauché. He finally remade his will to specify that the repayment of that loan would be the first money to be paid from his estate. Plauché, the former Creole shipwright who was by then an American citizen, became deputy mayor of New Orleans in 1828. These facts, like earlier information on the relationship, were made available to me by Dr. Mark Plauche Ryan.

271 *"Fellow-Citizens": The Letters of President Andrew Jackson*, vol.2, 118–19.

272 *ominously called Bayou Bienvenue*: Remini, *Battle of New Orleans*, 65–70.

272 *However, the city…price paid was incredibly low*: Facts and impressions in this chapter are drawn liberally from the books cited above and from two others: Wilburt S. Brown's *The Amphibious Campaign for West Florida and Louisiana*, 1969, *and* Donald Barr Chidsey's *The Battle of New Orleans*, 1961. The words, opinions, and conclusions in the chapter are entirely my own.

BIBLIOGRAPHY

Books

Adams, Henry. *History of the United States of America during the Administrations of Thomas Jefferson.* New York: Literary Classics of the United States, Inc., 1986.

Ammon, Harry. *James Monroe: The Quest for National Identity.* New York: McGraw-Hill Book Co., 1971.

Asprey, Robert. *The Rise and Fall of Napoleon Bonaparte, vol. 2.* London: Little, Brown, & Co., 2001.

Barbé-Marbois, François, Marquis de. *Histoire de la Louisiane et de la Cession de cette Colonie par la France aux États-Unis de l'Amérique.* Paris: 1829.

———. *Our Revolutionary Forefathers: The Letters of François Marquis de Barbé-Marbois, during His Residence in the United States as Secretary of the Foreign Legation, 1779–1785.* New York: Duffield & Co., 1929.

Barck, Otis T. *Colonial America.* New York: Macmillan & Company, 1968.

Bernard, J.F. *Talleyrand.* New York: G. P. Putnam's Sons, 1973.

Brant, Irving. *James Madison: Secretary of State 1800-1809.* Indianapolis: The Bobbs-Merrill Company, 1953.

Brodie, Fawn M. *Thomas Jefferson: An Intimate History.* New York: W.W. Norton, 1974.

Brown, Stuart Gerry. *The Autobiography of James Monroe.* Syracuse, NY: Syracuse University Press, 1959.

Bryan, George S. *The Spy in America.* Philadelphia: J.S. Lippincott Company, 1943.

Castelot, Andre, *Napoleon.* New York: Harper & Row, 1971.

Chidsey, Donald Barr. *Louisiana Purchase.* New York: Crown Publishers, 1972.

Congress Quarterly. *Guide to Congress.* 4th ed. Washington, D.C.: 1991.

Dangerfield, George. *Chancellor Robert Livingston.* New York: Harcourt, 1960.

Davis, Edwin Adams. *Louisiana, The Pelican State.* Baton Rouge, LA: Louisiana State University Press, 1975.

Gilman, Daniel C. *James Monroe.* Boston: Houghton Mifflin, 1883.

Hansen, Harry, ed. *Louisiana: A Guide to the State.* New York: Hastings House, 1941.

Harrison and Gilbert, eds. *Thomas Jefferson, Word for Word.* La Jolla, CA: Excellent Books, 1993.

Haswell, Jock. *Spies and Spymasters.* London: Thames and Hudson, 1977.

Hatcher, William B. *Edward Livingston.* Baton Rouge, LA: Louisiana State University Press, 1940.

Herold, J. Christopher. *The Age of Napoleon.* New York: American Heritage, 1963.

Hine, R.V. and Faragher, J.M. *The American West.* New Haven, CT: Yale University Press, 2000.

James, Marquis. *Andrew Jackson: Portrait of a President.* Indianapolis: Bobbs-Merrill, 1937.

Keats, John. *Eminent Domain.* New York: Charterhouse, 1973.

Larkin, Jack. *The Reshaping of Everyday Life.* New York: Harper & Row, 1988.

Madelin, Louis. *Talleyrand.* New York: Roy Publishers, 1948.

Malone, Dumas. *Jefferson the Virginian.* Boston: Little, Brown, & Co., 1948.

McCullough, David. *John Adams.* New York: Simon & Schuster, 2001.

Meade, Robert D. *Patrick Henry.* Philadelphia and New York: J.B. Lippincott Co., 1969.

Morgan, George. *The Life of James Monroe.* New York: AMS Press, 1921.

Remini, Robert V. *Andrew Jackson: And the Course of American Empire.* New York: Harper & Row, 1977.

———. *The Battle of New Orleans.* New York: Penguin, 1999.

Roberts, W. Adolphe. *The French in the West Indies.* Indianapolis: The Bobbs-Merrill Company, 1942.

Rogozinski, Jan. *A Brief History of the Caribbean.* New York: Facts on File, Inc., 1999.

Rosen, Gary. *American Compact: James Madison and the Problem of Founding.* Lawrence, KS: University Press of Kansas, 1999.

Rutland, Robert Allen. *James Madison: The Founding Father.* New York: Macmillan Publishing Co., 1987.

Sheldon, Garrett Ward. *What Would Jefferson Say?* New York: Perigee Book, Berkley Publishing Group, 1998.

Sinclair, Harold. *The Port of New Orleans.* Garden City, NY: Doubleday Doran, 1942.

Sprague, Marshall. *So Vast So Beautiful a Land.* Boston: Little, Brown, & Co., 1974.

Tallant, Robert, *New Orleans,* Boston: Houghton, Mifflin Co., 1952.

Talleyrand-Périgord, Charles Maurice de, *Talleyrand in America as a Financial Promoter,* trans. Huth and Pugh, (Washington, DC: 1942).

Taylor, George Rogers, ed. *The War of 1812.* Boston: D.C. Heath & Co., 1963.

Taylor, Joe Gray. *Louisiana: A Bicentennial History.* New York: W.W. Norton & Co., 1976.

Times of London. *The Times Atlas of World History.* London: Times Books, Ltd., 1983.

Wall, Joseph Frazier. *Alfred I du Pont.* New York: Oxford University Press, 1990.

———. *Iowa, A History.* New York: W.W. Norton & Co, 1978.

Wallace, Anthony F.C. *Jefferson and the Indians.* Cambridge: Harvard University Press, 1999.

Winsor, Justin. *The Mississippi Basin.* Boston: Houghton Mifflin, 1895.

———. *The Westward Movement, 1763-1798.* Boston: Houghton Mifflin, 1899.

Journals

Bowman, Albert H. *Diplomatic History, Journal of the Society for Historians of American Foreign Relations,* 1, no. 3: 257–70.

Letters

By far the most important source of direct and personal information about the exchanges of ideas among the persons who negotiated the Louisiana Purchase are the more than two hundred letters that were gathered when the U.S. Congress marked the 100th anniversary of the event by ordering research to gather correspondence that illuminates the many contacts that occurred over a period of roughly three years, creating a virtual roadmap of the path to agreement. It was also a month-by-month record of the hopes, tempers, courtesies, and discourtesies that were current among the nine principal players.

INDEX

ABOUT THE AUTHOR

Charles A. Cerami is the author of eleven books, including *Benjamin Banneker: Surveyor, Astronomer, Publisher, Patriot* and *A Marshall Plan for the 1990s*. Cerami's articles have been published in *The Atlantic Monthly, Playboy, New York Times, Foreign Policy, The Spectator* (of London), and *Swiss Review of World Affairs*. He lives in Washington, D.C.